Strategies for Meeting the Information
Needs of Society in the Year 2000

Strategies for Meeting the Information Needs of Society in the Year 2000

by
Martha Boaz

Libraries Unlimited, Inc.
Littleton, Colorado
1981

12478

LIBRARIES UNLIMITED, INC.
P.O. Box 263
Littleton, Colorado 80160

Library of Congress Cataloging in Publication Data

Main entry under title:

Strategies for meeting the information needs of
    society in the year 2000.

    Includes index.
    1. Information services--Social aspects--
Addresses, essays, lectures.   I. Boaz, Martha
Terosse, 1913-   .
Z674.7.S76   025'.063   81-11751
ISBN 0-87287-249-1   AACR2

PREFACE

People may question the practicality of planning for changes that will occur over a 20 year period, but history indicates that many of our current problems might have been avoided through such pre-planning; the energy crisis is just one dramatic example. We know today that information and knowledge are basic resources and that they have a profound influence on us all. In our information-centered society, constant changes in computer hardware and software, and in communications equipment provide us with increasingly rapid and inexpensive access to information services. Many advantages and many problems have become associated with these services. The articles in this book attempt to outline some of the problems and to suggest strategies for developing information technologies that can be controlled and that can be used constructively and efficiently.

The general outline of the book centers upon practical plans for meeting the information needs of society with emphasis on user needs, economics, technology, and legal issues. Specialists and authorities in their fields, by invitation from the editor have contributed the chapters in this book. Brief notes on these contributors are provided at the end of the volume. Each has his or her own style of writing and point of view relating to one of the following topics: the information explosion, the major national and international societal problems whose resolutions require information services, user needs, the particular information needs of business, the trend toward personal computers, expected advancements in computer technology and telecommunications during the next 20 years, telecommunications and value systems, the place of the author in the coming information society, regulatory factors that may affect the flow of information, and the financing and governance of information networks of the future. All of these articles indicate how essential it has become to plan for and to give careful direction to our information technology resources.

Martha Boaz

TABLE OF CONTENTS

THE THIRD REVOLUTION:
The Information Explosion —
Information Access in the Year 2000

by

Martha Boaz, Research Associate,
Center for Study of the American Experience
and
Dean Emeritus, School of Library Science
University of Southern California

The Information Age is here. The information explosion and the data communications revolution which erupted in the United States is moving around the world. Information systems freely traverse national boundaries and major future trends point to activities toward delivery of information rather than production of goods. In the material that follows attention is given to some of the general trends and problems in technological developments with particular reference to education and libraries and to the need for planning for the future.

Society has gone through various stages of development, from a primitive state to a very sophisticated highly civilized world. Histories of society that cover its various stages of development during the last several hundred years have established the following periods: a pre-industrial society, which depended primarily upon raw materials; an industrial society, which resulted from the replacement of hand tools by machine and power tools and from the development of large-scale industrial production; and a post-industrial society, which is organized around information and its use as a basis for organizing the flow of knowledge. Some people speak of the current age as the Postindustrial Revolution; others refer to it as the Information Revolution.

It is generally recognized that information and knowledge are basic resources that have profound influence on the world. Developments in informational technology--the nervous system of society--are transforming an industrial age into an information-centered age. The systematic arrangement of theoretical knowledge will be the basic resource for guiding and shaping society's future structure.

Note: Some of the material in this article was used in a lecture given at Louisiana State University (LSU) in October 1979 and is used here by permission of LSU.

Importance of Information

In his book, The Third Wave, Alvin Toffler says,

> The most basic raw material of all--and one that can never be
> exhausted--is information, including imagination.... With
> information becoming more important than ever before, the new
> civilization will restructure education, redefine scientific
> research and, above all, reorganize the media of communication.[1]

Information can be one of the most important influences shaping
society. It can furnish facts, report (or develop) feelings, establish
trends, which, if communicated, may affect decisions and actions that
influence the world. Access to information in the postindustrial society
is the key to all social roles--work, citizenship, recreation, and
others. This suggests that access to information may become a social
right, something like free education or equal opportunity, with
legislation designed both to ensure access to information and to
protect the privacy of the user.

Burt Nanus, professor and director of the Center for Futures
Research at the University of Southern California describes five
information revolutions: 1) the invention of language; 2) the invention of writing and then printing; 3) the introduction of mass media,
including newspapers, radio and television; 4) the invention of the
computer; and, 5) the marriage of telecommunications and computers.[2]
Through the fifth revolution, which was precipitated by enormous
complexes of computer hardware and software and communications
equipment, millions of people now have access to extensive information
services rapidly, inexpensively, and in varied environments.

Another university professor, Russell L. Ackoff, also talks of
revolutions:

> We are going through an intellectual revolution that is as funda-
> mental as that which occurred in the Renaissance. The Renaissance
> ushered in the Machine Age which produced the Industrial Revolution.
> The currently emerging intellectual revolution is bringing with it
> a new era that can be called the Systems Age which is producing the
> Postindustrial Revolution. I believe these changes give rise to
> most of the crises we face and simultaneously offer whatever hope
> there is for dealing with them effectively.[3]

Ackoff is concerned with the concept of systems and calls attention to
expansionism, which turns from ultimate elements to wholes with
intellectual parts, to systems.

He goes back to 1949 when Claude Shannon, a mathematician at Bell
Laboratories,

> turned attention to a larger process of which language was a part,
> communication. He provided a theory that formed the basis for what
> came to be known as the communication sciences. Almost simultane-
> ously another mathematician, Norbert Wiener, of the Massachusetts

Institute of Technology, placed communication into a still larger
conceptual context, <u>control</u>. In so doing he founded <u>cybernetics</u>,
the science of control through communication.[4]

The <u>system</u> concept has logically become an important factor in planning
holistically for the present and for anticipated future societies.
Technology has changed the world from isolated regions to one
community. John McHale, commenting on this fact, says,

> In terms of information environment, our world has shrunk swiftly,
> in just over two generations, from one whose surface was still
> incompletely known and whose peoples were fairly remote strangers
> to one another, to one which is a continuous neighborhood, in
> which, theoretically, no person is more than a few hours distant
> from all others and in which communications may be practically
> instantaneous. Man-made satellites encircle this neighborhood
> many times in one day, and the repercussions of decisive events
> affecting any part of the human family are swiftly felt around the
> globe.[5]

Technology has brought about more change in society than has any
previous force. Because of it there is more wealth, more products,
more consumption of products, more education, more communications, and
more travel.

If predictions become facts, any user of information systems will
soon be able to secure information in seconds on law cases, on lists of
symptoms for diseases, individual medical records, prices on any
product or service, a computation of the distance to the nearest star
and other facts. There will be computer access to education, to
libraries, to various services, to entertainment, and to many other
important fields of knowledge.

Technological change has been written about and discussed at
length. Alvin Toffler, in his book, <u>Future Shock</u>, emphasizes the rate
of acceleration of this change and says that society's inability to
adapt to the increasing rate of change is the most critical problem of
our times. Because of the increasing speed of technological change,
problems arise more rapidly than before and, by the same token, they
require quicker answers than ever before. Unfortunately, our society
is not capable of giving ready, quick answers.

The speed of technology has decreased the effectiveness of experience because the latter is too slow. According to Ackoff, "The time
lag between stimulus and response brought about by reliance on experience permits crises to develop to a point at which we are forced to
respond to them with little relevant knowledge."[6] He continues: "An
increasing portion of society's responses are made out of desperation,
not out of deliberation. Antipoverty, antidiscrimination, anticrime,
and antinarcotics measures recently taken in the United States are
examples."[7]

Current Trends

A survey of the literature discloses some of the current trends and accompanying problems for users of scientific publications. These include: 1) the enormous volume of material being published, 2) the accelerating cost of publication, 3) the increasing specialization in science and technology, and, 4) the delays in getting information out through customary channels.

F. W. Lancaster, in studying the information explosion finds rather startling figures in relation to these trends. The material which follows attempts to summarize Lancaster's findings.[8] Publication in the field of periodical literature in science and technology in the British National Lending Library of Science and Technology grew from 26,325 periodical titles in 1965 to 49,440 in 1974. A report of the National Science Foundation, in 1964, based on a sample of 262 scientific journals, indicates a 52% increase in a decade. Another report indicates that the number of pages printed by the American Institute of Physics doubles every 8 years and has done this since 1940. Other figures show that the total number of scientific and technical articles published in scholarly journals in the United States advanced from 105,932 in 1960 to 155,345 in 1975. The number of new books in hardcover form published in the field of science increased more than 40% in a ten-year period. The number of patents issued in the United States in the period between 1960 and 1974 was 60% of the total number of U.S. patents issued through 1960. These figures represent only the growth of primary literature. The secondary literature has been growing rapidly, too, with figures from one abstracting and indexing service showing a dramatic increase in the number of abstracts and indexes issued. In addition to the growth in numbers, there is increasing specialization and fragmentation in the scientific papers which are published. This may mean that an individual researcher will have to examine and pay for a large number of irrelevant articles before finding one that is useful.

The point of the above figures is that there has been and continues to be a large annual increase in the quantity of literature published in the scientific and technical fields. And, while the publications have grown exponentially, the time that a scientist or researcher has for reading the material continues to be more or less the same year after year. Better, more efficient, and speedier ways of selecting and locating those specific items of relevance to a particular researcher have become essential. Further, the cost of literature has increased dramatically. According to Lancaster,[9] this is partially because the publishing industry is still very labor-intensive and its labor costs have been largely responsible for price increases. Postal rates have also increased in the publishing field, with the estimated increase between 1962 and 1980 being 110%. Price increases in materials is another large publishing cost item. One report gives a dramatic increase of 232% in the cost of a technical report from 1966 to 1974, if bought in paper copy, and an increase of 97% in microfiche. A specific example of cost increase is the case of Chemical Abstracts (CA). The subscription price of CA was $12 a year in 1940; it is now more than $4,200 a year, which almost precludes private individuals' subscribing to it and makes it mainly available only to the richest institutions.

Since Johann Gutenberg's Mozarin Bible was printed in Europe from movable type, around 1456, most formal channels of communication have been in the form of printed documents on paper. Today there is a trend toward replacing paper-based publications with electronic alternatives, and one possibility is the use of computers for centralized storage of data, which can then be used at terminals in various locations. Scientists have discovered a number of electronic forms which have similar features in their storage, transmission, and retrieval systems and paper is being replaced by digital form documents, microform, television images, or a combination of these. Through the many systems, users now have access to a wide range of external bibliographic resources.

In commenting on a paperless information system, Lancaster says that there is strong need for such a system by the intelligence community: "The need exists because the volume of documents routinely processed by this community amounts to several thousand each day, a considerably greater number than those processed by the largest science information systems, and because these documents need to be disseminated, evaluated and acted upon very rapidly."[10] Lancaster calls attention to the work of the Central Intelligence Agency toward a largely paperless information handling system which will send intelligence messages in digital form to on-line viewing stations and will permit the recipient to discard or store messages, index them, comment on them, or bring them to the attention of other users. This prototype system, named SAFE (Support for the Analyst File Environment), has, according to Lancaster,

the potential for keeping a major segment of the intelligence community more thoroughly and more swiftly informed than ever before on current developments and on significant events documented in the accumulated literature of the past. A more thoroughly and swiftly informed intelligence community is likely to produce improved intelligence analysis and reporting which, in turn, could have significant impact on problem solving and decision making at the highest level.[11]

Information International

An international look at the growing information industry shows a large increase in information occupations: "A multicountry study being conducted by the Organization for Economic Cooperation and Development (OECD) has found that, across an important sample of the industrialized nations of the world, more and more people are employed in information activities."[12] The nations involved are Austria, Canada, Finland, France, Japan, Sweden, the United Kingdom, the United States, and West Germany.

The above facts lead to the list of hypotheses which follow. There will be no attempt to prove or disprove these specifically; they are

simply listed as general statements and as a basis for other
generalizations which follow.

Hypotheses: 1) The physical volume of knowledge and its accelerated rate of growth will require increasingly skilled organization
and sophisticated technological control of knowledge in order to make
it accessible, in a useful form to actual and potential users. 2) Such
accessibility will increasingly be the key to participation in the
progress and services of our society. 3) Without thoughtful and
responsible anticipation of alternative "information futures," the
evolution of institutions and systems for providing such accessibility
is likely to be less successful than society might otherwise expect.
4) Major breakthroughs are needed in the scientific and technical
information delivery infrastructure and delivery systems. 5) Information users will increasingly demand better services and will evaluate
them on a cost-effective basis. 6) Innovations in technology and
services must be accompanied by appropriate behavioral, organizational,
institutional, and social innovations. 7) Advances in the use of
technology are likely to be governed by nontechnical issues (i.e.,
political, administrative, behavioral, legal, and regulatory questions)
rather than technology itself.

Problems and Advances in Modern Technology
In the Information World

Technology may have both beneficial and adverse impacts. Although
the advantages seem to outweigh the problems, there may be serious
unfavorable consequences of the use of modern technology in the information world. According to the many people who have written on this
topic, these include: the loss of privacy, which is one of greatest
concern to a large number of people; dehumanization of the individual;
exploitation of the information poor by the information rich, specifically the increasing information dependency on the part of the
information poor nations; and information overload. These are just
a few of the many problem areas.

Privacy of information and compensation for information can be
assured by law, but all of this will have to be carefully planned in
order to protect individual and corporate rights, and the protection of
the individual or of a company or organization is a serious problem.
There is no international agreement on the protection of privacy across
national borders.

Other policy matters that must continue to be considered include:
protecting publishers and authors and their copyright rights; ensuring
accuracy of information provided by the communications systems; establishing charges that are fair to persons who need information, and at
the same time paying the persons or companies who supply the information; and providing high levels of service throughout the library
or information agency.

The enormous volume of information may finally become an overwhelming torrent, an "information glut." When computers become as
common as television sets in the home, they will have to be built to
serve the individual. For example, computers can be designed for

individualized services, for products, materials, and services, for
students in academic institutions, for employees in certain types of
occupations, and for almost any service that anyone wants.

The problem of information overload may lead to the banding
together and coalescence of small, strong, exclusive groups. Efforts
may be made to restrict access to information, and to control events
and people by certain types of information. Technology can be used to
concentrate power and to manipulate political and economic decisions,
to regiment people and to subvert the basic values of society. It will
be unfortunate if information technology is taken over by the government and the resulting power becomes tyranny. At present, development
and regulation are splintered and disparate. Again in the area of
privacy, the use of computers in integrated information systems, by
local governments, has brought on a problem in the protection of
sensitive data. Local governments face great difficulty in attempting
to balance the confidentiality of personal data with the duty of providing open access by the public to government. A USAC report on
Local Government Information Systems: A Study of USAC and the Future
Application of Computer Technology questions the wisdom of using a
department governed by a privacy policy as the enforcer of that policy.
The report lists elements that should be included in a well-drawn plan
for assuring the privacy, security, and confidentiality of data:[13]
1) a provision for controlling the collection of data, 2) a plan for
technical safeguards to keep data secure, 3) a means for controlling
access to data, including an individual's access to his or her records,
4) a mechanism to keep sensitive data confidential to protect both
private and public interests, and, 5) a plan for assuring the integrity
of the data.

The use of computers involving the sensitive areas of invasion of
privacy and questions of illegal and nonethical use may lead to the
licensing of computer professionals. According to C. V. Ramamoorthy,
the Society of Certified Data Processors has already initiated a move
for industry-wide licensing of that group: "They have drawn up and
sent to all state legislatures a draft resolution that would declare
DP 'a learned profession to be practiced and regulated as such.'"[14]
This leads to the matter of accreditation and to that of establishing
suitable accrediting agencies to evaluate and license the educational
programs that prepare people for the profession. Another possible
problem is that there may not be enough people with adequate knowledge
and skills to educate the next generation in the use of technology.

Ramamoorthy, after studying Bureau of Labor Statistics reports,
summarizes the forecasts of employment demands and trends in computer-
related industries in the 1980s and then comments on the educational
needs to satisfy these.[15] In summary and abbreviated form these are
as follows: 1) The cost of computer manpower is mounting; as a result,
the manufacturers will incorporate into their equipment functions currently being performed by computer personnel. 2) By 1980, data communications, minicomputers, and microcomputers are expected to be
extended to many more uses. 3) Easier-to-use programming languages are
expected to be available by the end of the decade, and packaged programs
are likely to be extended to a greater variety of applications. 4) The
wide diversity in educational backgrounds and preparations for computer

jobs is expected to diminish over the next decade. 5) Employers find
computer science and data-processing capabilities the most lacking
qualifications in the backgrounds of their computer personnel. 6) Major
improvements to computer education and training needed to facilitate the
availability of better qualified computer personnel include: (a) a
larger number of qualified teachers, (b) consistency of subject matter
in similar course offerings, (c) more rapid dissemination of information on computer technological advances to educational institutions,
and (d) techniques for determining the ability of computer products
from different companies to work in the same system. Two of the major
conclusions from these findings are that there will be 1) great demand
for properly qualified computer science and engineering graduates, and
2) an enormous need for continuing education programs to re-educate
professionals in the evolving technology. This re-education will
include retraining the teachers in institutions that do not have
research-oriented graduate programs.

Apparently, there are no technological barriers to the development
of any new advanced systems, but there are institutional, economic, and
behavioral problems. In forecasting the future, Joel D. Goldhar, who
is in the Division of Science Information of the National Science
Foundation, foresees a scientific and technical information (STI)
delivery system that is "capital intensive." Goldhar notes that

The traditional lines between primary publishing, secondary publishing, library retrieval and retailing-delivery services begin to
blur, and vertically integrated information services organizations
are being formed. The emergence of resource sharing networks,
information brokers, and other tertiary organizations which provide needed filtration, condensation, and validation services in
an effort to beat the combined information-overload and cost-
squeeze problem further complicates the institutional picture.[16]

Needs

Several persons have expressed the need for a national information
policy to guide and control information systems. Such a policy would
improve the progress and development of information and protect the
public against unfair commercial profit, manipulation for gain or
power, and invasion of privacy.

Responding to concerns expressed about the uses of technology,
Congress, in 1972, established the Office of Technology Assessment
(OTA), which was to assess and advise Congress on the impacts--both
beneficial and harmful--of the applications of scientific and technological knowledge. Russell W. Peterson, former director of the OTA, is
concerned about interlocking technological and social forces; he says,
"not only does technology affect society, so does society affect technology."[17] As an example, he points out that "the industrial revolution
was spawned through the application of technology, but industrialization
in turn markedly influenced the nature and rate of technological change.
This contributed to the industrial boom of the 1920s which floundered
into one of the world's most serious depressions in the 1930s leading
to a redirection of our science and technology toward meeting the basic

needs of the people. We also know that technology creates new weapons of war and war sparks major research and development."[18] The positive approach of research in technology should be to use it to improve society and the quality of life.

Technological Trends

New technological developments since 1964, says Walter S. Baer, "have primarily been applied to improve existing communications serv- ices rather than to create new ones. Television transmissions by satellite across the oceans is one of the few examples of a new com- munications service introduced since 1964."[19] Other observations by Baer note that "technological advance in telecommunications has been incremental and often invisible to those outside the field,"[20] and "even after new telecommunications technologies have proved economi- cally advantageous, they take a long time to diffuse into widespread use."[21] This statement is expanded by the comment, "A time scale of twenty years or more from commercial introduction to mature saturation seems typical for a system-oriented and highly regulated industry such as telecommunications."[22]

Baer points out that the growing use of information processing in communications systems is a result of improvements in performance, size of computer hardware, and lowered cost: "the costs of information- processing and storage units have fallen by a factor of three every two years or so for the past 20 years--a total cost decrease of more than 10,000 fold."[23] This means that a few hundred dollars now buys the equivalent of several million dollars in the mid-1950s.

Another specialist, Lewis M. Branscomb, vice president and chief scientist of IBM, provides information about the enormous changes that have taken place in the computer world and looks ahead to likely future changes. He says,

On the basis of the growth indicated, the computer of the year 2000 will contain the data memory equivalent of 16,000 human brains--the equivalent of a university population. While I am at it, I might add another improbable figure to this project. That figure is cost. If today's largest computer costs $5 million, and the cost per bit of online memory and per circuit of logic is decreasing at the rate of only 21 percent a year, then in 2080 the cost of a computer with the power of today's big machines will be extraordinarily low--in fact, 15 billion times lower, or down to 3/100 of a cent.[24]

Branscomb predicts other startling developments: "the computer of the future will not have to be approached by push-button or typewriter key or a punched card. It will respond to speech... In the next 100 years much information that is stored today may not have to be stored at all. It may be cheaper to reconstitute or reacquire information from basic elements each time the information is needed."[25] Walter Baer gives other dramatic figures:

By the early 1980s continuing improvements in LSI technology should yield commercial logic devices with roughly 60,000 components per chip. These micro processors will be able to execute four million instructions per second--roughly four times the speed of micro processors today and 100 times faster than the small computers of the early 1960s. The cost of such devices depends critically on the number produced, but with volume production, they should cost less than $100 by the early 1980s. Smaller capacity micro and processors that now cost $10.00 to $20.00, such as those used for programmable calculators and television games, should be available to manufacturers for between $1.00 and $5.00.[26]

Another interesting note was that "LSI memory costs are dropping even more rapidly than those of microprocessors, so that one expects to see LSI memory chips available in the early 1980s for 30 cents per thousand bits or less."[27]

Mass production of the miracle chips have already made possible computer systems that sell for less than $800.00. Eventually, according to an article in Time Magazine of February 20, 1978, these will be used so extensively that the household computer will be as much a part of the home as the kitchen sink. An interesting application of miracle chips is being checked into by Bell Telephone Laboratories; this would turn the home telephone into a burglar alarm, fire alarm and intercom. Another experiment reported by another company would allow telephone subscribers, for about $100.00 a month, to carry their telephones wherever they go in the metropolitan area and make or receive calls--even while walking along the street. Studies indicate that the amount of information stored and transmitted through many sources will increase and be available to more and more people and that more specialized information will be available to specialized audiences at low cost figures.

Communications networks more closely geared to users' changing needs are forecast for the 1980s. Those "intelligent" networks will readily adapt to user requirements. Personal computers are being marketed already, and they will be used more and more in the future. The personal computer has been defined as a small, desk top computer intended to meet business, professional and home uses and is priced from $15,000.00 down to a few hundred dollars. According to Dataquest, a Menlo Park research firm, Tandy Corp's Radio Shack subsidiary has shipped out about 100,000 of its TRS-80 personal computers.[28] Thus we know that the personal computer is on the market. Progress in information technology holds untold great promises, if used rightly; used wrongly, advances in the field could be very disruptive.

The major charge to today's society is to devise methods for controlling technology and to plan for future control--to use the benefits, to curb the problem areas, to ask how the future has been shaped by what has already happened. Persons who are making decisions now will have a powerful influence on what happens in the next 25 years. They will determine the future channels of information technology and will thereby be shaping the future society.

Education in the New Information-Technology World

Problems

The academic world is changing. Academic institutions and specific campus settings, have in the past, been centers for educational programs. This is likely to change. The days of the cloistered campus are gone. The cost of education has increased greatly in the last 15 years and many schools are facing fiscal crises. Educators anticipate a continued cost increase with only a small percent of the cost being borne by the students. As a consequence, educational institutions may have to find new sources of revenue or they may have to change programs, settings, and methods for delivering educational services.

The required shifts in education may change the primary settings of university courses from large campuses and multiple buildings to a few buildings, or even to sets of individual and group consoles. Academic courses may be formatted into packaged audiovisual materials or into televised or computerized delivery systems relying upon interactive access to computers.

Students may have more freedom to select courses according to their interests and may depend less on formal degrees. Instead, they may stop school at any time and receive certificates showing their records of performance. Colleges and universities will be forced to cut programs, dismiss faculty and staff, and find other ways for transferring information to students. Faculty may not be needed on the campus but may be required to give more care to well-prepared materials for educational network presentation.

Increased costs are due to several things: new courses, more expensive equipment, new technology, higher personnel costs, expensive physical plants, increasing demands for services, and general inflation. The biggest educational costs are in personnel/labor areas. Because of deficits and increasing costs, tuition and other charges have increased to the point that many students are unable to continue their educational programs, thereby causing further drops in income for the institutions.

Forecasts call for continued declining enrollments, increased competition for students and rising costs among colleges for the next 20 years. Inflation continues to outdistance endowments and rising tuition costs to diminish college attendance of middle and low income families. Serious job shortages already exist and thousands of graduates, including Ph.D.'s, face uncertain futures; higher education faces austerity and change.

Another growing problem for academic administrators is the amount of time spent in complying with the multitude of government regulations. One well-known university recently spent 60,000 hours of faculty time and an approximate probable cost of around 12 million dollars administering five federal programs in one year. New methods for keeping records of student performance, faculty competence and administrative services will possibly supplant the current systems of colleges and universities in these functions.

Education--Changes

Academic institutions have been slow to change because they have not been under aggressive competitive pressures to make their activities cost effective. There is more pressure today, by the governing bodies, to change this pattern, but progress is slow and the extensive adoption of electronic media and automated library services are very gradual compared to the practices of business, but budget deficits and more demands from society may compel the educational institutions to become more innovative and adaptive to emerging possibilities.

"Impending changes may seem odd in the present context of the economic depression, raising unemployment and cutbacks in educational funds," says John McHale, but "we should recall that many of these current dilemmas have arisen specifically from failures to anticipate change and to plan effectively in the longer range of unexpected contingences."[29] This leads to the conclusion that education definitely needs to be restructured.

Education should be thought of as a process in which information is transformed into knowledge. In the future this process will likely not be limited to rigidly scheduled units of subjects, exercises and grades; rather, a systems age educational program will need to be designed which emphasizes interactions and interdependence, focusing upon the learning process itself. We should expect a shift in emphasis: from learning facts to learning how to learn and to discovering the means and methods for locating what one needs to know, when the information is needed. Students are living in a machine age, they must learn to use and control machines, but they must also learn to do what a machine cannot do.

Russell Ackoff, speaking about education, says, "An educational system should (1) facilitate a student's learning what he wants and needs to learn, (2) enable him to learn how to learn more efficiently, and (3) motivate him to learn, particularly those things he needs in order to satisfy his own desires and be socially useful."[30] A student with the knowledge gained in this process, should acquire understanding and wisdom that will be beneficial to the individual and to society as a whole.

Information and knowledge are often used synonymously. There is a difference. Information may be a single fact or many unrelated facts. Knowledge is ordered, structured information. The main thrust of this paper is focused on the technological system by which these are communicated.

There is a current move at Harvard to reinstate the core curriculum, which requires students to meet academic requirements in five broad introductory areas, and to substitute this curriculum for 80 to 100 highly specific courses. The program requires that students show proficiency in writing, mathematics, and the use of computers, and attempts to bring purpose and coherence to the liberal arts. This is not a matter of returning to the traditional curriculum, as it was interpreted 25 years ago, but of providing a set of perspectives broad enough to enable students to observe, learn, and understand for the rest of their lives.

According to Derek Bok, president of Harvard, the state of secondary education was one of the forces that influenced Harvard in developing the core curriculum.[31] Bok deplores the decline in high school educational standards over the last 20 years and he thinks that college courses put too much emphasis on the passive transmission of knowledge through lectures and reading and not enough on wrestling with important problems. He is concerned that many of the brightest students come to Harvard without ever having written one or two substantial papers. It is expected that Harvard's concern and leadership will stimulate change at other colleges and universities across the nation.

The past pattern of going through school in an uninterrupted pattern--from elementary school, to high school, to college, to the university, and often to graduate school--is likely to change. After finishing high school, students will probably work for several years before going to college. They may also plan work-study programs, attending school one year and in alternate years working in business or industry or the community. More older people will be returning to school, some of them for renewal of vocational training or in order to become informed of new occupational opportunities; others will be specializing in research and highly refined professional studies. As society and technology change, people will have to continue learning and re-training in order to "keep up" in their own fields. There will be more incentives and more requirements for "continuing education" and for several careers within one lifetime.

In many cases academic institutions will discontinue having the professor meet students in a classroom setting; the educational material will be in prerecorded program or audiovisual form. Faculty time will be released for more research, for improvement of educational programs, and for community service. In addition to faculty changes in assignments, there may be changes in administrative structure, with computers being programmed to carry out high level planning and management functions.

The student's progress can be monitored by the computer. The strong school and departmental structure of today's universities will probably be changed and weakened as the dependence on physical proximity diminishes and as the reliance on technology increases. It is likely that professional educators will resist extensive use of technology, but in time they will be forced to use it, and, as they experience it in a future setting which will be different from that of today, they may welcome it.

The student will be allowed to proceed at an individualized pace and will use the technologically recorded course for information which may be issued to the student personally or stored in the library. Specific questions will be answered and the student's work monitored by a computer, which will also provide an analysis of the student's progress, tabulate a general score, and make suggestions for further study.

Professional schools may leave universities and be affiliated with organizations or businesses that specialize in the schools' professional work. This might apply in schools such as engineering or business;

there might be specialized research units and research degrees such as those now given by companies like the Rand Corporation. Universities will undoubtedly be faced with competition from commercial corporations, and educational institutions in their present forms may undergo radical changes. Thus, information technology will provide a channel for universal education, but not in the formal way of the past. Rather, it may become associated with hitherto noneducational institutions.

Library Education

Library schools and library/information science programs will change, and they should. The library school curriculum will place more emphasis on information science and machine-readable resources, on systems and management. The relatively small number of courses in these fields now will be extended. In addition to the increased general technological content, more attention will be paid to telecommunications technology and to working with potential customers and users of the services. It is hoped that library schools will affiliate, in cooperative relationships, with schools of communications, engineering, and business, in cooperative relationships, and in programs using the expertise of each of these professional fields.

Following trends in other professional schools, library schools will probably depart from the traditional schedule format, formal class meetings, and other academic customs and strive for individualized, self-paced study, geared to the student's needs.

Education--Recertification Requirements

In the future, many of the services performed by professional people will be different from those of today. As a result, according to Ackoff, "many professionals and sub professionals will require repeated requalification... Degrees will become less meaningful and many will become irrelevant. Licenses and certificates requiring periodic renewal are likely to become the rule."[32] With the heightened acceleration of technological change, employees will be required to update their knowledge and skills continually and to be re-trained in fields where technical obsolescence is a continuing factor.

Information technology is simplifying the learning process, and in some cases, shortening the period formerly required for learning certain types of material. For example, in factual content classes, students can spend less time on memorizing and more time on other educational processes such as learning how to learn. Someone has said that portions of education will be transferred from a "services" to a "goods" industry through the use of "media packages." This is a likely trend.

Negative Aspects of Technology

The impersonal, dehumanized characteristics of technology will have to be countered and plans developed to teach humanistic values and to develop individual growth. As educational choices proliferate, so should the individual's ability to choose in light of defined values.

The decentralization of education's physical settings, and of the educational process itself, will undoubtedly have negative effects on mutual objectives, social exchange, and group planning. People who are shaping the future should be aware of these problems and design plans which will counteract the negative elements. Experiments and trial runs of educational innovations should be tried out in restricted exercises before broad implementation is required.

Changes in education will have to come about because of a series of changes in other areas. These include: changes in values in society, the availability of funds and other resources, and the changes in technology which affect education.

The Library in the New Information Technology World

Will there be libraries in the year 2000? If so, will we have the same type of library that we have today? Statements have been made that imply the demise of libraries, and although most people who have lived in the library world would like to refute the inference, it behooves the library profession to get busy, check facts, look ahead, and anticipate what may happen in the information technology age, and to investigate possible relationships between libraries and other institutions. What actions will be needed to change the professional from one dealing primarily with print on paper to one working extensively with electronic media? This is a question that may cause considerable consternation.

There are two main facets of the problem says F. W. Lancaster:

1. How will the library apply electronics to the handling of electronic materials?
2. How will the library apply electronics to the handling of printed, microform, and other materials, assuming that materials of this type still require processing, and how will the electronic processing of these materials be integrated with the electronic processing of the electronic materials?[33]

As Lancaster notes, the first question requires more attention, for the latter activities are already being carried out in libraries in auto-mated acquisitions, check-ins, circulation, and similar procedures.

Some other questions for libraries and librarians, according to Lancaster are:

(1) Will a library "own" a collection of electronic materials (i.e., data bases for which it has paid certain access rights) or will, essentially, all libraries have equal access to all materials on a pay as you go basis? (2) If the latter, will there be need for libraries at all? That is, will there be some people who need to access data bases and data banks through libraries because they have no other access to the necessary terminals? Will libraries be able to offer services to users that they could not receive by going directly to data bases through their own terminals? (3) If libraries own electronic collections, how will these collections be selected and acquired?...

(4) If libraries do not own collections of materials, they presumably will have no responsibility for the bibliographic control
of these materials. Which organizations, then, will assume the
responsibility for cataloging and indexing operations?[34]

These and other questions are ones which require attention.

Libraries--Problems

Libraries do have a major responsibility for information transfer
and for providing all types of materials, particularly research
materials, to persons who desire them when they need them. But
libraries have problems now in providing the services expected of them.
The reasons lie in the growth of the literature, in the cost of publications and equipment, and in rising personnel costs. Salary figures
are the largest cost item in any library budget and always present a
problem. It would seem that any solution to these problems would be
better than continuing "as is."

The move in libraries from book storage to computer storage and
retrieval will be a slow and expensive process. Budget items now
listed for personnel and books will be transferred to equipment and
for rental services to data bases in other locations, (but this will
be true of the conversion of files in business and service organizations
as well.)

There will be problems of integration of the processing of electronic and printed materials and there will be people who do not have
their own terminals, or, if they have terminals, may not have high
speed printers. Thus it is likely that there will always be a need
for libraries. Libraries will be centers that will have data banks and
electronic services as well as trained personnel to assist and serve
persons who desire these various services. Local materials will
probably be collected and provided to users in traditional form, and
information specialists will guide and assist users searching for
materials and in their use of particular information.

Lancaster says that librarians in the electronic world will
probably play a more significant role than they do now in the training
of scientists and others in the use of machine-readable resources. He
thinks that training, in fact, may become a major activity of the
librarian by the year 2000.[35] He notes, however, that there is no
reason to suppose that librarians need to continue to operate from
"libraries," for as we approach a completely electronic system there
will be less need for libraries as physical entities within walls:

The librarian of the year 2000 may well be a freelance information
specialist, working from an office or from the home, to whom others
turn for help in the exploitation of the rich variety of information
resources available. In this environment, "consulting the
librarian" would mean using a terminal to contact an information
specialist.[36]

Librarians should not fear these changes. The information world
will expand and become richer, and the librarians'/information

specialists' status within it will probably be higher and their services more recognized as they work within the great information network world. Sad to say, the library, logically one of the institutions most concerned and involved with information technology, has not been much involved with its development.

If librarians are willing to face facts, they will admit that the library is not used as much as it should be. Many students and faculty members do not use libraries, and libraries are expensive to maintain in view of the cost and this relatively small use.

It will be a blow to librarians' vanity to learn that Carole Gantz and Joel Goldhar of the Office of Science Information Service, National Science Foundation, think literature surveys should be done by the innovator-inventor rather than the librarian. Gantz and Goldhar, reporting from the results of their study, write:

Of those interviewed who had a project which required a literature search within the last year, only a very small number used librarians as either a first step or for an entire literature survey, although a few others used librarians as intermediary steps.... One suggestion is an improvement in literature search formats to make them more responsive to users.[37]

Gantz and Goldhar also write that,

Subsequent phases of these studies will undoubtedly lead to suggested changes in the form in which literature is accessed, indexed, and retrieved, in order to make it more accessible and available to researchers. The form should be determined by the function of information in terms of the user's needs at specific points in the innovation process, rather than having the form determined by the need of the librarian, bibliographer and archivist.[38]

In other surveys that have been made, it has been learned that science and research scholars depend on a small number of people for materials and information that will aid them in their research pursuits. Someone has given the title of "information gate keeper" to these key people who provide information services; often they have been colleagues or people within the same organization as the researchers.

In checking library use, evidence shows that physical proximity, convenience of access, and ease of use are the biggest factors in the use of information sources and services. Users frequently do not make great effort to get materials that are very troublesome to get. It is suggested that librarians/information specialists do research themselves on the information-seeking behavior of users and that they then design careful information-supply programs, based on the findings of their studies. The new type of librarian will probably be a subject specialist as well as an expert in the business side of scientific and technical information. This person's subject field education and expertise in STI will have to constantly be updated.

The Library and Information Center of the Future

Librarians should develop more initiative and, libraries, instead of depending on outside vendors, could produce their own technological systems. At least they could plan to have systems and networks that are compatible with each other. They might even prepare packages and products to be marketed in order to provide operating money for the library. A point to remember, if librarians do go this way, is that, due to the progress in technology, materials needed on a very current, up-to-date basis are put into media form that is faster than the printed pages. For this reason, books are becoming less important in the fields of science and technology, and although the traditional library will continue to exist, there will be and already are different requirements made for it in certain areas. Methods for acquiring library materials, for accessioning them, for storing and for servicing them are being provided through high speed facsimile, reproduction, and communications devices. There will be more microforms and computer-based data banks. The automatic acquisitions, storage and retrieval systems may cause the present day library to become obsolete or to be retained mainly as a historic treasure. (In spite of these predictions, I feel sure that books will continue to be important and that people will still continue to read books, in book form.)

Dramatic changes will come about in the future in libraries and information centers. One writer says

> We are already very close to the day in which a great science library could exist in a space less than 10 feet square. Right now a single on-line terminal can give a small organization, or even a single individual access to perhaps 50 different data bases. Within a short time, several hundred will be accessible on-line.[39]

The book in its present form as the main repository of stored information will probably be displaced, in practical situations (usage) by cassettes, which can be inexpensively duplicated. A student will be able to buy or borrow these cassettes as well as small audiovisual playback machines. The card catalog, the journal, and the book stack as we know them today will be obsolete, several years hence. The use of "copy" facilities will provide for the purchase of printed or microfilm copies of pages, articles, or books at a fraction of a cent per page. The need for borrowing library materials will be greatly reduced.

Library Networks

Libraries have available to them machine-readable data bases and online processing, which provide extensive information resources from far distant geographical locations. Library networks make it possible for the smallest library to have access to the largest information centers and to get the information quickly from anywhere in the world.

The movement toward computerized networks of libraries will expand. With declining costs in the communication of data, it will be feasible

for more and more small, individual libraries to join the large
national and international library networks. Libraries will have
computer terminals that will enable users to have access to data bases
and systems in other libraries in regional, national, and international
networks.

With a diversity of materials and services libraries can provide
a variety of services, involving not only the traditional books,
periodicals, newspapers, but also audiovisual and art materials. They
can be centers for the most advanced and sophisticated forms of communication media. They can be centers where children have nursery and
child care services thus freeing the parents to shop or dine out, knowing the children are safe; and libraries can be centers for many other
activities. In the future, when education may change from the
traditional professor-taught courses and classroom setting, libraries
may become the educational centers and the cores of education processes.
Libraries may serve as sites for information teleconferences so that
persons who need information may consult online information systems in
distant locations. Teleconferencing is a very important development,
for it can involve networks of experts (as well as information systems)
to whom queries can be addressed and from whom authoritative and
informed answers can be obtained. These are only a few of the items
that can be provided, for the types of services libraries could provide
is almost limitless. Librarians are urged to identify functions that
library/information centers may perform in a society in which electronic
communication may become the main channel of information.

Notes

[1]Alvin Toffler, The Third Wave (New York: William Morrow & Co.,
1980), p. 368.

[2]Burt Nanus, "Information Science and the Future," Bulletin of the
American Society for Information Science, vol. 2 (March 1976), p. 57.

[3]Russell Ackoff, Redesigning the Future (New York: John Wiley,
c1974), p. 8.

[4]Ackoff, Redesigning, p. 12.

[5]John McHale, The Changing Information Environment (Boulder, CO:
Westview Press, c1976), p. 92.

[6]Ackoff, Redesigning, p. 5.

[7]Ackoff, Redesigning, p. 5.

[8]F. W. Lancaster, Toward Paperless Information Systems (New York:
Academic Press, 1978), pp. 66-103.

[9]Lancaster, Toward, pp. 66-103.

[10]Lancaster, Toward, p. 3.

[11]Lancaster, Toward, p. 49.

[12]"Information Sector Growth," Information World, vol. 1, no. 2 (March 1979), p. 17.

[13]"Data Privacy, A Problem for Localities," Information World, vol. 1, no. 2 (March 1979), p. 12.

[14]C. V. Ramamoorthy, "Trends and Perspectives in Computer Science and Engineering Education," Proceedings of the IEEE, vol. 66 (August 1978), p. 875.

[15]Ramamoorthy, "Trends," p. 877.

[16]Joel D. Golhar, "Obtaining and Using Information in the Year 2000," IEEE Transactions on Professional Communication, vol. PC-20, no. 2 (September 1977), p. 126.

[17]Russell W. Peterson, "The Challenge of Technology," Christian Science Monitor, (Wednesday, January 31, 1979), p. 17.

[18]Peterson, "Challenge," p. 17.

[19]Walter S. Baer, "Telecommunications Technology in the 1980s" (pamphlet) (Santa Monica, CA: The Rand Corporation, December 1978), p. 2.

[20]Baer, "Telecommunications," p. 2.

[21]Baer, "Telecommunications," p. 3.

[22]Baer, "Telecommunications," p. 4.

[23]Baer, "Telecommunications," p. 4.

[24]Lewis M. Branscomb, "The Ultimate Frontier," Data Processor, vol. 23 (February/March 1980), p. 8.

[25]Branscomb, "Frontier," p. 8.

[26]Baer, "Telecommunications," p. 5.

[27]Baer, "Telecommunications," p. 6.

[28]"Personal Computers," Datamation, (March 1979), p. 93.

[29]McHale, Changing Information, p. 46.

[30]Ackoff, Redesigning, p. 79.

[31]John J. Goldman, "Harvard Chief Takes Lead in Basic Reform," Los Angeles Times, Part 1, (May 28, 1979), p. 9.

[32]Ackoff, Redesigning, p. 94.

[33]Lancaster, Toward, p. 154.

[34]Lancaster, Toward, pp. 154-55.

[35]Lancaster, Toward, p. 158.

[36]Lancaster, Toward, p. 158.

[37]Carole Gantz and Joel Goldhar, "The Role of Scientific Communication In the Process of Technological Innovation," Information News and Sources, vol. 7 (October 1975), p. 245.

[38]Gantz and Goldhar, Role, p. 245.

[39]Lancaster, Toward, p. 163.

THE MAJOR NATIONAL AND INTERNATIONAL SOCIETAL PROBLEMS AND ISSUES WHOSE RESOLUTIONS REQUIRE INFORMATION SERVICE IN THE YEAR 2000*

by

John Naisbitt
Senior Vice President, Yankelovich, Skelly and White
Publisher, The Trend Report

In our research for corporate clients, we have uncovered ten power-ful trends which are restructuring the United States, and to varying degrees, all the other developed countries of the world. The force of these trends--or mega-trends--is so strong that we feel they predict, and in some cases, constitute, the major societal issues both nationally and internationally. In addition, these ten trends serve two key functions: 1) they determine the major areas requiring increased study and information service by the year 2000, and 2) they provide the basic structure within which to organize the huge amounts of information generated as we move toward the new century.

Let me first list the ten trends, and then return to each of them for a more detailed discussion.

1) The United States is rapidly shifting from a mass industrial society to an information society, and the final impact will be more profound than the nineteenth century shift from an agricultural to an industrial society.

2) There is more decentralization than centralization taking place in America--for the first time in the nation's history; the power is shifting not only from the president to the Congress, but--less noticed--from the Congress to the states and localities.

3) We are now a truly global economy because of instantaneously-shared information, and the world is deeply in the process of a redistribution of labor and production. As part of this process all of the developed countries are de-industrializing.

4) The American society is moving in dual directions of high tech-high touch. The introduction of every new technology is accompanied by a compensatory human response--or the new technology is rejected.

---

5) There are the beginnings of a job revolution in America, a basic restructuring of the work environment from top-down to bottom-up.

6) Ageism has replaced racism and sexism as the society's major anti-discrimination preoccupation. The recession of concern regarding racism and sexism will last for from five to ten years.

7) Equal access to capital will be the new rights issue, follow-earlier claims to equal access to education and health care.

8) Throughout the United States, notions of "appropriate scale" are reshaping our physical and organizational environment.

9) Issues of corporate governance--involving questions of leader-ship of American companies--will have an important impact on business in the '80s.

10) The most important trend in this century is the continuing shift of the United States from a representative democracy to a participatory democracy.

Before dealing with each of these structural changes, I will briefly outline our methodology. In developing the Trend Report for clients we rely almost exclusively on a system of monitoring local events and behavior. We are overwhelmingly impressed with the extent to which America is a bottom-up society, and so we monitor what's going on locally rather than what's going on in Washington, or in New York. Things start in Los Angeles, in Tampa, in Hartford, in Wichita, Portland, San Diego, and Denver. It's very much a from-the-bottom-up society.

The tracking concept employed in determining these trends has its roots in World War II. During the war, intelligence experts sought to find a method for obtaining the kinds of information on enemy nations that public opinion polls would have normally provided. Under the leadership of Paul Lazersfeld and Harold Lasswell, a method was developed for monitoring what was going on in these societies that involved doing a content analysis of their daily newspapers.

Although this method of monitoring public thinking continues to be the choice of the intelligence community--the United States annually spends millions of dollars doing newspaper content analysis in various parts of the world--it has rarely been applied commercially. In fact, we are the first, and presently the only group, to utilize this concept for analyzing our society. We have been doing content studies every day since 1970 of the 150 major newspapers in the United States.

The reason this system of monitoring the changes in society works so well is that the "news hole" in a newspaper is a closed system. For economic reasons, the amount of space devoted to news in a newspaper does not change over time. So, when something new is introduced into that news hole, as it is called, something or a combination of things has to go out or be omitted. The principle involved here can be classified as forced choice within a closed system.

In this forced choice situation societies add new preoccupations and forget old ones. We keep track of the ones that are added and the ones that are given up. Evidently, societies are like human beings: I do not know what the number is, but a person can only keep so many problems and concerns in his or her head at any one time. If new problems or concerns are introduced, some existing ones must be given up. We keep track of what preoccupations Americans have given up and have taken up. We are keeping track of the changing "share of the market" that competing societal concerns command.

The information collected on various issues or topics is not extrapolated, but is used to look for patterns. For example, there are five states in the United States where most social invention occurs. The other 45 states are, in general, followers. California is the key indicator state; Florida is second, although not too far behind; with the other three trend setter states being Washington, Colorado and Connecticut. An example of this phenomenon is provided by a look at who the governors are in these five states. Connecticut and Washington are the only two states where women have been elected governor in their own right. The other states have elected the "new" politicians: Graham, Lamm, and Brown. The new politics has little to do with the old liberal-conservative dichotomies. Rather, it has to do with appropriate scale, decentralization, fiscal conservatism, and a lot of experimentation.

Now let's look at the trends.

1. <u>The United States is rapidly shifting from a mass industrial society to an information society, and the final impact will be more profound than the nineteenth century shift from an agricultural to an industrial society</u>. In 1950, 65% of people working in this country were in the industrial sector. That figure today is around 30%. That is a dramatic change. (In 1900, it stood at 35%.) In 1950, the number of people in the information sector of the society--information occupations--was 17%; it now exceeds 55%. Information occupations are those involved in the creating, processing, and distribution of information, including banks, stock markets, insurance companies, education, and government.

For years we have been hearing that we are moving into a service society. Yet the service sector (absent information occupations) has remained relatively flat--about 11% or 12% for decades. (The character of these service sector jobs has changed--we have few domestics today and a lot of people in fast food jobs--but their ratio to the work force has remained fairly constant.) It is clear that the post-industrial society is an information society.

One of the important things to notice about this shift is that the strategic resource in the industrial society was capital; the strategic resource in the post-industrial information society is knowledge and data (and that's not only renewable; it's self-generating). That explains the explosion of entrepreneurial activity in the United States. Because the strategic resource is now what is in our heads, access to the system is much easier. Not only will we see an impressive increase in the creation of new small firms, but if large institutions are to survive, they will restructure to encourage entrepreneurial activity within their institutions.

Now, the mass instrumentalities that were created, that were consonant with the industrial society, are now out of tune with the times. Just as in 1800 the fact that 90% of the labor force were farmers dictated the societal arrangements of the day, the fact that most of us were in industrial occupations until recently dictated the arrangements of a mass industrial society--which are now out of tune with the new information society. Let me give you three examples. 1.) Labor unions. In 1950, with 65% of the work force in this country in the industrial sector, more than 30% of the workers in the country were members of unions. That's now 19%. There's no way that's going to do anything but continue to go down, as we move more and more into the information society. 2.) A late entry in mass industrial society, network television. Network television started down last year, and it is on a long, slow, irreversible slide downward. I will discuss that more later. 3.) National political parties, which had their heyday in the industrial society, exist today in theory only. Things like department stores and national chain stores, which are in tune with the mass, industrial society, have been yielding over the last decade and a half to things like boutiques. This phenomenon, the breaking up of mass instrumentalities, you'll see everywhere.

Starting a year ago, the number one occupation in the United States became a clerk, replacing the laborer, and the farmer before that. Farmer, laborer, clerk: a brief history of the United States. (What comes after clerk? I can't decide whether it is soldier or poet.)

In connection with this shift to an information society it is important to notice a powerful anomaly developing: as we move into a more and more literacy-intensive society, our schools are giving us an increasingly inferior product: this is a powerful mismatch. SAT scores (the tests to qualify for college) have been going down each year for more than a decade. We all experience that our young people are not outstanding when it comes to writing and arithmetic. Consider this: for the first time in the history of the United States, the generation that is graduating from high school today is less skilled than its parents. Lastly, with the basic restructuring of the society from an industrial to an information society, the traditional groupings of goods and services won't work any more. That is why the economists are almost always wrong. And they will continue to be as long as they rely on the old indices. We need new concepts and new data if we are to understand where we are and where we are going.

2. <u>There is more decentralization than centralization taking place in America--for the first time in the nation's history: the power is shifting not only from the president to the Congress, but--less noticed--from the Congress to the states and localities</u>. Trends move in different directions, at different speeds. They have different weights. They have different life cycles. About three or four years ago, the heft and feel of the movement toward decentralization became greater than the heft and feel of those forces toward continued centralization. The two great centralizing events in America's history were the Great Depression and World War II, plus the centralizing impact of industrialization. We are now receding from these centralizing influences.

You remember, in the '50s and into the '60s (and beyond) we began
to celebrate individual diversity more than we had celebrated it before.
In the '60s, we started to celebrate ethnic diversity. Polish, as well
as black, is beautiful. We started to celebrate our ethnic restaurants,
which of course had been there all the time. (An extraordinary thing
happened, by the way, in the late '60s. We gave up the myth of the
melting pot. For years we had taught our children in fourth grade
civics (or thereabouts) that America was a great melting pot, as if we
were all put in a giant blender and homogenized into Americans. Now
we have given up that myth and recognize that it is our ethnic diversity
that has made us such a vital, creative country.) Then a phenomenon of
the '70s was jurisdictional diversity, geographical diversity. We have
no national urban policy today because a (top-down, master plan)
national urban policy is out of tune with the times. The only national
urban policy that would be in tune with the times is the national urban
policy that would respond to local initiatives. It is an inappropriate
question to ask, "Are we going to save our cities?" That's an either/
or formulation. It doesn't work in the new multiple option society.
The point is, we'll save some of our cities; we will not save others.
We'll save some of our cities a little bit; we'll save others a great
deal. And it will all turn--again--on local initiative. That's also
why we're not getting a national health policy, because you can't do a
top-down monolithic kind of policy anymore because of the growing
diversity in the United States.

Now, where we feel centralization continuing most painfully is in
government regulations, as we well know. And that's changing. That's
really bending back. It was a Republican, Nixon, who opened China. A
Democrat never could have done that. And I think just so, the Democrats
are the only ones who're going to be able to at least get the deregu-
lation started, because Republicans would come under too much pressure.
You know about the airlines, and you know about the trucking industry,
which I thought would be the last to go, the railroads, radio. The
watershed in this, I think, was in February of 1978, when the U.S.
House of Representatives voted against a consumer protection agency.
What was not, I think, sufficiently underlined at that time was that
the first and second term Democrats voted 43 to 37 against establishing
that agency. More and more, we are going to see the political left and
right meeting on this issue of being against big government and against
government regulations. And that's part of a larger power shift, too,
that's going from the president to the Congress, and from Congress to
the states, which means more state regulations.

Proposition 13, I think, has to be understood as having a lot more
to do with the initiative trend, or the referendum trend, than it has to
do with taxes. We are submitting to the political process questions we
never submitted to the political process before. The watershed on that
was Proposition 15 in California three years ago, when the citizens in
California voted on whether or not to build a plant (a nuclear plant,
but nevertheless, a plant). We have never submitted that kind of
question to the political process before. Business got very involved
in that because they had so much at stake. And in the process they
helped to legitimatize this notion of submitting such a question to the

political process. There is no end to it. Last November, more than
400 questions were voted on around the country. There have been many
votes on where we can and cannot smoke. Five jurisdictions last year
voted on using or not using public funds for abortion. Two cities
voted on South Africa. Long Beach, California, voted on whether or
not to have an oil tanker terminal, and, later, on the color of street
lights. We never voted on those kinds of things before, but we're
going to see more and more of this. It's a part of this larger,
"direct democracy." We'll be voting on a great range of new things,
at times "leapfrogging" the traditional political process.

In America, the large, general purpose instrumentalities are
folding everywhere. An early sign and instructive analogue of this
was the demise of Life, Look, and The Saturday Evening Post, the huge
circulation, general purpose magazines, nine years ago. That same year,
300 special purpose magazines were created, most of which are still
being published. Four hundred or so were added the following year, and
so on. There are now more than 4,000 special interest magazines being
published in the United States, and no general purpose magazines. This
phenomenon is an analogue for what is going on in the United States.
Two years ago the National Association of Manufacturers and the United
States Chamber of Commerce announced they were going to merge for all
kinds of wonderful reasons, none of which was true. They were going to
merge in order to survive. About a year ago they announced that they
couldn't negotiate the merger, so now, presumably, they're going to die
separately (except that the Chamber has lately become much more responsive to the grass roots, which may save it). The American Medical
Association, another umbrella organization, is getting weaker as the
groups within it--the pediatricians, surgeons, etc., and the county and
local medical groups are getting stronger.

A year ago two big labor unions, the meat cutters and the retail
clerks, merged to form a huge union--for survival. That's the dinosaur
effect: they get larger just before they go under. (We haven't noticed
it, but there have been 50 mergers of labor union in the last eight
years.)

These kinds of umbrella organizations are out of tune with the
times, just as network television now is becoming. ABC, CBS, and NBC
will be the Life, Look, and Post of the '80s and '90s. Back to the
magazine analogue, network television will lose ground to new options:
the incredible array of cable, videodiscs, and new special-interest
networks--a Spanish language network, the all-sports network, the all-
news network, the BBC in America network, etc. My guess is that by the
end of the '80s, the three big networks may have fewer than half the
viewers they have today.

The cross-over in politics came in 1976--a Presidential year--when
the number of people contributing to special interest groups, like
"Save the Dolphins" exceeded the number of people who contributed to
the umbrella Democratic and Republican parties combined. That trend is
continuing. The two great American political parties now exist in name
only. We have a Congress filled with independents. We may get some
new political parties, but in tune with the decentralization of the
country, they will be local political parties, not national. We already

have the Right-to-Life party on the ballot in New York State; we will
have other local special-interest parties developing in the United
States.

The magazine analogue is also instructive in connection with
leadership. In the United States, we have all noticed a dearth of
leadership. We have no great captains of industry any more, no great
university presidents, no great leaders in the arts, or in civil
rights, in labor, or in politics. It is not because there is any
absence of ambition or talent on the part of those who would be
leaders. We don't have any great leaders any more because we
followers are not creating them. Followers create leaders--not the
reverse--and we followers are not conferring leadership as we did in
the past. We are now creating leaders with much more limited mandates:
closer to us and on much narrower bands. In the old Taoist model of
leadership, "find a parade and get in front of it," we who would be
leaders in America are finding much smaller parades--and many more
of them.

3. We are now a truly global economy because of instantaneously-
shared information, and the world is deeply in the process of a redistribution of labor and production. As part of this process all of the
developed countries are de-industrializing. The other side of relying
on less centralized political authority is the growing world economic
interdependency. Sir Arthur Clarke said that the two inventions that
accounted for America's swift economic growth were the telegraph (later
the telephone) and the railroads. Similarly, the two great inventions
that are making us a global village are the jet airplane and communication satellite. In another way Marshall McLuhan captured the sense
of interdependence when he recently said, "there are no passengers on
spaceship earth. We are all crew."

We are now a truly world economy because of instantaneously shared
information. We have wiped out the "information float." And we are
now deeply in a process of re-sorting out who is going to make what in
this world. As part of this process all of the non-communist, developed
countries are de-industrializing. Even Japan (the most flexible country
in the world) is getting out of the steel business and the shipbuilding
business; she knows that in these markets (which are at saturation
worldwide), South Korea will outdo her in steel and ships will be more
economically built by the new shipbuilders: Brazil, Poland, and Spain.

The United States and the rest of the developed countries are on
the way to losing the following industries: steel, automobile, rail-
road equipment, machinery, apparel, shoe, textile, and appliance. By
the end of the century, the Third World will make 25% of the world's
manufactured goods. The end of the century is only 20 years away.
Remember when President Kennedy was inaugurated? That is how far it
is to the year 2000.

We developed nations are probably going to kill ourselves competing
over steel and cars, when we should be moving in other new areas as the
Third World takes over the old tasks. That is why the Chrysler bailout
was so important. That bailout is a big step down; the path of turning
the U.S. automobile industry into an employment program, just as Britain
turned its automobile (and steel) manufacturing into an employment program. We have to see Chrysler, and the other automobile companies in

a world context. Consider: In the world automobile market we are
reaching saturation; it will soon be a replacement market. There are
now 86 countries that have automobile assembly plants. Japan takes 13
man-hours to build a car; the U.S. takes 30 man-hours. Imports passed
Ford and became number two to General Motors in 1979 with 20% of car
sales in the United States. But in the bellwether state of California
imports were 50% of car sales last year. It has been part of the
conceit of the U.S. automobile companies that they never diversified.
They thought they would go on forever. Now even Henry Ford is getting
out while the getting's good.

Yesterday is over. We have to look to the new technological
adventures: electronics, bio-industry, alternative sources of energy,
mining the seabeds. We have to work out policies (or at least let the
marketplace do it) to make the transition from the old to the new. By
the way, how reliable is the Dow-Jones as a barometer to the economic
health of the society or stock market with all those companies from the
dying industries on its list? Like the economists, they need a new
index.

4. <u>The American society is moving in dual directions of high
tech/high touch. The introduction of every new technology is accompanied by a compensatory human response--or the new technology is
rejected</u>. With the introduction of television, for example, came the
group therapy movement, which, in turn, has led to the personal growth
movement and the human potential movement. (Watching TV in bed with
someone is, of course, very high tech/high touch.)

Similarly, the high technology of the medical field (brain scanners
and heart transplants) has led to a new interest in the family doctor
and neighborhood clinics. A novel high tech/high touch example is
citizen band (CB) radio: people using this technology to get in touch
with another human being--anybody! And, moving closer to our offices,
the high technology of word processing has initiated a revival of
handwritten notes and letters. The high technology of chemistry and
pharmacology produced the pill, which led to a revolution in life
styles (away from either/or to multiple-option). Jet airplanes have
led only to more meetings. A poignant example of high touch/high tech
is how the high technology of life-sustaining equipment in hospitals led
to a new concern for the quality of death (and to the hospice movement).

Whenever institutions introduce new technology to customers or
employees, they should build in a high touch component; if they don't,
people will try to create their own or reject the new technology. That
may account, for example, for the public's resistance to automation and
electronic accounting. Electronic Funds Transfer (EFT) is failing
everywhere.

The high technology of the computer has been somewhat intimidating
to many of us, but now I see its high-touch potential: "computer as
liberator." Let me explain. A company with 40,000 employees has always
treated those 40,000 the same; it had to because that was the only way
it could keep track of them. And that has been unfair, because people
are different. Now with the computer to keep track, that company can
have a different arrangement with each of its employees as to relation
of salary to retirement benefits, work hours, job objective, and so

forth. And that is the trend: each of us having an individually-tailored contract with our employer. Also, the computer will outmode the hierarchical system of organization (and that is liberating!). We had to have a hierarchy in order to keep track of everybody and what they were up to. Now with the computer to keep track we can restructure to horizontal organizations of many small entrepreneurial groups. The pyramid has been outdated by the new technology.

    5. There are the beginnings of a job revolution in America, a basic restructuring of the work environment from top-down to bottom-up. Whenever pressing economic trends converge with changing personal values, you get change in a society. That's why we can start to look for some revolutionary changes in the workplace. A whole new attitude toward American workers is on the way. And it could result in a revitalization of the spirit of work and America's sagging productivity.

    Here's the situation: The productivity growth rate is on a dismal downswing. Last year was the worst for productivity improvement in the nation's history. At the same time, over the last two decades, personal values have been changing radically; there's a growing demand for more satisfaction from life. Workers feel it, too. Their psychic pain is reflected in their low productivity. They are sick of being treated like machines in the service of increased productivity. Workers refuse to produce and even deliberately sabotage the products they make. They are no longer content with the traditional remedies offered up by labor unions, such as more pay, four-day weeks, better health benefits. What they really want, like everybody else, is deep human satisfaction from their work.

    But industry had no compelling need to give it to them--until now. These dropping productivity figures will finally force industry, in economic desperation, to give more than token attention to the mental health of workers. The workplace is in for a good shaking up. And the American worker is about to be saved by one of the most unlikely forces in society--call it humanization, personal growth, "the human potential movement," participatory management, the values of the '60s. Call it whatever, it is about to converge with the economic necessity of the '70s and '80s to rescue the American worker from a deadened existence. For one thing, American industry is beginning to eye the way Japanese companies are run. Japan's productivity runs circles around ours. As I mentioned earlier, it takes Japanese workers 13 man-hours to build a car, compared with 30 man-hours for American workers.

    It's often mistakenly thought that Japanese workers are so productive because they perform like robots, ever subservient to authority. The opposite is true. Unlike American workers, the Japanese are given enormous freedom both to plan and to execute their work and solve problems alone without the help or interference of managers. The plants are run not from the "top down" like ours where managers deliver orders, but from the "bottom up" where workers make many crucial decisions. Fully 90% of Japan's industrial work force is organized in work groups of 8 to 11 people. The whole theory is: the workers know their jobs better than anyone else, and given a chance, workers will be creative and self-motivated. Interestingly, the Japanese developed some of their management techniques from the theories of our own humanistic psychologists, such as the late Abraham Maslow.

When the Japanese use their techniques on American workers, the changes are astounding. The Japanese Matsushita Company several years ago took over a Motorola plant near Chicago and began to produce Quasar TV sets. The company retained 1,000 on-line workers but dismissed half of the 600 supervisors and managers. Within two years, production doubled and the reject rate of sets dropped from 60% to 4%. Moreover, through good quality control, the company reduced its annual warranty costs from $14 million to $2 million. Just think, too, of the countless consumers who were spared the frayed nerves of dealing with defective products. That alone is an important contribution to the nation's sanity.

Our workers are not stupid or lazy. They, like everybody else, want a chance for more personal satisfaction. And they are about to get it--even if the trigger is such an eye-glazing event as lower productivity figures. U.S. industry leaders may not understand such a trend as changing personal values, but they do understand dropping productivity.

Because of how economically interlaced the United States is with the rest of the world, the only weapon it has against inflation that is in its full control is productivity improvement. As Peter Drucker says in his new book, Managing in Turbulent Times, (Harper & Row, 1980) productivity improvement will be management's most important task for the '80s. And in this regard, for the '80s, creative management will be more important than creative technology.

6. Ageism has replaced racism and sexism as the society's major anti-discrimination preoccupation. The recession of concern regarding racism and sexism will last for from five to ten years. In the United States, concern about racism started to recede about eight years ago and concern about sexism started to recede about two years ago. There's sort of a tolerance box in the United States society--we can only handle so much concern, or so much information, or so much attention in connection with discrimination. And that box in the '60s, was almost completely filled with concerns about racism. About eight years ago, concerns about racism in this society started to recede, and that box started to fill up with concerns about sexism. Two years ago concerns about sexism started to recede in this society. And that box quickly filled up (perhaps two-thirds full) with concerns about ageism. And I think that recession in concerns about sexism and racism will continue for four or five years, as we are more preoccupied with concerns about ageism. Part of the ageism concern, of course, led to the delay of mandatory retirement from 65 to 70. The next Congress, I'm pretty sure, is going to wipe it out altogether. There's going to be no mandatory retirement in the United States, just as there is none in the bellwether states of California and Connecticut. At the same time, early retire-ment is a very strong and continuing trend. They're both there--multiple-option. Ralph Tyler used to say, "You can tell if you're being educated if your options are increasing." And the reverse, if they're decreasing. And that's why he was concerned about specialization. In fact, there's new evidence that shows that your I.Q. actually goes down in the process of getting a Ph.D. We all suspected that. In any case, multiple-options. Even though concerns about sexism are in recession, that doesn't mean we're not going to be concerned. That means that

there's a readjustment of priorities. And in that concern about
sexism in this society, we're moving from the point of equal pay for
equal work to a new idea that's being pushed called "equal pay for
work of comparable value." Why should a carpenter get more than a
nurse? Well, we know why a carpenter gets more than a nurse; because
men are carpenters and nurses are women, and men decide. Why should a
dog-catcher get more than someone in a daycare place? These are the
new questions that are being asked.

Business is wholly unprepared for a complete removal of mandatory
retirement in the United States. Many companies in the United States
are already operating in a slow-growth mode. Some are even in a no-
growth mode. One of the biggest problems created in such circumstances
is the slow down in promotions. When a company is growing very fast,
with people being promoted all the time, the place practically runs
itself. But how do you manage an institution where you can't promote
people? Or where promotion comes very slowly.

Our universities are trying to manage in a negative-growth mode.
The tenure system is going to eliminate an entire generation of
scholars because there is no place for them. If you add to a slow- or
no-growth mode the end of mandatory retirement (no matter how much you
sweeten the incentives to leave early, many people will exercise an
option to stay on), you have complicated tremendously the task of
running an institution. It further dries up the principle incentive
for good performance: promotion.

Many different kinds of incentives are now being studied as a substitute for promotions, the principal traditional incentive for good
performance. Sabbaticals are one possibility. For example, entire
work forces could be given a tenth-year, or eighth-year sabbatical.
However, there are more imaginative approaches, and I think the end of
mandatory retirement will catalyze many rearrangements in our work
force. One intriguing idea would treat a new occupation or career as
an incentive. Consider a person who is, say, 44 and a lawyer, but who
would rather be a designer. The problem has always been that such a
person can't afford, financially, to go back. There is the possibility,
however, for the person to have a transitional period, during which to
consult backward and apprentice forward, but staying at about the same
salary.

It appears, therefore, that the end to mandatory retirement will
bring with it many changes in the present arrangement of dividing life
into separate periods of education, work, and retirement. The question
is, how do we, both as individuals and as a society, get out of these
"three boxes of life," which are more or less entirely unrelated. There
are very few specialists looking at all three of these divisions and
their relationship to one another. But I think the end of mandatory
retirement and some powerful economic reasons will force us to look at
them. In 1945, 35 people were in that middle box for every one person
on social security. Last year, the ratio was 3.2 to 1, a ten-fold
change in 30 years. The amount of work relative to the population has
shrunk so much that the people in the middle box are going to have to
share their work with those in the other two boxes, the young and the
old; and while they are sharing, and not working, they have to have
options to do other things.

7. <u>Equal access to capital will be the new rights issue, following earlier claims to equal access to education and health care</u>. During the '50s and '60s in the United States, equal access to education was demanded as a right. This was followed by demands for equal access to health care. Now a new equity issue is emerging: a push towards equal access to capital. This is manifested by what has happened to that phenomenon called red-lining. Within a relatively short period of time, this method of grading investment risks has gone from something considered to be a solid business practice to something that is now illegal in many parts of the country. In essence, the question comes down to this: why should <u>you</u> get money to buy a house when <u>I</u> can't get money to buy a house?

As to other areas of the economy, there have been hearings in Washington on whether or not the government should be involved in apportioning the increasingly limited capital pie--in deciding which companies should have access to capital. The question being posed here is: Why should <u>your</u> company get money when <u>my</u> company isn't getting any? And in the area of consumer credit, more and more credit is being advanced as a right, to women, the young, and the poor.

8. <u>Throughout the United States, notions of "appropriate scale" are reshaping our physical and organizational environment</u>. Notions of appropriate scale ricocheted through this society as fast as I have seen anything move. It started four or five years ago with E.F. Schumacher's book <u>Small is Beautiful</u> (Harper & Row, 1976), which advocated inter-mediate technologies--e.g., technologies that can increase output without decreasing employment levels. For example, he saw that the use of big combines and chemicals in India to accelerate agricultural production knocked 99 out of every 100 farmers out of work. What the Indians needed, Schumacher concluded, was to increase their technology just a little bit (an intermediate technology, a better plow), so that production would go up without reducing the work force. Notions of intermediate technology were soon broadened in this country to appropriate technology, and then, interestingly, to appropriate scale.

What is the appropriate scale of anything, let alone technology? What is the appropriate scale of government? To raise an army, it is surely federal; whereas for public welfare it may be neighborhood. As to appropriate scale for corporations, if the activity involves putting gas in an automobile it is the neighborhood service station; but if it involves exploration, appropriate scale becomes, by comparison, huge, like raising an army. In general, if corporations start from where people are, they are more likely to be understood and to have their ideas accepted.

9. <u>Issues of corporate governance--involving questions of leader-ship of American companies--will have an important impact on business in the '80s</u>. Corporate governance is going to be a big issue for business in the '80s. That'll be expressed at two levels. One level is on the composition of the Board of Directors, a lot of people pushing for a Board of Directors to be entirely composed of independent directors with only the CEO being on the board, and not serving as chairman. And the other part of corporate government has to do with the way decisions are made inside a corporation. Without going into that, let me just say that those are going to be big issues in the '80s for business.

10. <u>The most important trend in this century is the continuing</u>
<u>shift of the United States from a representative democracy to a</u>
<u>participatory democracy</u>. Let me tell you what I mean by the shift
from a representative democracy to a participatory democracy. In a
representative democracy, you elect someone for two, four, or six
years. And they go out and represent you. And then come back, and
if you think they've done a good job, you reelect them. If not, you
turn them out. Participatory democracy says, "Okay, we've elected you
to represent us, but if anything comes up that impacts on our lives,
you've got to check with us." Now what happened about a year and a
half ago is that almost unconsciously, companies said "Hey, wait a
minute." (By the way, it was some companies, because here again, it's
not either/or, it's multiple-option.) Some companies said, "Wait a
minute, we're participants, too." And companies started to become
more and more assertive about things that impacted on their corporate
lives. And that is entirely in tune with the times. In the meantime,
some of those things that we call corporate social responsibility are
being put on the shelf, as we really, in a much more participatory way,
engage the society and speak out and become assertive about those
things that impact on our corporate lives. As I said, that is
entirely in tune with the times.

As we move further into a participatory society, we must
increasingly often ask the key guiding question of such a society,
namely: should the people whose lives are affected by a decision
be part of the <u>process</u> of arriving at that decision. This question
applies whether we are dealing with our children, our spouses, our
employees, our customers, or the citizens of a society.

The decade of the '80s will be very exciting and uncertain. We
must make uncertainty our friend. It is, among other things, the only
certainty we have. In the decade of the '80s, we will be restructuring
our society from an industrial to an information society; we are
decentralizing at home while at the same time we move into a truly
world economy where the redistribution of production spells opportunity
for all of us; we are becoming an increasingly high touch world as we
continue to push high tech; we are becoming a multiple-option, highly
market-segmented society; and we will be a more participatory society
with greater opportunities for each of us to realize his or her
potential. In short, we will be a much more complicated society, and
the period of working through the structural changes will be painful,
but we will be a more interesting, creative, and nourishing society.

TELECOMMUNICATIONS AND VALUE SYSTEMS:
Policy Issues for the Information Society

by

Richard Byrne   and John E. Ruchinskas
Acting Dean   Research Associate
Annenberg School of Communications   Annenberg School of Communications
University of Southern California   University of Southern California

We are living in an era of unprecedented growth and change in human communication, a technological renaissance. New applications of computing and telecommunication technologies are flowering all about us, revolutionizing our ability to create, store, retrieve, manipulate, transmit and receive information.

Human communication capabilities have changed technologically more in our own lifetime than in the 40,000-year history of our species. Whether we call it the "post-industrial society,"[1] "the information economy,"[2] "the third wave,"[3] or the "new world information order,"[4] there is clear recognition that we are entering a new historical era as a society. We are changing from an economy based on the manufacture of goods to one dominated by the production and delivery of services, and most of those services will be the creation, transmission, and manipulation of information, a shift largely enabled by advancing communications technologies.[5]

However, it is not simply our economic system that is undergoing change. No fact of our existence can escape the impact of changing communications technology. Our work environments, our educational institutions, our modes of doing business and conducting the affairs of government, and even our home lives are changing dramatically. In 1900 approximately one in every ten workers handled information, with the remainder handling physical goods. Now one in every two workers handles information, and the percentage is rapidly increasing.

Specific Communication Technologies

This steep acceleration curve of new technological communication capability makes it hard to imagine what extraordinary optical, chemical, mechanical, and electronic breakthroughs may appear soon. Things are moving so fast that we feel our solutions to problems may be obsolete before we can work them out thoroughly. One certainty is that most technologies discussed here will seem simplistic or self-evident by the time they are considered by the reader.

Popular earlier technologies continue to exert their appeal. Commercial television broadcasting is watched by ever-increasing numbers of people for ever-increasing lengths of time. However, a newer form of television viewing, "narrowcasting" by cable television, is augmenting

broadcast television, and in some ways offering it a direct challenge
for viewership.

Despite an inhibitive regulatory environment for almost a decade,
cable TV now reaches 20% of American households. Bidding for new
franchises is furious, and cable subscribers' current choices from
among 20-40 viewing options pales in the face of proposed 100 channel
systems. Local broadcast signals are supplemented with regional
channels, satellite retransmitted "Superstations" from around the
country, and a host of information and other interactive services.

The Qube system in Columbus, Ohio, has provided a working example
of these emerging systems, allowing viewers to interact with a central
computer via a numeric keypad attached to their sets. The audience can
immediately react to a presidential speech, tell a talk show host when
to move on to the next guest, or order products by shopping at home.
Subscribers can have burglar and smoke alarms attached to the system to
monitor their homes, automatically notifying police and fire departments
in case of trouble. Other locations have used these systems to have
town meetings, with each citizen voting from the home.

The simple technology involved in distributing television over a
wire is being revolutionized by computers that can interact with
subscribers, by satellites that broadcast dozens of channels to
inexpensive earth stations, and by increasingly sophisticated telecommunications systems that allow more and more channels to be carried
on the same physical wire.

Elsewhere, the change is even greater. Cable TV is being joined
by rapid diffusion of videocassette recorders offering an alternative
means of distributing entertainment programming. Videogames also
compete for the television screen, offering the "viewer" more and more
options and control over the television viewing experience. The passive
viewer may now become an active programmer, participant, and even
producer through these distribution and playback technologies.

Developments in teletext and videotex systems offer a new world of
information to the consumer.[6] Broadcasters can insert hundreds of pages
of information into the standard TV signal, allowing home viewers to
read information about news, weather, airplane departures, civic affairs,
or current entertainment events on their home television sets. Videotex systems, through which users link their TV sets or more complex
"integrated video terminals" to local or remote computer data banks via
telephone, offer access to hundreds of thousands of pages of text. Such
systems provide a sort of "800" electronic information window.

A videodisc, a lightweight plastic disc no larger than a long-
playing record, is recorded and scanned for playback by a low intensity
laser. Forty billion bits of data can be stored on one side of one
disc, the equivalent of a color and sound motion picture, or 54,000
still photographic frames. The videodisc can be used for individualized instruction, record storage, or home entertainment. One videodisc
can hold the approximate content of the complete Encyclopedia Britannica,
the Bible and the Sears and Roebuck catalog with pages to spare.

The combination and availability of these technologies in our homes
is causing our entertainment and information options to explode, our
leisure activity patterns to be challenged and our household tasks
reshaped. Daily household business is changing in the face of "smart"

machines which regulate and program themselves. Sewing machines and microwave ovens can be controlled and monitored by a combination of computer and telecommunications feedback. We not only can pre-program our entertainment devices through presently available home computers, but also can alter our physical environment by linking our heating, cooling, and lighting systems. Prior concepts of household chores are changing, as is our ability to create a sensory environment in the home that matches our habits and our whims.

Relatively inexpensive cameras contain microminiaturized integrated circuits in the form of electronic "chips," which permit them to set their own shutter speed and their own aperture. They can choose between either option. They can focus themselves in the dark. They can set off a flash, measure the light, and automatically stop exposure when it is perfect. When combined with a motor drive, such a camera can be sent merrily off for you on a summer vacation. You won't even need to accompany it. You will save on meals and housing, and the pictures will be perfect.

In the realm of work, the office of the future is likely to see far less paper movement and far more electron movement.[7] Electronic messaging systems are quickly becoming cost efficient compared to transporting mail, and offer instantaneous message delivery. Tele-conferencing as a substitute for travel is an increasingly considered option.[8] The telephone system is handling an increasing amount of data transmission already, and individual terminals are able to access and utilize massive stores of data. The same satellites that provide tele-vision transmission and the possibility of direct broadcasting to the home currently allow businesses to move data faster and less expensively than ever before.

The home may become less of a leisure environment and more a central location for our overall life. Telecommunications links already offer a select few workers the opportunity to transmit their work to the central office electronically while physically staying at home. A new rural society may result, linked electronically with business, educa-tional, and cultural centers. This circumstance would have profound impact on patterns of social interaction, as well as savings in consumption of energy resources.

Through a concept called "convergence," these communication media are also interacting and blending in unprecedented ways. Hand calcu-lators, combined with computer games and television sets attached to "modems," can use a telephone link to connect with other similar home-based microcomputer systems, or even to large mainframe computer instal-lations. Those comforting old days when an adding machine was an adding machine, a television set was a television set, and a telephone was a telephone, and that was that, are gone forever.

These changes in communication technology are creating parallel yet opposing trends toward centralization and decentralization. The decreasing cost of transmission, continued diffusion of computer tech-nology and increased efficiencies in switching and data base management are all driving the creation of massive computer networks. Remote locations and stores of data are increasingly linked by computer and telecommunications technologies, creating a degree of control and centralized knowledge unimaginable in past eras. Plain old telephone service may soon be transformed in conjunction with an integrated video terminal to provide a powerful home communications facility linked to the center and capable of instantaneous delivery of electronic mail and message systems, combining facsimile, office automation, record and graphic communications.

Yet, each of these same advancements in computer technology further enables the individual user to concentrate computing power at a local location, or within the terminal itself. Mini and micro processors now allow individual users to perform tasks that formerly required massive main frame computers. Computing power is affordable for the small user, who no longer needs to be affiliated with a large organization to gain access to main frame computer systems. The emerging phenomena of teleconferencing, computer-conferencing and distributed work centers also point toward a decreasing role of a central location, and an increase in individual flexibility and choice.

Technology has created the opportunity for both scenarios, allow- ing greater centralization and control of knowledge, yet also encour- aging decentralization and user flexibility. Clearly, the determining factor is not the technology itself. It is the application of that technology.

Listing all the burgeoning new technologies would occupy more space than is available in a single volume, but a summary of the general areas of most explosive expansion may be useful:

Highpowered direct broadcast communication satellites

Broadband fiber optics

Powerful and inexpensive computers

Telephonic technologies

Micro and Miniprocessors

Cable television

Videocassettes

Videodiscs

Cybernetics

Microminiaturization

Electrochemistry

Digitalization of imagery and sound

Magnetic bubble memories

Superspeed computers

Large scale circuit integration

Teletext

Computer graphics

Voice synthesizers

Voice recognition systems

Human- and machine-readable information retrieval systems

Plasma terminals with touch sensitive fingertip scanning

Voice actuated access systems

Digital image enhancement and analysis

Holographic photography

Holographic data storage and retrieval

Large scale computer-based telecommunication networks

Throughout the communications field, the trend is toward cheaper, smaller, lighter, yet more powerful hardware. Transmission and storage costs are decreasing, while capabilities have increased a hundredfold in less than a decade. These tools are more energy efficient and are non-pollutive, offering a contrast to prior trends in technological development.

All of these technologies are currently market driven, and the marching order seems to be, "Get them out there!" There is little evidence that serious consideration is being given to the impact of these technologies on the quality of life of their owners and users. Science and technology are providing the equipment and the capability to link that equipment in striking new ways. But we have not yet developed the human means of coping with these powerful new social forces.

What effect will widespread use of these technologies have on human relationships? What assets will we gain, and what risks do we face? What myths will be established or destroyed, and at what cost to us?

Values Systems

Since the beginning of human experience, concepts like the good, the virtuous, the true, and the right have inspired and guided all people. Some believe that values are divinely proclaimed, and thus absolute and fixed. Others believe that values spring from the necessities of each time and place. In either case values are ideals that represent beliefs about ultimate goals and modes of conduct. People live their lives according to their values, and govern the methods and manner in which they strive to accomplish their purposes. Values stand behind our every choice and action.

Much care has been taken with the scholarly analysis of values and valuation.[9] Many commentators on value systems agree that there are usually a small number of global, or "terminal" values, which form the central core of an individual's value system. These are closely held personal values of high salience in important life choices. Examples of such global values might be self-respect, freedom, equality, family security, social recognition, comfort, or pleasure.

There are also a larger number of domain specific, or "instrumental" values, which shape experiences in specific situations. In economic, social, or religious transactions, a person may be influenced by the values of ambition, helpfulness, honesty, imagination, independence, affection, politeness, or responsibility.

Societies also have value systems. One dramatic change in recent years has been the erosion, or transformation, depending upon your point of view, of a unified value system in the United States. While this country has always been a melting pot, it is now marked by diverse values amounting to chasms between generations and different special interest groups.

Specific Values Associated With Telecommunications

Telecommunications technologies in general are seen to have certain essential values. In a period of rising costs and declining resources, communication is displaying a linear decrease in costs, and an exponential increase in the capability to store and transmit data.[10] Timeliness, speed, convenience, linkage, and social efficiency are commonly attributed to telecommunications, and are seen as significant benefits. The assumption is that a better informed and more effective populace will result, with increases in both productivity and satisfaction.[11]

Major influences have also been wielded on American value systems by the content of telecommunications. American public and private life has obviously been shaped in part by broadcast television, both in commercial advertising and in dramatic programming. The common message is that the ideal is to be young, attractive, powerful, and sexually athletic. The stream of dream imagery from television changes our images of ourselves, and aspects of that disparate reality become actualized in public behavior.

The effects of current broadcasting, and of future telecommunications, are profound, and extremely difficult to measure or predict with precision. Certainly the disintegration of some aspects of the mass society, the growth of alternative lifestyles, social dislocations, cult-based religion, and loss of respect for older hierarchical command systems are due in part to the role of the media. How can we prepare for the ultimate implications of an environment filled with new and different media forms?

Context for Telecommunications

Key questions in examining the future of telecommunications are, "Who is the user?" and "What is the context in which that user will use the new technologies?" The "user" will not be an amorphous, androgynous "consumer," but will be a specific human being using different technologies in different settings for different purposes each day. The user may be a knowledge worker, a technician, a representative of a larger group, a novice entering a complex system, or a consumer in the home. Each user will have a different level of sophistication, and will have different social expectations.

Conflicts in processes and priorities will arise from these user distinctions.[12] At the international level the free flow of information, so important, at least in principle, to Americans, will not be seen as benign. Unbalanced information flow in a global information environment will stimulate charges of cultural imperialism and the development of quota systems and regulatory controls. Contention about the importation of distant signals and varying forms of transborder data flow, which at one time were issues of concern only to bordering nations, now occur world wide, due to the 44,600 mile child's hop made possible by the satellite networks girdling the earth. Some officials in each country will lead the drive to buy in to the global information network, while others will press for cultural and economic autonomy and restricted borders. At any rate, communications may replace geography and transportation as the basis for organization of some governments.

At the level of the individual there are a multitude of questions that involve human values as constrained by social, economic, and political forces, as well as consumer demands.[13]

Will telecommunications reflect diversity and pluralism?

Will electronics be used for highly personal and private inter-action, and how?

Will fractionation of the public increase?

Will there be more or less work, and where?

Will telecommunications impact the increasing number of working women, and how?

Will communication alter transportation options?

Will the trend of increasing discretionary income continue?

What valuation will consumers place on entertainment and information?

What communication and information "rights" will develop, and at what costs?

Will instantaneous electronic polling prove to be a boon to democracy, or a threat?

Will the new rural society, former urban dwellers, have unattainable high communication expectations?

Will variable price sensitivity develop for communication per income, region, background, ethnicity and lifestyle?

What will the effect of new electronic social networks be?

Good News and Bad News

Clearly, there is no one mandated future, but rather many possible futures from which we can choose to create the actual events and effects which will occur. The essential point about futures scenarios is that each contains "good news" and "bad news," depending on our own conscious actions and the impact of those actions on our value systems.

All of life is yin-yang, bittersweet. While we read a book, we are not exercising strenuously, both of which may be desirable activities. While we play chess, we are unable to pay the piano, and so it goes. The key is to develop a balanced pattern of behavior that capitalizes on whatever opportunities are available and acknowledges our individual and group value systems to produce a state of satisfaction.

The high technology scenarios outlined here suggest that current trends toward mechanization and technological proliferation will accelerate. Increasingly, the gross national product of many nations will be based on information services. Generations will mature, comfortable with daily interaction with technological systems and, in fact, dependent upon them for gratification.

The good news inherent in a high-technology scenario is impressive indeed. Tutorial computers may provide completely individualized education in the school and in the home. Telemedicine via satellite may bring the state of the art in diagnosis and treatment from the urban centers to the most remote rural areas. Home information centers may offer an "electronic hearth" around which the family can reconvene and learn to grow together. Humans may feel greater self-esteem through increased competency and specialization, and increased inter-dependence. Accelerated international development may result from instantaneous interaction with other cultures. In fact, we may see the birth of the true global village, so long heralded and so seldom experienced.

The bad news lurking in a high technology scenario brings delight to the heart of the most committed doomsayer. A technological takeover may truly occur. As we rely increasingly on technology we become increasingly vulnerable to it. Havoc could result from power shortages and brownouts or from increased costs or arbitrary cutoff of power by the gatekeepers at the control centers. Apathy may be widespread as those outside the information elite turn the running of things over to the managers. Self-esteem of those deprived of access to technology could drop to an all-time low. White collar crime would undoubtedly escalate. Teleconferencing run amok could eliminate the human touch. Cultural and economic effects of information pollution may make environmental pollution pale to insignificance. The information elite may be reduced to an even smaller number of people, and the gap between the information haves and information have-nots may expand to become unbridgeable. We may produce a generation that knows everything about computers, but little about human relationships. Cut off from our cultural, spiritual and ancestral roots, we could drift in electronic space.

Although most projections indicate that we are headed toward this kind of technology-driven future, which will result in a global communication-based economy, another scenario is possible, a world of low technology or no technology. Such a world might come about of necessity as a result of energy shortages and overdependency on massive, linked technical systems, culminating in ultimate system collapse. It might also evolve from choice, a conscious turning away from techno-logical alternatives and a move toward the Buddhist economics of E.F. Schumacher, which he called "technology with a human face."[14]

Again, such a scenario is replete with "good news" and "bad news." The good news might include a greater sense of self-reliance and personal competence, paralleling that of the high tech scenario but based in other skills. A reinforcement of family and kinship ties might accompany a refocus on humanistic values. The contrasting yet complementary characteristics of self-actualization and a greater sense of community might coexist as prime values in our culture.

The bad news of low technology is equally evident. We could deny the intellectual, economic, and scientific victories of the last hundred years and experience retrograde social development. We could deny the personal and cultural benefits of past technological advances. Isolation might result in an apathy which could rival or exceed that from high technology. Narcissism and self-centeredness would undoubtedly increase and could result in solipsism of unprecedented scope. Social alienation and cultural retardation would be ever-present dangers.

Conflicting Legitimate Interests

An additional complication is that the arena is filled with conflicting legitimate interests. There is no single, correct way to satisfy competing demands. Any law or regulation is wrong part of the time, and any law or regulation is wrong at different times. Economic efficiency contends with social benefits. The needs and rights of the individual must constantly be weighed against the needs and rights of the society. Distributed information processing decreases the role and significance of information centers, and jeopardizes a traditional method of production and distribution. Should regulations and commerce primarily serve the professional, or the informed and motivated consumer?

There are no simple answers in these deliberations, but it is clear that this is one of the most important fields for consideration in the development of public policy regarding telecommunications of the future. Who benefits? In what ways? Who supplies services? Who pays? And how much? How can the inevitable conflicts be resolved best?

Agenda for the Future

Once we have a clear image of possible futures, it is critical that we commit ourselves to a preferable future. We should do all we can to blend the best of all the scenarios. Each of these and many others we can posit will exist in varying degrees in various cultures and in various parts of the daily experiences of each individual. The key is to select and use the appropriate technology for the task and the personal values of the user. A person may work in a high technology environment and seek the solace and comfort of a traditional home filled with antiques, peace, and quiet. Others may work in fields that have not changed in essence for generations, but enjoy at home the latest state-of-the-art advances in videodisc recording, complete with large-screen video playback and interactive information systems.

Some analysts assume a kind of technological determinism: "The future is coming; hope you know when to duck." This ignores the genuine influence which we can exert in creating that world of the future. The choice is not between humans and technology. What can the individual, the organization, the policymakers, the citizenry at large do to capitalize on the inherent benefits of these scenarios? What can we do to avoid their most disquieting aspects?

First, we need to identify the full range of stakeholders, both informed and unwitting, and engage the opinion leadership of each group.

Serious and accurate dialogue should occur at every level of the information enterprise: research, policies, management, production, operations, distribution, supply, support, consumption and utilization.

Recommendations for Stakeholders

This essay is intended to sketch the outlines of the technological present, and suggest trends for the near future. It is hoped that stakeholders in these issues will engage in the necessary dialogue to develop value-based criteria for future communications policies. Needed and desired actions will grow out of such deliberations. However, some preliminary indications of useful actions may serve as a stimulus to the reader for independent, personal actions.

For communication planners:
Develop long range and short range communication plans.
Become aware and stay aware of the state of the art in communications.
Learn to use values clarification techniques.
Identify conflicting legitimate interests and pay special attention to them.
Don't violate long-range goals in short-term decision making.
Read journals and literature outside technical fields which show the direction and intensity of social changes.
Alternate the long and short views; think about the big picture often.
Constantly reevaluate goals and objectives in light of users' needs.

For producers, directors, and information "creatives":
Think about the users, or the audience.
Create programming to fill specific unserved needs.
Present diversity, and provide alternatives.
Challenge old assumptions.
Recognize emerging patterns in social behavior.
Be enthusiastic; be playful.
Press for your best at all times.
Expect a transformation in attitudes, illusions, beliefs, myths, value systems, and ultimately in the quality of life.

For researchers:
Identify values represented in the process and content of telecommunications.
Track convergence and divergence of values.
Identify unserved communication, entertainment and information needs.
Develop formative and summative evaluation techniques to a higher degree of refinement.
Study how communication technologies are diffused and adopted in various user groups.
Continually monitor developing media usage patterns.
Evaluate the impacts of changes in policies and resource allocations.

For educators:

>Recognize that educational institutions must adapt to accommodate to telecommunications in some ways.

>Assist educational institutions to make appropriate applications of technologies to the process of facilitating learning.

>Avoid the seductive tendency to "accommodate" by simply emulating the style and technique of popular media.

>Study the advances being made in self-paced, self-instructional modules commercially available for in-home use.

For parents and consumers:

>Recognize communications as an issue and area of personal concern.

>Develop personal competency in values clarification of some practical kind.

>Plan consumption and use of telecommunications with family members.

>Be selective in communication activities, and be an active participant with involved family members.

>Learn from your children, who understand the media environment intimately.

>Be a critical consumer, and an active advocate for improved communication programming in all media.

>Have clearly in mind what you would prefer to see in communication media, and express your views to responsible authorities.

>Develop plans with your family for enriching, rewarding personal activities not connected with communication media.

Conclusion

The human species is crossing one of the Great Divides in our history. The communication revolution of the past 50 years has irrevocably changed the nature of the world. We have new perceptions of the physical universe and our place in it, since communications technology has shown us the extraordinarily slow and fast phenomena, the infinitely small and huge aspects of our place in space. Our new skills and experiences are creating new langugages, myths, beliefs... in short, new humans.

We have before us an astonishingly rich range of potential choices. The actions we all take, individually and in concert, will determine whether we have succeeded in choosing for the welfare and fulfillment of human beings or merely for the care, feeding, and greater glory of machines.

Notes

[1]Daniel Bell, The Coming of Post-Industrial Society (New York: Basic Books, 1973).

[2]Marc Porat, The Information Economy (Washington, D.C.: U.S. Department of Commerce, 1978).

[3]Alvin Toffler, The Third Wave (New York: Morrow, 1980).

[4]Jonathan F. Gunter, The U.S. and the Debate on the World Information Order (Washington, D.C.: Academy for Educational Development, 1979).

[5]James Martin, Future Developments in Telecommunications, 2nd ed. (Englewood Cliffs, NJ: Prentice-Hall, 1977).

[6]Daniel Bell, "Teletext and Technology: The Coming of Post-Industrial Society," Encounter, June 1970, pp. 9-29.

[7]Robert Johansen, Jacques Vallee, and F. Spangler, Electronic Meetings (Reading, MA: Addison-Wesley, 1979).

[8]Jack M. Nilles, F. Roy Carlson, Jr., Paul Gray, and Gerhard J. Hanneman, The Telecommunications-Transportation Tradeoff: Options for Tomorrow (New York: Wiley, 1976).

[9]John Dewey, Theory of Valuation (Chicago: University of Chicago Press, 1966); Abraham H. Maslow, The Psychology of Being (Princeton, NJ: Van Nostrand, 1962); Milton Rokeach, The Nature of Human Values (New York: Free Press, 1973); Milton Rokeach, Beliefs, Attitudes, and Values (San Francisco: Jossey-Bass, 1968); W.H. Werkmeister, Man and His Values (Lincoln, NE: University of Nebraska Press, 1967).

[10]Ithiel de Sola Poole, ed., The Social Impact of the Telephone (Cambridge, MA: MIT Press, 1977).

[11]Jacques Ellul, The Technological Society (New York: Vintage Books, 1964).

[12]Gordon Thompson, A Memo From Mercury (Ottawa, Canada: Bell Northern Research, 1977).

[13]Rob Kling, "Alternatives EFT Developments and Quality of Life: A Theoretical Analysis," Telecommunications Policy, March 1979, pp. 52-64.

[14]E.F. Schumacher, Small Is Beautiful (New York: Harper & Row, 1973).

Bibliography

Bell, Daniel. The Coming of Post-Industrial Society. New York: Basic Books, 1973.

Bell, Daniel. "Teletext and Technology: The Coming of Post-Industrial Society," Encounter, June 1970, pp. 9-29.

Dewey, John. Theory of Valuation. Chicago: University of Chicago Press, 1966.

Ellul, Jacques. The Technological Society. New York: Vintage Books, 1964.

Gunter, Johnathan F. The U.S. and the Debate on the World Information Order. Washington, D.C.: Academy for Educational Development, 1979.

Johansen, Robert, Jacques Vallee, and F. Spangler. Electronic Meetings. Reading, MA: Addison-Wesley, 1979.

Kling, Rob. "Alternatives EFT Developments and Quality of Life: A Theoretical Analysis," Telecommunications Policy, March 1979, pp. 52-64.

Martin, James. Future Developments in Telecommunications. 2nd ed. Englewood Cliffs, NJ: Prentice-Hall, 1977.

Maslow, Abraham J. The Psychology of Being. Princeton, NJ: Van Nostrand, 1962.

Nilles, Jack M., F. Roy Carlson, Jr., Paul Gray, and Gerhard J. Hanneman. The Telecommunications-Transportation Tradeoff: Options for Tomorrow. New York: Wiley, 1976.

Poole, Ithiel de Sola, ed. The Social Impact of the Telephone. Cambridge, MA: MIT Press, 1977.

Porat, Marc. The Information Economy. Washington, D.C.: U.S. Department of Commerce, 1978.

Rokeach, Milton. Beliefs, Attitudes, and Values. San Francisco: Jossey-Bass, 1968.

Rokeach, Milton. The Nature of Human Values. New York: Free Press, 1973.

Schumacher, E.F. Small Is Beautiful. New York: Harper & Row, 1973.

Thompson, Gordon. A Memo From Mercury. Ottawa, Canada: Bell Northern Research, 1977.

Toffler, Alvin. The Third Wave. New York: Morrow, 1980.

Werkmeister, W.H. Man and His Values. Lincoln, NE: University of Nebraska Press, 1967.

USER NEEDS FOR INFORMATION IN THE YEAR 2000

by

Burt Nanus
Director
Center for Futures Research
University of Southern California

It is hard to imagine a broader charter than that of this chapter. We are all users of information, and our need for information differs with every one of the many roles we daily assume--worker, parent, citizen, decision maker, patient, teacher, consumer, judge, etc. Moreover, information itself is a strange commodity, for although it has definable costs of production and distribution and is of undeniable value to a user, it has peculiar properties which make it very difficult to generalize about it. For example:

1.) It is not homogenous like electricity or grain, but rather is extremely heterogeneous, with virtually infinite variations in response to individual conjunctions of supplier, processor, user, and channel of communication.

2.) It is rarely of value in itself, but rather requires a context, structure, or model within which it can be interpreted.

3.) Demand for information is a function of such variables as age, perishability, convenience, reliability, source, etc., as well as more traditional economic variables such as cost, quantity, and availability of supply.

4.) The role of information in an organization is so central to its management and functioning that it must be viewed as a fundamental factor of production like money and manpower.

5.) Both suppliers and users of information often need special protection by means of government intervention such as copyright and patent laws, privacy legislation, and fraud statutes.

The problem of assessing user needs in the future is further exacerbated by the fact that the environment of user needs is rapidly changing. Virtually everything in the social environment affects user needs and in turn is affected by information usage. Since the larger society and its dynamics are very complex and subject to fundamental change due to both chance occurrences and deliberate human interventions, there is no way to be comprehensive about an examination of user needs.

Nevertheless, we will try here to identify some important major trends in three domains--social values, economics, and business practices--and to make at least an initial attempt to interpret their significance for user needs.

Social Values and User Needs

American values are in transition. The cultural paradigm that has predominated over the past two centuries--namely "progress through economic growth"--is now being called into question by a large part of the population. This has happened not because of the failure of the economic growth paradigm, but because of its overwhelming success and the consequences of that success. This has been called by Willis Harman "the fundamental dilemma of industrial civilization," which he describes thusly:

> The basic paradigm that has dominated the industrial era including emphasis on individualism and free enterprise; material progress; social responsibility mainly the concern of the government; few restraints on capital accumulation; etc. . . ., has resulted in processess and states (e.g., extreme division of labor and special- ization, cybernation, stimulated consumption, planned obsolescence and waste, exploitation of common resources). . ., which end up counteracting human ends (e.g., enriching work roles, resource conservation, environmental enhancement, equitable sharing of the earth's resources). The result is a growing and massive challenge to the legitimacy of the present industrial system.[1]

The evidence of disaffection with the prevailing paradigm is abundant in America. High crime and divorce rates, urban blight, the failure of the educational process, the drug culture, television's success with "escape programming" (e.g., violence, soap operas, game shows), alienation and resentment directed toward government and other large institutions, etc. This discontent has resulted in large-scale experimentation with new social values ranging from communes to wife swapping to religious revivalism. Even those who are not given to radical experimentation share a feeling that all is not well with our quality of life. Energy, air, and water can no longer be considered free goods; the losers in the society are no longer powerless to press their demands (e.g., terrorists, New York blackout riots); unfettered technology has been shown to be a mixed blessing (e.g., nuclear plants, DDT, SST), and economic success seems unable to reduce unemployment or underemployment, prejudice, crime, alienation, and other ills.

As a result of these forces, there is a widespread search for alternative cultural paradigms to supplement or displace "progress through economic growth." Some have proposed a new humanism, envision- ing a society built upon cooperation, as opposed to competition, through the expansion of volunteerism, community development, consumer coopera- tives and other forms of mutual support mechanisms. Others have advocated voluntary simplicity, characterized by rugged individualism in an attempt to return to a simple life style, one that is more under the direct control of the individual. There are proposals for a return to theological orthodoxy or for a paradigm based on a more harmonious relationship between man and nature through the use of "appropriate technology." Still others focus on the quality of life, emphasizing a more balanced approach to human existence with economic criteria second to human criteria such as self-fulfillment at work and leisure, environmental enhancement, cultural enrichment and the primacy of human concerns over technical or economic concerns.

At the moment, and probably for the next two decades, all these paradigms (and others) will be competing for primacy, and no single one is likely to reach the consensus that was apparent for decades with the prior economic growth imperative. This suggests that the values domain for the next decade could be characterized as follows:

1.) Continued social conflict and discontent, accompanied by a good deal of social experimentation with new value systems.

2.) Increased government involvement in all aspects of society as the economic growth imperative weakens and the demand for more government planning to achieve noneconomic ends increases.

3.) A shift of concern from the concept of independence toward the concept of interdependence, with an accompanying shift from competition toward cooperation in dealing with social issues.

4.) More concern with the quality of life, living in harmony with nature, and the "recycle society."

5.) Increased emphasis upon work as self-fulfillment and the development of human capital as opposed to physical capital.

6.) More diversity and pluralism, with temporary shifting communities of interests.

7.) Lowered expectations with regard to material consumption and a concomitant emphasis upon more humane social institutions, with increased intellectual and spiritual interaction.

8.) Increasing emphasis on continuing education, life-long learning, multiple careers, and other means of assisting individuals to develop meaningful work and life trajectories.

In general, these developments are favorable to the rapid increase in user demand for information because information services tend to be nonpolluting, energy-efficient, mind-expanding, and enhancers of group interaction. Attitudes toward information services are likely to be mixed, with both dislike for depersonalizing technology and excitement about the opportunities for learning and exploring relationships with others. The ways in which these values impact upon user needs are shown in Figure 1.

Figure 1
Values Forces Affecting User Needs for Information

Effects on User Needs for Information

TRENDS	More Plentiful	More Accurate	More Reliable	Faster	Cheaper	More Accessible
1. Social Experimentation, Conflict	X					X
2. Increased Government Involvement	X	X	X		X	X
3. Greater Interdependence	X		X			X
4. Quality of Life, Recycle Society	X	X			X	
5. Development of Human Capital	X		X		X	X
6. Diversity and Pluralism	X					X
7. Lowered Goods Expectations	X					X
8. Emphasis on Meaningful Work Experiences	X					X

The values trends suggest that user needs for certain kinds of information services will increase substantially. Two classes of services are likely to receive particular impetus. The first is recreational services such as computer games, cultural programs on demand, and remote library access, since these applications are consonant with the trends toward an improved quality of life and self-development. The second class is educational services that include the whole range of applications that can be designed to enhance human awareness, such as computer-aided school instructions, adult courses via terminals, preschool language instruction, drill and practice exercises, and the like. The drive toward widespread participation and interaction suggests that providers of information services will be required to accommodate a very broad spectrum of users, including many who have little experience with computers. This may also involve needs to develop new capabilities to allow disenfranchised users greater access to information, including minority groups, prisoners, handicapped persons, and less educated people.

Economic Framework for User Needs

For the next two decades, economic growth will likely occur at a much slower rate than historic increases in GNP because of resource, environment, and energy constraints. For the same reason, inflation is expected to continue at a higher rate than in the past decades. There may be a slow transition to economic stability in the developed countries as more resources are diverted to developing countries in order to preserve world economic order. While absolute poverty may decrease, the gaps between rich and poor are likely to increase unless real efforts are made for more equitable wealth distribution.

Recently, the mix of jobs and products has been shifting toward information-related activities. Not only has the information sector of the economy grown faster than the total economy during the last 40 years, but the internal bureaucracy of governmental/business managers has grown at the same pace. The U.S. economy is now more complex, dynamic, and regulated than it has ever been before. Shifts in economic structure occur slowly, and it is likely that these forces will continue. As a result, the general climate for information services will continue to be favorable. Some of the specific economic trends that may impact upon user needs are suggested below.

1) Service Industry Expansion. It is well known that the agricultural and industrial sectors of the U.S. economy have been declining as a percentage of the entire economy at the expense of the services sector. What is not so generally known, however, is that the information occupations portion of the services sector has been the major factor in the increase of service occupations. The very rapid growth in both the demand and supply of information coincided approximately with the introduction of the computer. This dramatic increase in information services has prompted some scholars, such as Daniel Bell, to declare that we are already a "knowledge society" and that information will be the principal commodity in the modern post-industrial society. In fact, many of the services that have been growing most rapidly, such as education, communications, banking, insurance, and

legal services, are nearly entirely information-based. There is every reason to expect that the trend toward an information-based economy will expand even further in the coming decades.

2) <u>Resources Shortages</u>. In the long run, global demand for scarce resources--energy, water, arable land, certain metals and minerals, etc.--will lead to shortages that may place real limits on productive output. Within the next two decades, steadily increasing global demand for resources is expected to drive prices up so that certain commodities, such as oil, will become very expensive in comparison with others. The economic impact of this development will be to make information services, which are resource-efficient, more attractive than other products and services in the general economy. It may also lead to substitutions of information and labor for capital and energy where such substitutions are possible--e.g., substituting communication for transportation or sophisticated inventory control systems for buffer stocks.

3) <u>Environmental Cleanup</u>. The next two decades will, almost certainly, see a continued emphasis upon environmental responsibility, as industries, governments, municipalities, and every sector of the economy attempt to clean up the deleterious effects of prior production processes and to prevent further environmental degradation. The partial conversion from oil to coal alone will cause greatly increased environmental expenditures in all steps of the process from extraction to transportation to consumption. Many of the processes involved in cleaning up the environment require information services such as environmental monitoring, analysis of environmental impacts, process control, emission testing, and research and development.

4) <u>Government Expansion</u>. The government sector of the economy continues to expand as citizens demand services in such areas as crime prevention and control, recreation, job creation, urban planning, and education. Nearly all increases in government services are reflected in either increased labor costs or increased information processes, and the government is widely recognized as both the largest consumer and largest producer of information services in the U.S. economy. As our society becomes more complex, government's reliance on information services is likely to increase by an order of magnitude because of taxpayer pressures to hold down personnel costs.

5) <u>World Interdependence</u>. The world is becoming increasingly interdependent for trade, resources, and political stability. One result of this increasing interdependence is the burgeoning of multinational computer systems, defined as computers in one country linked to computers, data bases, or users in one or more other countries.[2] Such systems are already widely used for purposes as diverse as banking, airline reservations, multinational management information systems, news services, the space program, production and logistics operations, etc. In the coming decades, perhaps half of all foreign exchange operations will be carried out on multinational computer systems, and there will be a greatly increased use of such systems in multinational corporations for marketing, manufacturing, logistics, and credit functions. These world networks will very likely interface with domestic information services in the United States.

6) Expanded Technology Investment. Business and government investments in research and development activities, in general, are expected
to increase in response to the need for new technical approaches to
some of the above problems. Consumer investments in certain technologies will also increase, particularly information and communications
technologies. Recognizing the great expansion of capability per dollar
in computers and telecommunications, it is evident that there will be
a massive expansion of installed technical capability in these areas.

The net effect of these economic trends is to expand greatly user
demands for information, as suggested in Figure 2.

Figure 2
Economic Forces Affecting User Needs for Information

	Effects on User Needs for Information					
TRENDS	More Plentiful	More Accurate	More Reliable	Faster	Cheaper	More Accessible
Inflation					X	
Resource Shortages	X		X	X	X	X
Environmental Cleanup	X			X	X	X
Government Expansion	X	X	X		X	X
Government Regulation	X	X			X	X
Employment Expansion	X					X
World Interdependence	X				X	X

Users will be especially interested in information services that expand
citizen access to government services. Also in demand will be all those
information services required to make more careful use of high cost
energy, land, water, air and other environmental resources, and to
coordinate the vast bureaucracies established to control them. This
is likely to stimulate the development of many large, geographically
dispersed information networks.

The Business Environment and User Needs

Most observers expect business to continue to be influenced strongly
by pressures generated by general worldwide inflation, increased international competition, rising wages in excess of productivity increases,
and increased government involvement in all aspects of business. In
addition, however, certain business trends are particularly important
to users of information services.

1) Fractionation of Mass Markets. In the last two decades, mass
markets have gradually crumbled, with increasing attention to individual
treatment of smaller market segments. Symbolic of this trend has been
the growth of specialty retailers and franchise outlets, the death of
mass market magazines such as Look and Life, increasing participation in
crafts and folk arts, the growth of special interest publications, and

the shortening of product life cycles. The fractionation of mass markets applies to many products and services--automobiles, breakfast foods, etc. It does not apply directly to the field of information services because here a mass market has never appeared. However, information services themselves may facilitate the further fractionation of markets by permitting individual products and services to be custom-tailored to individual needs and specifications. Products can be customer-tailored to user needs by program-driven machines, and advertising can be tailored to fit a community or individual's stored profile.

2) <u>Loss of U.S. Mass Production Initiative</u>. U.S. industry made its most dramatic contributions in this century by pushing mass production techniques further than any other nation. However, within the past several decades, mass production operations have migrated to areas of low labor costs. Thus, for example, Korean shirts, Japanese electronics, Italian shoes and Hong Kong toys have swept into the U.S. marketplace from abroad. While some mass production still takes place in the U.S., the next two decades will probably see a continuation of pressures from abroad on these industries. On the other hand, the United States seems to have an edge in certain high technology products such as computers, space satellites, aircraft, and large engineering projects where information is the major factor of production.

3) <u>Greater Accountability of Business</u>. In the next two decades, business is likely to become subjected to even greater pressure for accountability to its various publics--consumers, the workers, stockholders, and the government. The trend toward greater accountability has received stimulus from consumer movements, reported corporate abuses such as payoffs, OSHA, and the SEC. Greater accountability almost certainly means additional information services to record transactions and to report progress in meeting regulations and objectives.

4) <u>Organizational Complexity</u>. Recent trends in real time systems, work design, project management and conglomerate corporations have led to increasing complexity of organizational forms in order to cope with increasing complexity in the environment. New organizational forms such as franchising, sales and leaseback arrangements, office condominiums, and the like, promise to continue to introduce new levels of complexity into organizational designs, each of which adds new information requirements. Similarly, longer lead times, coupled with shorter product life cycles and higher investments required for major strategy moves raise both the stakes and the uncertainty in business decisions, thereby increasing the information content of many of these ventures. At every stage there must be reports filed, alternatives tested, impacts assessed, markets surveyed. This greatly expands the need for informational activity of all kinds--message transfers, access to technical and regulatory information, use of computer-based decision-assisting tools, etc.

5) <u>Increased Computer Sophistication</u>. With educational levels continuing to rise and many more women in the work force, consumers have both the income and the knowledge to be more sophisticated in their purchases, implying an increased need for information services. One result of this need might be a very rapid growth over the next decade

of the use of computers in the home for recreational, educational, and business purposes.

Business trends suggest greatly expanded user needs for information in the private sector, as shown in Figure 3.

Figure 3
Business Forces Affecting User Needs for Information

TRENDS	Effects on User Needs for Information					
	More Plentiful	More Accurate	More Reliable	Faster	Cheaper	More Accessible
1. Fractionation of Mass Markets	X	X	X	X	X	X
2. Information--Cheapest Factor of Production	X				X	X
3. Increased Accountability	X	X				
4. Organization Complexity, Sophistication	X		X	X		X
5. Increasing Consumer Sophistication	X	X	X	X	X	X

Fractionation of mass markets, the increased demand to customize information services, greater accountability, and other similar requirements mean that there will be many more information users, and much greater interaction between and within businesses. In fact, user needs in this area may be so strong that information access borders on being a right. Until recently, large businesses have tended to benefit most from the use of the computer, since only they could afford the high installation costs and conversion delays. Now that computers are almost universally available, private networks are one of the few remaining barriers limiting the competitiveness of small businesses. While primarily small businessmen are likely to fight for public support in gaining access to information, all businessmen are likely to demand strict policing of information system use so that crime and other forms of abuse can be kept to a minimum. As businesses become deeply committed to information system offerings, they are likely to insist upon reliable, responsive and secure service.

Conclusion

We have reviewed, in a general way, some of the forces that will shape user needs for information in the year 2000. It appears that the major theme is a need for increased access to information as a fundamental requirement of successful societal adaptation to change in the next two decades. At the same time, users will need protection from the potential abuses of an information-based society--distortion or manipulation of information, fraud, violations of privacy, information overload, and exploitation of the information-poor by the information-rich. A focused national concern for managing the evolution of information services in the interest of social excellence and user protection now seems to be a matter for high national priority.

Notes

[1]Willis Harman, "Notes on the Coming Transformation," in The Next Twenty-Five Years, edited by Andrew A. Spekke, (Washington, D.C.: World Future Society, 1975), p. 18.

[2]Burt Nanus, Leland M. Wooton, and Harold Borko, The Social Implications of the Use of Computers Across National Boundaries, (Montvale, NJ: AFIPS Press, 1973).

THE INFORMATION NEEDS OF BUSINESS WITH SPECIAL APPLICATION TO MANAGERIAL DECISION MAKING

by

Paul Gray
Chairman of Management Science and Computers
Edwin L. Cox School of Business
Southern Methodist University

The Nature of Business Decision Making

Business managers spend a significant portion of their time making choices among alternatives, that is, making decisions. These decisions always deal with the present and the future of the firm, since the past is known and cannot be changed. Because the future is not certain, the outcomes of each of the alternatives considered in decision making cannot be predicted precisely; that is, each alternative contains some degree of risk. Typically, managers seek to maximize return on investment and, at the same time, minimize risk of loss. These are usually conflicting objectives since the outcomes with higher anticipated return usually have higher risk associated with them. Since managers want to reduce risk wherever possible, they seek as much relevant information about the future as possible.

These essential elements of alternatives and uncertainty-induced risk are the rationale for the existence of managers since, if there are no choices to make and no risk involved, there would be no need to hire someone to make decisions. Information provides a way of determining the alternatives available and of assessing the associated risks.

The information needs of business can be divided into three parts:
1) record keeping
2) management of ongoing operations
3) strategic planning

The record-keeping function is basically historical. It involves collecting routine repetitive data such as inventory levels, sales, accounts receivable and payables, credit ratings, and the like. Although often involving large expenditures and currently increasing at a rapid rate to cope with the increasing regulation of business, record keeping is done at the lowest levels of the organization and is not central to the decision process. It does, however, provide a perspective and framework that guides decision makers insofar as they assume the past will continue into the future.

The management of ongoing operations, usually performed at middle management levels, is concerned with day-to-day phenomena. Here information is needed on the current situation, and decision rules, be they rules of thumb or advanced techniques generated from Management Science, are applied routinely and repetitively. The decisions involve such mundane questions as how many inventory items to order and when to order them, routing and scheduling of items through production lines, management of waiting lines, pricing to meet challenges from competition, hiring and firing of personnel, and supervising the record keeping functions.

Strategic planning is the role of top management. Here information is needed that describes current alternatives, future possibilities, the societal and business environment, the competitive and political environment both here and abroad, new technological developments that may pose threats or provide opportunities, as well as the historical and operating information that describes the company and its capabilities. Strategic planning decisions determine the future of businesses. In this article we will focus on the strategic planning aspects of businesses and the evolving information environments that are changing the way in which strategic planning is being done.

Central to these changes are the revolutions in both computer technology and telecommunications. Our discussion therefore begins with a review of the changes taking place in these areas.

From Data Bank to Decision Support System

When a new technology is introduced, it tends to look and be used like the technology it replaced. The early automobile, for example, looked like and was used in the same way and over the same roads as the carriage with only the horse replaced. So it was with computers. The initial computer applications were for recording and organizing information. They simply mechanized existing record and filing systems. Examination of what computers are used for in business shows that a large fraction of the usage is for entering information, merging old information with new information, and sorting information into retrievable form. Thus, computers find major application as data banks. These data banks are essentially lists, whether they are customer records or parts lists or the New York Times Index. The data bank approach emphasizes the collection and maintenance of very detailed data about various aspects of a business. It is typically geared to supporting record keeping and specific routine operations (e.g., inventory, ordering, billing, accounting) rather than supporting management decision needs.

The concept of a data base proved to be the step forward needed to make the information in the data bank useful for operational decision making. A data base is an integrated non-redundant collection of stored information.

A simple library catalog analogy will help in understanding the data base. In a conventional library card system, information about a particular book is kept in several places including subject, title, and author indices. Each new entry or change (e.g., replacement by a new edition) requires changes in several locations. In the data base approach, all data on each volume held are kept together on a single "card," which contains the author, title, call number, publisher, publication date, acquisition date, subject categories, etc. Inquiries made of this data base can be in terms of author (e.g., H. Melville), subject (e.g., whaling), date of publication (e.g., last three years), and, most important, any combinations of these categories. The computer provides a complete listing of all entries that meet the criteria of the inquiry.

Thus, a publisher trying to decide whether to reissue <u>Moby Dick</u> can rapidly find out about competing editions as well as other competitive aspects of the market.

Integration and non-redundance are the key characteristics. No longer does a firm keep separate records for accounting and finance and personnel and marketing and production, with great overlap and duplication; rather, it maintains a central information file that can be used by all parts of the organization for both operations and planning. Data bases have many advantages, two of which are important to us here. First, they assume that changes need to be entered in only one place (e.g., a female employee marries and changes her surname or a selling price is changed) not in several places (e.g., personnel records, payroll, or catalog and billing). Second, a data base can be used to assist various parts of an organization, from routine operations to decision making. In providing information for decision making, the data base is the backbone of a management information system.

A management information system provides an organization of past, present, and projected information about both the internal operations of the firm and its external environment. The purpose of this organization is to condense and filter data in such a way that it becomes information usable in decision making. The management information system typically is used to generate reports managers can use to solve problems. Thus, in a good management information system, the focus is on decision-oriented reports rather than routine aggregations of information. However, such systems are rare. Among the reports typically generated by an information system are regularly scheduled documents that record inventory levels, provide project budget status, and summarize sales and orders booked. More important for top management are the exception reports that forewarn of difficulties and crises and the special study reports that are designed to answer specific questions. Figure 1 (see page 68) lists the information that may be included in a sophisticated management information system.

Management information systems were developed during the 1960s. By 1967, a reaction had set in. In a famous, provocative paper, "Management Misinformation Systems,"[1] Ackoff argued that the problem in management information systems was not the conventional wisdom that managers were receiving too little information and that they all would be right if only enough information could be stored. Rather he believed that managers were receiving too much data, which overwhelmed them and actually hindered the decision process. He felt that a good information system did not just provide information, but provided perspective as well, highlighting what is important and eliminating what is trivial. The fetish for having but not using computer printout that develops in some corporations is illustrated by the story, perhaps apocryphal, that in one company the president one day inserted a $100 bill in the middle of the printout received by each of his 13 vice presidents daily. By the end of the day, only one of the 13 bills had been discovered.

Figure 1
Contents of a Management Information System

INTERNAL INFORMATION   Examples:

    Activity Information   Production scheduling, inventory
                                          control, credit management

    Status Information   Work in process, customer
                                          accounts

    Resource Information   Personnel, materials, facilities

    Resource Allocation Information   Capital budgets, personnel
                                          assignments

    Planning and control   Plans, budgets, variance reports

EXTERNAL INFORMATION

    Politics and government   Political, legal, legislative
                                          developments regulations,
                                          monetary and fiscal policies

    Society   Demographic, cultural, societal
                                          trends

    Economy   GNP, economic indicators

    Technology   New products and processes

    Supplies and Suppliers   Raw materials, labor,
                                          subcontractors, energy

    Competition   Prices, products, market share

    In institutional terms, the typical management information system has come to be a provider of large amounts of detailed data to middle managers. Such systems do not really resolve the problem of assisting in top level decision making. The decision support system approach (see, e.g., Keen and Scott-Morton[2] or Alter[3]) adds the idea of providing decision rules and decision models tailored to the specific decision facing a specific manager. Decision support systems are designed to use the decision maker's understanding of the problem and judgments in an interactive, computer-based process leading up to a decision. This is a much more sophisticated approach in that it implies that merely providing information is not enough; the information must be tailored to the problem and must be coupled to the specific decision and decision maker; that is, it must take the human factor into account.

Decision support systems provide a strategy for making computers useful to top management in firms, where the decisions to be made are rarely routine and where the decision tasks are relatively unstructured. The implementers of decision support systems have come to the realization that the computer and information environment must adjust to the manager, not vice versa. Thus, for example, good decision support systems accept input and translate output into the language of the decision maker. Furthermore, the emphasis is on support. The information and suggested actions are viewed as aids to the evaluation process of reaching a conclusion, not the definitive answers to be accepted blindly. In the view of Keen and Scott-Morton the decision support system is a scratchpad for the manager in which the manager is able to create alternative solutions to the problem and use the leverage of the computer to determine the anticipated results of each alternative. Because of the ability to deal with "what if" types of questions, decision support systems require both a strong data base and a computational capability that allows processing the information in the data base.

Telecommunications and Information

The changes in information storage and retrieval for decision purposes has been aided immensely by the advances in telecommunications. These advances have included the use of telephones for data transmission and for computer conferencing (discussed below) and the introduction of satellite communications in routine business operations. In information terms this growth in telecommunications services has meant that both centralization and decentralization could take place. By sending information over long distances to centralized computers, it became possible to make decisions at headquarters that were previously made in the divisions and field offices of a company. Some argue that we are seeing an erosion of the decisions made by middle managers and that the trend to centralized decision making on routine operating questions will accelerate. Such a trend would have serious implications for the mix of skills required by business.

At the same time that there is a centralization of decision making there is also a trend toward decentralization through "distributed" data processing. In distributed data processing there is decentralization of information and information handling made possible by using a network of computers interconnected by telecommunications. Each organizational unit has its own minicomputer or microcomputer system to handle its own data needs and can communicate both with the central computer and with other computers in the distributed network. From an information standpoint, distributed data networks introduce some redundancy but enable local, autonomous operations and hence improved service.

Interior Versus Exterior Information

Most of the business information referred to thus far has been information generated within the company about itself. Organizations do not exist in a vacuum. They operate in a competitive environment that is impacted by and impacts on society as a whole. Thus, businesses require large amounts of information about the external environment. This information ranges from technical developments to actions and intentions of competitors, to present and anticipated government regulations and taxes, and to local, national, and global political developments, to name just a few. Strategic planning involves consideration of both the abilities of the organization (finances, capital investment, human resources) and the external environment. In those companies where strategic planning is advanced, environmental scanning is practiced regularly and large libraries of information are kept about the world outside the company.

Managing Crises

Information needs become most acute in time of crisis. Crises arise in all organizations from time to time, even the best managed ones. They may be the result of external actions (e.g., an oil embargo) or internal failures (an accident such as Three Mile Island). They almost never repeat; that is, each is seemingly new and involves unique circumstances. At the time that a crisis occurs, decision making and planning activities are suddenly compressed in time. It is no longer possible to examine a problem from every possible angle or leisurely to gather additional data. Actions have to be taken, and they have to be taken now. Here, the organization with an information system in place and with its people trained to cope with crises will, in most cases, do better than the organization that works by the proverbial seat of the pants under such conditions.

The key to successful crisis management is having the information needed to make decisions in a form that relates to the new problem being faced. The time compression implies that most of the information needed for the decisions must already be available. Furthermore, the decision makers have almost no time available for learning. To use the approach of trying to fight the current crisis by what is known from past crises is not likely to work; it is analogous to the general who tries to fight the next war like the last one. History almost never repeats. Therefore, decision makers must have training that enables them to cope with future crises. Contingency planning based on alternative future scenarios is one approach to such training.

The development of scenarios about the future is a developing art. Scenarios are not science fiction. Rather, they are carefully thought out extrapolations of the present into the future. A good scenario has three characteristics:
- it must be possible
- it must be plausible
- it must be consistent
"Possible" refers to feasibility. The scenario should not call for conditions that are not technically feasible, such as travel faster than the speed of light, or are not economically feasible, such as capital expenditures that are ten times the ·GNP in constant dollars. A possible scenario may still not be plausible; that is, it may not be believable. The user of the scenario must feel that the situation forecast, although far different than the current situation, could take place. Finally,

the scenario must be internally consistent. A scenario, for example,
should not include both a ban on nuclear power plant construction and
a tripling of national nuclear power use.

Scenarios can be written in two forms, tomorrow's newspaper and
tomorrow's history. In the newspaper form, the conditions that exist
at a particular point, for example on January 1, 2000, are described
and it is assumed that the reader either knows or does not care what
happened between now and then. In the history form, the scenario
describes the sequence of events that "occurred" between now and then
as if the events were being chronicled by the historian of the year
2000. In either case, the preparation of scenarios involves knowledge
of the past and considerable information about the possible events
that can happen in the future.

It can be anticipated that businesses working to survive in an
ever more uncertain future will undertake multiple scenario generation
and development of contingency plans for them. The INTERAX system,
developed at the Center for Futures Research of the University of
Southern California, is typical of the management training that can
be done to cope with crises. In the next section we describe INTERAX
to indicate the range and scope of planning information and training
that is beginning to come on the scene and that will be much more
evident in firms over the coming years.

INTERAX

The INTERAX system[4] generates alternative futures by using
analytic models and human analysts in an interactive simulation.
Each simulation produces a single possible scenario. The procedure,
illustrated in Figure 2, is based on the following underlying
assumptions:

1) The future is not predetermined, but involves both uncertainty
   and human will.
2) Existing trends will continue unless natural limits are
   approached or external changes occur.
3) External changes are uncertain as to their nature, timing,
   and magnitude of effect.
4) The desirability of social conditions is a value judgment
   that does not obey fixed criteria.

Trends are physical, social, and human processes that describe the
state of affairs under investigation. These trends may be quantitative
(e.g., gross national product, population) or qualitative (quality of
life). Physical changes (e.g., scientific breakthroughs, nuclear
accidents) are inherently uncertain and not fully controllable. Social
changes are the results of policies taken by various organizations in
an attempt to manage evolutionary conditions.

In INTERAX, trends and physical changes are described through a
computer-based analytic model, whereas social changes are based on the
deliberations and decisions of people simulating interest groups and
decision makers.

Figure 2
Scenario Generator

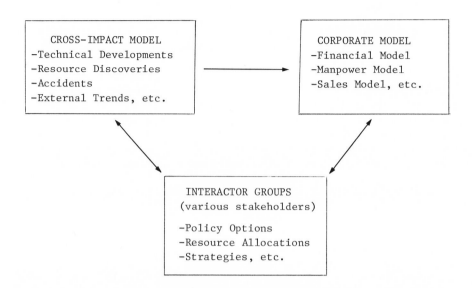

The corporate model describes the way the company works in terms of variables routinely used in the firm to evaluate performance. The Interactive Financial Planning System, econometric models and other standard forecasting models of the firm are used. The corporate model generates information for fixed time intervals into the future.

The cross-impact model is a simulation model in which random numbers are used to determine whether particular events did or did not occur in a particular time interval. The occurrence and non-occurrence of events (e.g., a depression or commercialization of electric-powered cars on a mass scale) is used 1) to modify the value of trends (e.g., Gross National Product or automobile sales) and 2) to modify the subsequent likelihood of occurrence of other potential events (e.g., commercialization of steam powered cars). The cross-impact model determines the outcomes of events on a period-by-period basis. The simulation is interrupted after each period and all occurrences in that interval are reported. The model updates the likelihood of occurrence (that is, the probability) of each of the remaining events in light of the outcome in the prior periods and awaits the inputs from the interactors (i.e., managers) before proceeding to the next interval.

An interactive analysis proceeds through the following steps:

1) A long time (e.g., 20 years) is divided into shorter intervals (e.g., 2-year intervals).

2) Current conditions and expectations contained in the corporate and cross-impact model are reviewed by the interactors.

3) The interactors evaluate the data presented to them and decide on what policy changes, if any, should be made.

4) The policy changes are incorporated into the two computer models.

5) The computer models then determine which of the remaining events occur and projects trend values for the next interval. The results of this step become the new current conditions and expectations in Step 2, and the process is repeated for the next interval.

With the completion of all intervals, one possible scenario is described. The scenario describes which events occurred, what values the trends had, and the policy decisions that the managers serving as interactors made. A narrative is usually prepared that describes the rationale behind the policies chosen. If they try another run of INTERAX, different results will be achieved because of the use of the random numbers. For example, a particular scientific breakthrough may occur in one run but not in another; even if it occurs, it may occur at a different time and in a different relation to events and trends.

Attempting to manage an issue under constant uncertainty is similar to the situation faced by managers in the real world. The benefits obtained from trying to solve problems interactively as they unfold are a heightened awareness of the types of situations that may arise to thwart even well-conceived policy choices and an understanding of the follow-up actions that can be taken after the initial choices have been made. By running the model many times with different management groups, it is possible to develop a richer appreciation of the situations likely to be encountered in the future and to determine what responses are likely to work. As a result, the frequency of surprise is reduced when the transition is made to the real world under crisis conditions.

The use of a model such as INTERAX requires the generation of considerable information about a business and its environment. Typically, the INTERAX model will contain forecasts about several hundred potential events and trends, some dealing with the world in general and others industry or corporate specific. The services of consulting firms that specialize in forecasts can be used to obtain many of the external and some of the industry forecasts; others, however, have to be generated within the individual company.

Advances in Computing

Other developments in computing in the late 1970s are improving the ability to manage crises and improve long-range planning. We will focus on three developments here: personal computers, interactive planning systems, and graphic display of information. These developments, when combined with some of the other capabilities in computing and communication referred to earlier, make possible the developments in telecommuting, teleconferencing, and advanced decision rooms to be described later in this article.

Personal Computers

The continual miniaturization of electronics led to the development of minicomputers affordable by small firms and then microcomputers, usually referred to as "personal computers." These units are being sold in 1980 at prices starting at $500, with the most popular models and accessories running slightly over $1,000 for home and $4,000 for business use. Forecasts of the personal computer market indicate that cumulative sales by 1990 will be 25 million or more units, of which on the order of 5 million will be for business uses. While most of these units will be used for the more routine work of business, many will be used to assist middle and upper level managers in their planning efforts.

"Personal" is the operative word. Managers can, at a cost of less than a month's salary, have at their fingertips the basic planning data they need for their work. The typical office of the future will see a personal computer on most managers' desks. These machines will contain custom-tailored data bases and decision support algorithms. They will also be interconnected to the company's central computer system and able to gain access to "videotext" and other centralized information systems.

Videotext systems are data retrieval systems that allow individuals to access large data banks. These systems are being developed as network information services for both the home and the business market. In a typical system, large data banks are made accessible by phone lines at nominal cost. The provider of the network information service collects information and stores it in a central computer. Phone line inquiry brings the information up on the screen of the user. Videotext services offer the information sources that will be needed as part of the environmental scanning activity.

Interactive Planning Systems

With the broad dissemination of the personal computer, the problem of overabundance of information pointed out by Ackoff must again be faced. Managers must be able to put the information in context. The development of interactive planning systems provide one means for doing so.

Interactive planning systems refer to computer software that allows managers to perform planning activities in an online, real-time mode. Such systems, to be successful, must be able to use extremely simplified, natural-language instructions. Several such natural-language systems were developed during the 1970s and the trend toward increased use of natural-language programming concepts is well-established.

The Interactive Financial Planning System (IFPS) developed and marketed by EXECUCOMM of Austin, Texas, is typical of such systems. Figure 3 shows an example of a simple five-year forecast based on current values and assumed growth rates of ten percent in market and seven per-cent in selling price. Built-in functions compute net present value (NPVC), the measure of effectiveness for the problem. The important point of Figure 3 is not the specifics of this particular language or program; rather it is the idea that easy-to-use languages in which individuals can be trained in less than two hours are becoming available. Such languages promise to overcome the typical executive's fear of computers. Furthermore, these languages have "what if?" capability; that is, it is possible to examine a whole range of alternatives by asking the computer to change assumptions. In Figure 3, for example, the effect of a change in market share from 25% to 15% is examined. Uncertainty can be taken into account. In extensions under development, optimization routines to find the best answers are being developed.

Figure 3

```
MODEL MODEL2  VERSION OF  07/01/80  20 45
10 COLUMNS 1981,1982,1983,1984,1985
20 TOTAL MARKET=100000,PREVIOUS TOTAL MARKET * 1.10
30 MARKET SHARE=.25
40 MARKET=TOTAL MARKET* MARKET SHARE
50 SALES=MARKET*UNIT SELLING PRICE
60 UNIT SELLING PRICE=10.50,PREVIOUS UNIT SELLING PRICE * 1.07
70 CONTRIBUTION TO PROFIT =0.20*SALES
80 INVESTMENT=50000,50000,25000,0,0
90 PRESENT VALUE=NPVC(CONTRIBUTION TO PROFIT,.25,INVESTMENT)
END OF MODEL
     SOLVE
MODEL MODEL2  VERSION OF  07/01/80  20 45 -- 5 COLUMNS 8 VARIABLES
ENTER SOLVE OPTIONS
    ? ALL
```

	1981	1982	1983	1984	1985
TOTAL MARKET	100000	110000	121000	133100	146410
MARKET SHARE	.2500	.2500	.2500	.2500	.2500
MARKET	25000	27500	30250	33275	36603
SALES	262500	308963	363649	428015	503773
UNIT SELLING PRICE	10.50	11.24	12.02	12.86	13.76
CONTRIBUTION TO PROFIT	52500	61793	72730	85603	100755
INVESTMENT	50000	50000	25000	0	0
PRESENT VALUE	-8000	-8453	12785	47848	80863

```
ENTER SOLVE OPTIONS
    ? WHAT IF
WHAT IF CASE 1
ENTER STATEMENTS
    ? MARKET SHARE=.15
    ? SOLVE
ENTER SOLVE OPTIONS
    ? SALES,PRESENT VALUE
```

```
***** WHAT IF CASE 1 *****
1 WHAT IF STATEMENTS PROCESSED
```

	1981	1982	1983	1984	1985
SALES	157500	185378	218189	256809	302264
PRESENT VALUE	-24800	-41072	-34720	-13691	6118

Graphic Display of Information

In 1975, Henry Mintzberg, writing in <u>Harvard Business Review</u>,[5] observed, "I was struck . . . by the fact that the executives I was observing--all very competent by any standard--are fundamentally indistinguishable from their counterparts of a hundred years ago (or a thousand years ago for that matter). The information they need differs but they seek it in the same way--by word of mouth." The rapid advances being made in computer graphics are beginning to make this observation obsolete.

"Computer graphics" refers to the technology that converts numbers stored in the computer into pictorial form. One of the barriers to using computer-generated information has been the inability of people to absorb the large amount of data provided. By presenting the data in the form of graphs, managers do not have to sort their way through reams of printout to make sense of information.

The benefits of computer graphics are twofold: they save time and they improve decision making. By presenting information in pictorial form it is possible to find changes, interpret information, and communicate complex sets of findings to others more quickly, all of which reduce the time managers need to process information and permit them to examine a broader range of alternatives.

What computer graphics does is not new, since pictorial information in the form of maps, graphs, charts and drawings are a staple of management briefings. The change that is taking place is the ability to examine rapidly the effects of alternatives in a form that is easily grasped and acted upon.

A few examples of the use of graphics in decision making is helpful in understanding what they do. The following are among the applications reported by Takeuchi and Schmidt:[6]

- preparations of maps for reducing the uncertainties associated with oil exploration, thereby affecting decisions on where to drill
- selection of sites for new car dealerships
- determining the areas of best advertising opportunities
- planning of space allocation in shopping malls
- allocating police resources in high crime areas

The technology of graphics is improving rapidly and, at the same time, costs are going down. Two-dimensional and three-dimensional color graphic displays are routinely available both on stand-alone graphics computers and as accessories to both small and large machines. In the years ahead the trend to three-dimensionality can be expected to increase as holographic techniques are developed.

Telecommuting

Historically, most organizations have one or more central places of business, often at downtown locations. Each morning and evening, people travel to and from work, creating the traffic jams and other ills associated with urban commuting. In recent years it has become evident that the need to gather people in one place to work is no longer necessary for many corporations, particularly those that are in information-related businesses (e.g., insurance, banks). Examination of what people actually do in offices indicates that there are large armies of clerks who spend most of their time creating information that is stored in the computer or dealing with information generated by the computer. Since, as we have implied by our previous discussion, the computer can be anywhere and the people using the computer can use telecommunications to gain access to the machine, it is no longer necessary to collocate individuals who work for a particular firm. The concept of moving work to where the workers live rather than moving the workers to where the work is goes under the name "telecommuting."

Extensive studies of the substitution of communications for transportation[7] have shown that this form of business organization has economic advantages to both employers and employees, as well as having major implications for conservation of energy. In the basic concept, individuals go to work at a place close to where they live. If they change assignment, they merely change the data base with which they work. Supervision is split into two parts: local supervision of work attendance and work habits and remote supervision of work content through teleconferencing (see below).

Telecommuting is a significant new possibility that was made feasible by the new information technologies. It carries the concept of distributed computer networks one step further to the concept of distributing the data gathering and data dissemination functions of business decision making.

Teleconferencing

Teleconferencing systems are computer and telecommunications networks that allow video, audio, and data communications among widely separated groups of people. That is, teleconferences are electronic alternatives for groups meeting in person to exchange information and/or make decisions. Teleconferencing is a form of telecommuting. Such systems are available at three levels:

-audio teleconferencing, the extension of the conference telephone call to groups of people located in multiple conference rooms. Although a number of systems are in use, audio teleconferencing is probably a transient phenomenon. The most difficult problems in audio teleconferences are determining the order in which people are to talk and identifying who is talking.

-computer teleconferencing in which messages are exchanged via computer terminals. Computer teleconferences offer the capability for conferences that are extended in both time and space. Each participant in such a conference types messages into a common file and is able to read the messages of others. Because of the storage capabilities of the computer, participants do not all have to be present at the same time. This results in giving participants the ability to give measured, well-thought-through responses to the statements of others and provides a permanent record of what is said. Such conferences require a strong chairman to keep them on track. They open new vistas. For example, in one computer teleconference in which the author participated, effectively all the researchers in the world, including those in Canada, the United States and Europe, working on telecommuting were able to exchange views. Teleconferencing has also proved to be useful in a wide range of applications from the passing of routine administrative information to holding committee meetings to performing consulting without travel (i.e., a form of telecommuting) to crisis management.

-video conferencing in which participants sit in the equivalent of a television studio and can see one another. Such systems have been offered commercially in the United States (Bell Telephone's Picturephone® Meeting Service among 14 cities), England (Confravision), Canada, Australia, and Japan. Typically, such systems involve people coming to a public conference room located in the center of a major city, although privately run systems are used by some very large corporations. Video teleconferencing systems are, in a sense, attempts to reproduce conventional meetings for people separated in space.

Of the three systems, audio teleconferences are the least satisfactory. Video conferences have the advantage that they allow large communications substitutions for transportation since more people can participate and travel costs are eliminated (at the expense of rather high communications costs). However, video conferences, while they allow distant participants to be seen as they speak, are still qualitatively different from face-to-face meetings and require participants to adjust to this difference. Computer teleconferencing is perhaps the most innovative but also the one that is strangest to new users. It also seems better suited to people at staff level than to operating executives who, in present environments, live under high pressure and do not have (or think they have) the time to do the contemplative work necessary for conferences dispersed in space and time.

Teleconferencing systems are in their infancy and can be expected to have extensive development during the remainder of the twentieth century. Being a new communications medium, teleconferences are going through the same sequence as other new technologies, initially attempting to reproduce face-to-face meetings as faithfully as possible. However, teleconferences are really a new way of transmitting ideas and information. As such, we can anticipate that they will change over time and become a unique way of meeting the information needs of business.

The Board Room of the Future

The various developments discussed in this chapter: advances in computers and computer graphics, advances in telecommunications, telecommuting and teleconferencing, all come together in the executive decision-making facilities of the future.

In most business organizations, when members of the board of directors or groups of executives meet for making decisions, they gather in a room that is little different from the ones their predecessors met in a hundred or more years ago. Technology is evident only in the electric lights and perhaps a telephone. The only information they have available to them during the meeting other than what is in their heads is contained in a few memoranda or a notebook containing financial and other reports. They may receive verbal briefings with the aid of charts. The information, in short, is static and cannot be changed to consider the implications of new alternatives. Yet, as we have seen in this chapter, the new set of technologies provides capabilities for enhancing this information environment by providing:

-rapid information retrieval

-rapid evaluation of new alternatives

-visual display of complex information

-participation of individuals located at remote locations

A few companies have built advanced environments that make use of these capabilities and one or two experimental facilities are being developed at universities. In these "board rooms of the future," the physical environment is still very comfortable and plush. High resolution graphics terminals are used to display information to be seen by the group as a whole. Video screens project the faces of participants at remote locations. There is complete two-way transmission of information, and what is displayed at one site can also be seen at all the other sites. Individuals participating in these meetings may sit around a conference table as in the past or they may have their own table with both workspace and their own personal computer to allow them to obtain the data that they need during the deliberations.

The computing facilities for individuals would be set up to minimize the need for typing. "Touch screens" have been developed where alternative sequences of preset questions set up in menu form can be used to obtain answers to a wide variety of problems.[8]

In trying to assess how the new information technologies will be used in the advanced environment, we must return to the nature of decision making meetings. Consider the following scenario of a typical planning decision:

The manufacturing vice president proposes that a new plant be established overseas for producing semiconductor "chips," the heart of the electronic devices marketed by the company. He comes to the meeting with a set of briefing charts that outline the proposal in terms of its financial and human resource needs and the anticipated benefits to the company. He briefly describes the staff studies that considered various alternatives and presents a recommendation to invest $100 million in the Third World Country X.

At once a series of questions are asked: Is this expenditure necessary at all? What happens if the company tries to use its existing facilities? Is the government of X stable politically? Is the labor supply in X adequate in numbers and skills? What are the risks of expropriation? Why not build in Country Y which offers a subsidy for new industry? Would the company be better off building two smaller plants, one domestic and one abroad? How sensitive are the projected contributions to profit to the assumed growth in sales? How sensitive is the assumed growth in sales to changes in the national economy and the world economy? Are there technological developments on the horizon which, if they occurred, would make the proposed plant obsolete earlier than planned? The list of serious questions is large. For many, the manufacturing vice president has answers because of the staff work done in advance; however, some bring new consideration into play. It is in resolving these new issues that the enhanced information capabilities come to the fore.

If the question is one of fact, (e.g., the space capacity available in the company) the company's data base can be consulted. If a particular expertise is needed that is available at another company location (e.g., on competing technologies) the individuals with that expertise can be brought into the meeting by video or other teleconferencing. If new alternatives are to be considered (e.g., the Country Y option), the "what if" capabilities can be tapped and the answers displayed for all to see. The data can, in fact, be presented graphically and comparisons of the alternatives shown directly. Members of the meeting who want to explore an idea privately can turn to their terminals and ask the "what if" question without using up the time of the group or, as is often the case, exposing their ignorance to their colleagues. If the answer is favorable, the results can be displayed to everyone; if it is unfavorable no harm is done.

Eventually, a decision must be made. Here the electronic environment helps in overcoming the usual problems of committee action. Often the wishes of the chairman or other person of authority or the persuasiveness of a dominant personality sway the outcome. Individuals "go along" rather than following their best judgment. Sometimes the chairman makes the decision in a direction which is universally opposed by the other members of the board. By using anonymous voting, (with the results visible only to the ultimate decision maker, if so desired) consensus can be reached both for the problem as a whole and for many of its constituent parts.

The board room just described did not exist at the beginning of the 1980s; however, many of these constituent parts were available in facilities at various firms. The essential ingredient for achieving the full capability is the marriage of information with the computer and telecommunications into an integrated capability.

Notes

[1]Russell Ackoff, "Management Misinformation Systems," _Management Science_ 14 (December 1967), pp. B147-56.

[2]Peter G.W. Keen and Michael S. Scott-Morton, _Decision Support Systems, An Organizational Perspective_ (Reading, MA: Addison-Wesley, 1978).

[3]Steven L. Alter, _Decision Support Systems, Current Practice and Continuing Challenges_ (Reading, MA: Addison-Wesley, 1980).

[4]Selwyn Enzer, _INTERAX--An Interactive Model for Studying Future Business Environments_ (Los Angeles: University of Southern California Center for Futures Research, 1980).

[5]Henry Mintzberg, "The Manager's Job: Folklore and Fact," _Harvard Business Review_, July-August 1975, p. 49.

[6]H. Takeuchi and A.H. Schmidt, "New Promise of Computer Graphics," _Harvard Business Review_, January-February 1980, pp. 122-31.

[7]J.M. Nilles, et al., _Telecommunication Substitution for Transportation: Options for Tomorrow_ (New York, NY: Wiley, 1976).

[8]The avoidance of typing will be important probably through the mid-1990s while pre-computer-era trained managers are still active and in senior positions. Under any circumstance, the knowledge of computing required will be minimal, with the power of new languages helping to reduce dependence on these skills even further.

PRODUCTIVITY IN THE INFORMATION SOCIETY*

by

Vincent E. Giuliano
Consultant for Information Systems
Arthur D. Little, Inc.

Information Boosts National Production

Information handling is the most important economic activity in
the United States today. New information and communications technologies are driving the continuing transformation of our businesses,
institutions, and values. Among the benefits of this process of
transformation are increases in both personal and organizational
productivity.

Productivity is not a simple concept, but I use the term to
describe the capability of an individual, an organization, or the
nation as a whole to produce beneficial results. These include not
only goods and products but also services and situations that contribute to the quality of life. An investment that produces clean
air or clean water is regarded as productive, even if the "product"
is not in the market system.

In the last 20 years the United States has evolved from an industrial economy--one based mainly on manufacturing--to an information
economy--one in which the main concern is the generation, handling,
storage, retrieval, communication, and utilization of information.
Some 60% of the work force is now engaged in information work--what
managers, executives, professionals, brokers, salespersons, and white
collar workers do.

Three major waves of technological change--associated with computers, with telecommunications, and with office automation--have
combined in the last few decades to produce a basic transformation of
businesses and the economy. Manufacturing now accounts for only 22%
of the labor force, a decline of 3% from 1970, and farm employment
dropped from 4% in 1970 to 3% in 1979. The rate of technological
advancement has been so fast that even the most sophisticated organizations are still using mixtures of the basic office technologies of
the year 1900 (typewriters and file cabinets) together with the newer
electronic "paperless" means.

The transformation is affecting the basic nature of work for large
sectors of the population, and has led to a requirement to re-examine

---

*This article was originally published in Information World, vol. 2, 1980.
Reprinted by permission of the author. copyright 1980 by Vincent E.
Giuliano.

what we mean by productivity. We already have an information-oriented economy and, considering the whole of our work and leisure activities, an Information Society.

Productivity has received much attention recently in the United States. High productivity is essential if we are to achieve such objectives as overcoming energy and resource shortages, or ensuring equal opportunity for all of our citizens. If we as business managers or as policy planners want to increase real productivity, however, we have to start by taking a broad enough view of productivity to take into account what is going on in our information-rich society.

Yet, the concern over productivity has been largely off the mark. Economists, businessmen, and government policymakers have been concerned over certain distressing symptoms having to do with declining savings, lower rates of productivity increase than in European or Japanese economies, and declining capital investment rates. Here are some of the statistics of concern:

- The U.S. rate of consumer savings has for several years been significantly less than that in other advanced countries. In the U.K., West Germany, and France, the six-year average rate has been well over double that in the United States; in Japan, the rate is nearly four times that in the United States.

- Coupled with the declining savings rate is a decline in U.S. industrial investment. Business investment in new productive facilities, factories, and machinery averaged about 3% per year added to the existing capital base prior to 1973. The average has been closer to 1.75% per year increase since then.

- Capital formation growth rate for the United States, currently around 3.4%, is significantly lower than that for Japan (estimated about 6.7%) or Western Europe (estimated about 4%).

- Corporate debt appears to be accumulating faster in the United States than stockholder equity, while the ability to service that debt is increasingly coming under strain; so is corporate liquidity.

- Coupled with the above, there has been a significant decline in the rate of increase of U.S. (labor) productivity. Productivity has fluctuated with economic conditions, but tended to increase at an average rate of over 3% through the 1960s. That average rate dropped to 1.6% in 1977, .4% in 1978, and essentially zero in 1979.

- Precisely the countries that have the highest savings rates-- and the highest rates of capital investment--are the ones that are experiencing the greatest rates of increase in productivity. Productivity in the U.K., France, and West Germany (non-farm) increased at a rate of more than twice ours, and in Japan it increased at a rate of over four times ours.

- There is concern that lack of productivity increases is
  seriously jeopardizing the ability of the United States to
  compete in world markets and, eventually, our ability to
  maintain our capability to import what we need (like oil) and
  to maintain our standard of living.

The average Japanese production worker wage was 10% of the
average New England production worker wage in 1960, up to 48% in
1975, over 75% now and is projected to exceed 100% about 1983.
Industrial areas where the United States has lost the incentive or
is feeling heavy foreign competitive pressure include textiles, steel,
automobiles, TV sets, shoes, and shipbuilding. The Japanese are pre-
paring to take on the United States seriously in some of our strongest
areas, including computers.

This picture appears rather grim. In fact, the situation is not
as negative as it appears to be, and has important positive aspects.
This is because many of the economic measures we are used to employ-
ing are misleading when applied to an information-oriented economy,
making matters look a lot worse than they in fact are. Take the
savings issue for example. By savings, we mean money placed in
savings accounts in banks, savings and loan associations, and credit
unions. Money is put away or "saved" in many other ways today, housing
being a main one among them.

Savings and Investment

Residential properties are currently estimated to be worth about
$2.3 trillion, with mortgage debt at about $735 billion. Thus, owner
equity in homes is about 68%, a very healthy figure. Inflation is in
fact pushing this equity up significantly faster than the increase in
mortgage debt, as can be easily calculated. The result is preservation
of a healthy margin of homeowner equity.

As home prices increase, the amount of this equity is constantly
increasing by more than $250 billion a year, representing about $1,050
in yearly savings for every U.S. citizen. Also, a significant portion
of the aggregate $4 trillion debt (all types) is currently held by
individuals in the forms of corporate and government bonds, certificates
of deposit, and money market funds. For them, these instruments
represent savings.

As to capital formation and business investments, again it is
misleading to compare us with countries that are not yet as
information-oriented as we are.

- While the Western European and Japanese capital formation
  growth rates have been dropping since 1973, in the United
  States this rate has been picking up since 1975. It is now
  almost equal to the West German rate.

- Significant amounts of European, Japanese, and OPEC investment capital is flowing into the United States, and sophisticated foreigners see America as offering the greatest
  opportunity for profitable investments in an advanced country.

The work force has been expanding at a very high rate; 3 million jobs were created last year, and two out of three of those jobs were taken by women. Most of these jobs are in information-related activities, which require less capital investment than typical manufacturing or agricultural activities.

Even more significantly, human capital--investment in skills and knowledge of people--becomes ever more important in an information society, and the measures we use simply ignore the vast current rate of investment in human recourses. Some of this investment is through our educational system where college-level training is now becoming more and more universal. The United States invested about $150 billion in education in 1979; another $350 billion in other aspects of human investment are associated with adult education in all forms, travel, and, most significantly, on-the-job training and the learning that comes with high job mobility.

So the United States has lost its industrial manufacturing initiative for low and even medium-technology goods to foreign countries. One point of view is "So what, as long as the United States maintains a healthy economy with high-technology and service-related industries." The Japanese plan to compete with the United States in the computer business. They are likely to continue to find this difficult to do, because applications software is increasingly important, and there is some question as to whether their understanding of the details of Western business systems can be sufficiently complete and sophisticated to permit them to compete strongly with domestic firms in the applications software arena.

Several European countries have invested heavily over the last two decades in massive efforts to create national computer industries that would get the lion's share of the domestic computer markets, competing effectively with IBM. Their success has been minimal. One reason may be a lack of an information-age orientation toward innovation and business organization. At the risk of gross oversimplification, we might hypothesize that they tried to apply industrial organizational principles to creation of information-age businesses, and largely failed.

Some of the alarm about productivity currently being expressed stems, in my opinion, from misunderstanding of what is happening to the labor force as our information intensive economy develops. If my three teenage sons suddenly get jobs, productivity in my family (total income divided by total hours worked) would drop a lot, simply because my sons would earn less per hour than I do. This is no reason to worry that my family can no longer compete with other families; their work makes our family better off, not worse.

In the same way, our country is not necessarily worse off when we add workers while keeping our relatively high rate of productivity more or less constant. Gross national product, national income, personal income, family income, disposable family income--all have been going up in real dollar terms, with relatively minor business cycle fluctuations.

"Rear-view" Vision Limits Growth

The United States has been rapidly expanding its economy while its traditional industrial competitors have been concentrating on productivity increase. It has been busy expanding its information and service sectors, which are less capital-intensive. Thus, the overall scope and power of the U.S. economy has continued to expand in ways not reflected in traditional investment or productivity figures. The United States thus has a stronger, larger, and more flexible economy, with a large number of two-worker families. Real family income (since most families have two serious workers) has been going up much faster in the United States than personal income statistics suggest.

Competitiveness of the United States in world markets, on closer look, shows stronger U.S. economic power and strategic economic position than appears on the surface. In large part this is because the United States is proportionally less heavily invested in traditional manufacturing activities and more heavily involved with newer information and service activities than most of its major industrial competitor nations. This makes the United States relatively less vulnerable to competition from the rapidly industrializing third-world countries.

Another direction of misperception of the productivity issue is seeing the solution as investing more and more capital in manufacturing machinery and plants, even though the marginal contribution of capital to productivity is already precariously low for most U.S. manufacturing industries. It is a view of the situation appropriate to the past not the present.

We need a flip in the view from thinking about investment in manufacturing jobs where fewer and fewer of the workers are and where investment per worker is already very high, to investment in information jobs where more and more of the workers are and where equipment investment per worker is very low.

Whether a company is involved in farming, manufacturing, distribution, transportation, retailing, mining, or energy-providing, its management, marketing, inventory, distribution, and other operating controls are basically information-handling activities. The same holds for trade and professional associations, organizations dependent upon communications with their membership and with outside constituencies.

Most "work" in our society is information work, and most information work takes place in offices. Yet, the benefits obtainable through increasing productivity of office workers are not always in the attention span of management. There is a persistent rear-view mirror approach to looking at productivity that originated in the manufacturing-oriented society that once was. This view of productivity has looked mainly at cutting office costs that are visible, and has tended to ignore real but distributed benefits. Office and paper work activities are still seen as cost centers, as overhead. The only "real" production, according to this view, is on the factory floor; the rest is fluff to be minimized.

This rear-view mirror approach to productivity in offices is thus limited to cutting costs required to do the same old things. Focus is on decreasing resources input to the office (people, dollars, etc.) not on more or better output from people--the major limited resource in most information-handling organizations.

Cutting office costs is, in fact, often an important and valuable first benefit from automation attempts. It is also the most clearly definable one and has been the main historical justification for introducing word processing, for example. But cost reduction is only a first step in productivity improvement, and not the most important one at all.

Offices are where basic decisions are made that impact heavily on the viability, costs, and effectiveness of the rest of the organization. The office is the place where the timeliness of a decision or response can have immense impact. There plans get made, performance analyzed, and responses developed to deal with the changing external environment.

The office is the place where a high degree of automation can be realized extremely cheaply (in terms of equipment costs) compared with usual standards of investment associated with factory or farm automation. The office is the place in the organization where the activities with the highest leverage for profits exist, where the productivity of the rest of the organization can be most fundamentally impacted. What counts is the quality and timeliness of management activities, and these factors are measured ultimately in terms of corporate profitability, service to customers and growth.

What is going on now in increasing numbers of organizations is flipping the mirror around, from looking at office cost-cutting to looking at increasing management and organizational productivity. Some of the ways of creating a context for expansion of productivity through use of new office technology are:

- Expansion of the work place in location, to include home, hotel, client or customer's offices; that is, broadening the choice of places where information work takes place.

- Expansion of the work place in time; that is, making possible a 24-hour available work day.

- Reduction of information "float"; that is, decreasing the delay and uncertainty associated with information in the mail, in typing, in an inaccessible file, in an office that is closed, etc.

Driving the information society are some of the most dynamic high-growth industries in the United States today: companies that provide computer equipment (big mainframe systems, mini-systems, peripherals); suppliers of office automation equipment, including word processing, switching, copier-duplicator, facsimile, microform, and other systems; telephone companies and other communications equipment and service suppliers; remote terminal information service and data base access companies; and manufacturers of microcomputers, semiconductors, and "intelligent electronics" of all kinds. These are the industries where the United States has a technology edge, where it is a major net exporter, where the Soviet block countries are left far behind, where 25% to 40% annual growth rates have been sustained year after year, where innovation counts a lot, where many of the best jobs reside, where small high-technology companies still get born and grow to compete with corporate giants.

The economic vitality of these industries reflects their capability to generate profits and plow them back into growth. The total computer industry, today representing over $55 billion a year and into its third decade of existence, still is doubling its size every three to four years. IBM alone is currently investing at a rate of $7 to $9 billion a year.

Sectors of the computer industry, like small office computers, and distributed systems, are growing at even faster rates. "Personal" computers for office and home are experiencing over an 80% annual rate of increase in value of shipments, and as many as $60 million such units are expected to be in operation by 1990.

Productivity and Profits

Major sectors of our economy consist of information-handling and communications industries, including banking, insurance, education, consulting, broadcasting, publishing and all forms of government. These have been major growth industries in the '60s and '70s; they account for a big slice of our economy. They are among the biggest current employers of people entering the labor force, women in particular.

Some of these industries have already handsomely profited from productivity increases associated with use of the newer information technologies. Computer services provided to other organizations by commercial banks are reported to have grown to nearly $8 billion annually, and are growing at 18% to 20% per year.

Certain sectors of the publishing industry also report very high growth rates. Data base publishing--producing publications and search services out of computer-maintained data bases--has grown to be a $1.5 billion industry.

Many of the more successful data base publishers are able to produce 30% to 40% real pretax profits (i.e., funds available to invest in new products, in R&D, and in growth). Yet, several of the other information industries, such as book and journal publishing and education, are just beginning the information automation process, and have not yet realized most of the benefits.

The main partners sharing in the benefits of information automation are citizens who realize benefits of office and computer automation in a thousand unseen or unrealized ways--ways that contribute directly to convenience and quality of our lives. Electronic devices that speed us through checkout counters at supermarkets are examples; credit cards and the systems that back them are others. Each contributes to the productivity of our time, enables us to do things that might otherwise be impossible or at best draining of personal energy.

In the last few years I have spent an hour and a half cashing a travelers check in a bank in Sardinia, five hours (including travel to the one office open downtown) to change an airline flight reservation in Teheran, three hours trying (unsuccessfully) to locate the telephone

number of a certain government office in Moscow--all matters we take
for granted to be accomplished in minutes in the U.S. and in other
advanced countries.

I have also traveled between cities in the Middle East where there
were no means to identify the hotels and their available space without
actually going to them. One particular night, in Kerman, the experience in the hotel we did finally get was memorable in a way we did not
appreciate at the time. We have already grown accustomed to use of
computerized airlines, automobile rental, and hotel reservation
systems that make personal travel reliable.

Personal Productivity

The public also benefits immensely from personal productivity
increases. In 1950 a four-function electromechanical calculator cost
over $2,000 in today's equivalent dollars; today the electronic
version costs less than $10. Then the number of such machines in
use counted in the thousands; today it is in the tens of millions.
Benefits go not only to those officially in the work force but also
to students, retired people, housewives, people at sport or play.

The public also benefits from better resource utilization made
possible by information-handling technology and data bases, the only
resources whose costs are actually decreasing. The costs of all other
resources--energy, minerals, people, the environment--are increasing.
But these scarce resources can be made to go much further through
direct use of new information technologies, and through faster and
more informed decisions which are facilitated by office information
technologies.

Examples are all around; computerized temperature control in
office buildings saves energy without sacrificing comfort; microprocessors controlling automobile engines cut gas consumption without
sacrificing performance; teleconferencing can reduce personal travel
requirements; etc. Electronic communications can be more and more
substituted for physical transportation, saving both energy and
personal effort.

To put it another way, moving people takes a lot of energy; moving
physical packages of information (mail), considerably less, but still
a lot; and moving information electronically takes very little energy.

The public, employees and citizens in all walks of life, are the
greatest beneficiaries, through realization of higher quality of life.
The key has been increased productivity resulting in higher quality of
goods and services, more real personal choice, a pluralistic society
that really works, and an opportunity for people to realize themselves
in their own ways.

EXPECTED ADVANCES IN COMPUTER AND COMMUNICATIONS TECHNOLOGY DURING THE NEXT 20 YEARS

by

H. S. McDonald
Assistant Director and
Systems Architecture Research Consultant
Bell Laboratories

The entire technology of information processing is changing at such a rapid rate that definite projections of hardware costs or software capabilities in the year 2000 are virtually impossible. However, there are certain bounds and trends that will serve to moderate these changes. Before examining these bounds and trends, it is useful to examine what is driving these changes today.

Reasons for the Rapid Advances

The principle underlying reason for the very rapid advance is the development of integrated circuits on silicon substrates, which contain many tens of thousands of individual circuit elements that are interconnected with fine metal paths made by lithographic etching. The circuit elements are digital in the sense that they have a binary property of on or off. One circuit usually consists of several transistors and has the capability of storing one bit of information or acting on information to make a single decision to yield one bit of data. Dozens of these circuits can be combined to store or process enough bits of information to handle a character or a number. Enough of the clusters can be combined to process a string of characters representing a word of text. Enough components can now be placed on a single silicon chip to form an entire computer suitable for simple tasks such as controlling all of the timing and cycle sequences of a washing machine or a microwave oven. These devices are called microcomputers. Also, enough components can be placed on a chip to form the processor of a computer system that has the capabilities of minicomputer processors that sold for tens of thousands of dollars five years ago and for hundreds of thousands of dollars ten years ago. These chips are known as microprocessors. To go along with these microprocessors are chips that are capable of storing as many as 65,000 bits of information, about the contents of three pages in a book. In the laboratory, memory chips up to 256,000 bits have been demonstrated and reasonable people are predicting one million bit chips by the mid 1980s.

All of this process was made possible by the invention of the transistor in 1948 by Shockley, Bardeen, and Brattain at Bell Laboratories in Murray Hill, New Jersey, and by the subsequent work at Texas Instruments by Kilby in 1958, when the first collection of transistors

89

on the same silicon substrate was interconnected to form a working circuit. The transistor discovery came out of a fundamental study to understand the electrical properties of matter. The transistor as we know it today is several small adjacent patches on a very pure silicon crystal surface that has been treated with certain impurities such as arsenic or boron to change the electrical properties of the silicon just under the patches where the impurities have diffused down into the pure crystal. At the boundaries of several of these patches, or junctions as they are known to the device engineers, electrical phenomena are present that can cause amplification of an electrical signal. In less than a decade after the development of the transistor, the electron tube or vacuum tube became obsolete. Where the electron tube amplifier required watts of power the transistor amplifier required hundredths of watts; where the electron tube "wore out" after a few years the transistor had an almost indefinite life. The replacement of the $200 portable radio powered with several pounds of batteries by a $10 cigarette pack-sized transistor radio caused a major change in world communications.

In the 1960s, the technology was developed for making thousands of transistors on a single slice of pure silicon crystal by techniques similar to lithographic printing. By covering the slice surface with a light sensitive layer of photo-resist and then exposing this layer to light through a mask that contains patterns, selective patches of crystal surface are exposed. When placed in an oven with a gas containing certain impurities, the diffusion of these impurities makes the transistor. After covering the surface with an insulating layer and depositing a layer of metal, then a similar lithographic process can form a wiring pattern connecting the transistors when the exposed metal is etched away. By repeating this process more "wires" can be added until the transistors are interconnected to form a complete processor or memory. The key element to low cost is the batch fabrication of hundreds of thousands of transistors at one time by a sequence of a dozen processing steps on a five-inch slice or wafer of silicon crystal. As lithographic techniques are improved so the units can be made smaller then more can be put on a single wafer and the price will come down. Resolutions of one millionth of a meter are being achieved in the laboratory while current production is running about three to five times larger. In the quest for better resolution and the resulting greater circuit density, visible optics are yielding to X-rays which probably will yield to electron optics similar to the electron scanning microscope.

One fortuitous consequence of the quest for smaller size digital circuits is that speed goes up and power goes down as the elements get smaller. The result is that the complexity can grow until a complete subsystem is on a single chip and the power at moderate speeds stays within reason. In the fastest computers, however, the quest for speed has precluded using very large scale integrated circuit chips because of the heat removal problems. However, in 1980, the quest for smaller and smaller circuits in order to get more complicated chips is producing startling results. Every year for the past 8 or 10 years, the number of components that can be economically produced on a single chip has doubled and is expected to do so for many more years. There are limits, both theoretical and practical. As the circuit size shrinks, the amount of electrical charge representing the storage of a single bit gets so small that a passing alpha particle can disrupt it or induce disturbing signals in the wires connecting to the bit circuit. As the size shrinks the wires shrink to the point where the current density of the signals in the metal causes ion migration which can part the conductor. Practical limits are encountered for imperfections in the masks, the photo-resists, or even from dust on the surface of the silicon wafers. However, several orders of magnitude in complexity increase can be anticipated before these limits constrain the scaling to more dense circuits. It is not hard to imagine that the computer system that fits in a cabinet today will fit on a magazine-sized circuit board by the year 2000. A cabinet would hold a hundred of these computers and a high speed interconnect would allow them to talk to one another or to other computers in other cabinets connected by optical fibers. Such a network of computers, or as it is sometimes known "distributed processing," seems to be the direction most systems will take.

There is more to computing than just the processors and memories. Equally important are the mass data storage systems and the terminals that must interface with the user, usually over a communications system. The rapid advances in micro-circuit technology are also affecting the mass storage field. Due to advances in making very small magnetic heads that are used to read and write data on magnetic discs, the size of a bit on the platter is shrunk so that many more bits may be stored per platter. Improved head mountings and smoother, more homogeneous magnetic surfaces have also contributed to increased density. A recent survey published in the February 1980 issue of Datamation magazine reported the cost of storing one million bits for a month on a disc storage unit fell from $89.00 in 1964 to $1.91 in 1979 and is estimated to be $0.30-0.55 in 1990. At 30 cents a month per megabit, we can afford to store a great deal of information in a readily available form. In the latter decades the cost of owning information will be the cost of acquiring and updating it rather than the hardware rent to hold it. A similar story about magnetic tapes will also be true.

An improvement in the performance and cost of terminals is also under way and will continue at least into the 1990s. It is not as dramatic a change as computer processors, memories, or mass storage devices, because the process of printing is mature and cannot be scaled down. The human is not going to shrink by several orders of magnitude as did the circuits, so the size of the keyboard, screen and cabinet are fixed. The terminals should become "smarter" in that they will be able to be more forgiving such as in helping to correct mistakes or generally requiring less specialized training than today's interfaces require.

Communications technology is merging with computer technology in that for distributed systems communications becomes an integral part of the system. Also, in the communications plant itself, computer-like elements play a major role in the control, diagnosis of faults, and measurement aspects of communications. Although the change in communications has not been as dynamic as the change in computers, there have been major shifts, such as in the costs of long circuits, which have come down from several hundred dollars a circuit mile to several dollars a circuit mile through the successive introduction of carrier techniques, microwave signals, broadband coaxial cable systems, satellite links, and in the 1980s optical fiber links. The cost reduction is a combination of new technology and a larger amount of traffic to be carried. Even today, if a circuit to a single remote house is required, the pair of copper conductors is still the most economical way. Satellite antennas, microwave or infrared beams, or glass links are very difficult to make low enough in cost to support only a few circuits in an economical way.

However, one area has been undergoing a major change for almost the last 20 years and will continue into the last two decades of this century. That is the transmission of hundreds of circuits at up to tens of miles. With the advent of the transistor, small low powered amplifiers became available that could be placed about every 6000 feet in the man-holes along existing underground copper cable routes. These amplifiers were used to amplify digital pulses at about 1.5 million pulses-per-second to a level high enough that after the 6000 foot trip down the cable they were still large enough to be recognized, stripped of any noise or crosstalk, amplified again, and sent on to the next circuit. Such an amplifier for digital pulses is called a regenerator (or a regeneration repeater), and it is the reason that digital signals have been used for most of the new short-haul circuit growth of the communications plant. Two pairs of copper wire in a cable (one for talking in each direction) can be converted to carry 24 speech conversations using digital techniques by adding regenerative repeaters and by using digitizing terminals at the ends. Almost one-half of the trunk circuits between telephone central offices are now implemented using digital circuits. In some high growth cities such as Houston, Texas, 90% of these circuits are digital. The technique is now being used on the long feeder routes that carry subscriber links to the central office.

Digital central offices are proving to be an economical alternative to the mechanical switches used before. The prove-in of a digital central office is enhanced when most of the circuits are digital as the expensive digital terminals at the ends of digital circuits are no longer necessary. Sometime in the 1980s there will be enough digital feeders, digital central offices (or computer controlled offices with miniature switches that are capable of carrying digital signals), digital inter-office trunks and digital long distance circuits (the long distance switches are already mostly all digital) so that a major all-digital communications service will be feasible at an attractive cost over most of the country. Of course there are already many digital circuits in use today as well as many voice circuits that carry data using data modulated signals, but these are small compared with the potential for a nation-wide broadband digital service. Such a service will play a major role in supporting the type of distributed computing expected by the end of the decade. Even broader links will be needed by the end of the century.

There are some limits to the growth of certain modalities of communications systems. Back in the 1920s and 1930s, the number of telephone poles and overhead wires became a serious burden. The technology of buried cable and underground ducts holding multipair cable solved that problem. When the ducts became full, conversion to digital carrier helped. Optical links will free up more ducts. In long distance routes, the ether is becoming saturated around population centers so further microwave channels cannot be added. Coaxial cables or optical fibers carrying thousands of conversations in digital form is solving the ether congestion problem. The number of satellite "parking slots" are filling up and the solution lies in better satellites with scanning spot beams to increase the communications traffic that can be supported by a "parking slot."

In general, new technological solutions have been effective at relieving congestion as long as there has been an increasing demand so that the capital to pay for these solutions is available. However, as the demand is satiated and the embedded capital is in the hundreds of billions of dollars, paying for technological change becomes difficult. It is difficult to imagine that the voice communications market would more than double in units and triple in usage for the remainder of this decade. On the other hand, the data processing, data communications, and other data markets will grow at near saturation rates for the decade of the 1980s and at substantial rates for the rest of the century. It seems very important that, to this author, at least, prime priorities are the fostering of new technology and the incentive to invest in its installation in the communications plant, particularly in the coming digitalization of the plant from the subscriber to the central office. Very little if any of the recent technological advances in communications have "helped" voice and "hurt" data uses of the plant. On the other hand many advances will help data much more than voice. We should make sure to keep it that way.

The conclusion about the future hardware technology for both computing and communications is that growth in capabilities and reductions in cost will continue barring factors such as the inability to raise capital or regulatory or statuary constraints. The capabilities for the year 2000 will provide for ubiquitous computer terminals, networks of computers, access to very large data bases, and (hopefully) many new, as yet unforeseen, information appliances that can enhance the quality of our lives.

However, there is another technology that has recently emerged that might play the most dominant role in the information field. That is the technology of programming computers and systems of computers. The programs, or software as they are sometimes called, are the crucial part of the information system of the future. The programs determine the interface the user sees. The programs determine the capabilities of the system. The programs set the speed and availability of the system. Some of these systems are today so complex only a second program has a chance to diagnose trouble and return the system to operational status. It is interesting to note some of the benchmarks of demonstrations of programming progress. An incomplete listing follows:

1940-1950: Solutions to numerical problems far too complex for mechanical calculators.

1950-1960: Operating systems and job-related languages allow many people to use one computer--larger machines solve large problems.

1960-1970:   Many new applications for business and scientific
             uses emerge, i.e., election results analysis.
             Graphics, electronic music, and automated cartoons
             are made by computer. Time sharing and multiple
             user systems emerge. Many new user languages are
             invented. Artificial intelligence programs emerge.
1970-1980:   Very large and very small operating systems emerge.
             Chess programs achieve master's status. Word
             processing changes document preparation. Data
             base management systems control huge pools of data.
             Process control becomes almost all automatic. Net-
             works of computers allow resource sharing and
             electronic mail. Public data base services appear.

In the 1980s and 1990s it is expected that this progress will
continue and in particular advance on several important fronts. The
management of the human-to-machine interface is probably one of the
most important. In a typical large, automated data management system
for a large business it was found that 90% of the costs were due to
the personnel to operate, analyze, and manage the operations system,
and the remaining 10% paid for the space, power, computers, and
supplies. Better ways to increase the productivity of these people
is an obvious opportunity for new technology. Better terminals,
quick checks on the validity of data, automatic resolutions of dis-
crepancies are all being actively pursued toward this end. As the
computer systems of the future are able to respond quickly, access
more data, and process data locally, then interface programs can lower
the human costs of using automated information systems. The search for
easier-to-use computer programming languages is also a potentially
useful pursuit, and progress in the 1980s should be expected.

In nineteenth century mathematics better notations and conventions
added considerable economy of thought, which made understanding and
communications of problems and solutions much easier. As replacing
human muscle in production with machines was the challenge of the
nineteenth century, replacing human senses, simple memory and motor
skills in production is the challenge of the twentieth century. In
addition, replacing these skills in the "behind the scenes" places in
commerce, government, and service delivery systems can greatly improve
the value and reduce the costs of these systems. The information
system of the next century will give humanity a knowledge of the facts
about itself and its environment and means to use them that will at
least make clearer the consequence of actions or potential actions.

PRESTEL AND THE TREND TOWARD PERSONAL COMPUTERS*

by

Martha Boaz

The use of personal computers to communicate information to large numbers of people has universal possibilities. Current efforts to expand the scope and availability of personal computer services are described, with special reference to the PRESTEL experiment in England. The library profession should support similar efforts in the United States, and study ways in which personal computers can be used to serve the library community.

Computers have been widely used by business firms and other large organizations for a number of years, but it is only recently that people have started talking about having computers in their homes. Computers can be designed for individual uses: for students, for employees in certain types of occupations or professions, and for many other services. Experts in the field of technology predict that computers will soon become as ordinary in the household as the television set and the kitchen sink. This phenomenon is certain to also affect library services. The library profession should look into a tie-in with the home computer development and study its applications to library services.

The personal computer may become man's best friend according to John Gottfried, a free lance financial journalist who monitors the computer industry. The computer has the potential for a great many applications: "Using a unit called a modem, you can connect your computer to the New York Times Information Bank and draw out on your television screen any of 1.6 million abstracts from back issues of the New York Times or 60 other publications. The information is then stored in your computer's memory. Research that might have taken a week can now be done in three to five minutes of computer time, at a cost of $1.80 per minute. There is a similar program that allows you access to Dow Jones files for up-to-date information on any stock that interests you"(1).

Examples of specific services that are currently available are personal tax or mortgage calculations; direct purchase of goods or services by credit card; information about accident prevention, education, shopping, and many other types of information. The system can

---

*Reprinted from Special Libraries, vol. no. 71 (no. 7):310-314 (July, 1980). Copyright by Special Libraries Association.

even play a part in the democratic process with terminals that serve as voting booths.

Gottfried also describes more playful uses of the home computer. It can be programmed to respond to vocal commands, such as a request that the lights be dimmed or the front door opened or the morning coffee turned on. Computers are capable of this now but the programming instructions and mechanical devices have not been perfected. Yet, all indications are that personal computers will soon be as common as the CB radio.

British Post Office System--PRESTEL

The British Post Office is experimenting with a system that aims, eventually, to supply millions of homes and offices with equipment that falls into the personal computer category. The British Post Office, which pioneered the British viewdata system--the world's first electronic publishing system--has recently launched a public service called PRESTEL. This system offers a wealth of information for both home and business use by way of the television set and telephone. The PRESTEL service has been offered to residential customers in London since March 1979. Plans are underway to extend the service to London business users and, eventually, to users in Manchester, Birmingham, Edinburgh, and other parts of the country.*

The PRESTEL program is designed to convert the home or office television set into a terminal that can display graphics and words. The set is connected through the ordinary telephone to a central computer which can store hundreds of thousands of pages of information, ranging through news, stock market prices, encyclopedic information, timetables, theater guides, and almost anything published in books, magazines, or other printed form. The set has a remote control key-pad that resembles a pocket calculator. Each user is assigned a personal code number which is built into the receiver and is scanned automatically by the PRESTEL computer each time a call is placed. This number is used for identification and billing purposes.

Advantages of PRESTEL

One of the most valuable assets of the PRESTEL system is the ease of access to potentially unlimited banks of information. Although the volume is restricted now, the forecasts indicate a large growth potential. Even now the material is updated several times a day. Later it will go to a much faster system such as EPIC which is used by the New York stock exchange to provide continuous updating. Another advantage claimed for PRESTEL is that it is interactive. This means that the user who receives information can communicate with the computer which has the stored information.

---

*The author visited the PRESTEL headquarters in London in July 1979 and obtained information which appears in this paper.

Financing

Information sources for PRESTEL include independent organizations such as advertising agencies, publishers, airlines, and official bodies. These groups pay a fee to the British Post Office for the use of computer storage and, in turn, charge users up to ten pence for each page. The charges are totalled automatically by the computer.

By the 1980s, it is predicted that millions of homes will be equipped to receive information and that the cost for the individual home will be nominal. It stands to reason that if the personal computer system is to reach a mass market, cost will have to be brought as low as possible. This will be possible only if there is mass production and widespread use. The British Post Office plans to make PRESTEL available as inexpensively as possible so that it will be accessible to a large majority of people for home use. Usage charges can be reduced during off-peak hours.

Worldwide Use

Standardization of equipment is an item in the cost picture. If different countries use the same machinery the cost will be lowered and compatability of communication channels will be achieved. The British Post Office does not claim a monopoly on this system. One of the aims of PRESTEL is to ensure that international standards are adopted whereby all the systems are compatible with each other. The British system is being transferred to West Germany, Hong Kong, and Holland, but similar systems are being set up in France, Sweden, Canada, and Japan. It is indeed highly desirable to develop a universal terminal that can be used to link European, Asian, American, and worldwide systems. Its success will depend on a service that is open to competition, simple to operate, cheap, and international-transnational in scope. The competition will extend to the provision of hardware, the software (information), and to the service itself.

Introduction Into the United States

PRESTEL will be introduced in the United States during the first part of this year according to Insac Corporation, the company representing the system on this side of the Atlantic (2). It will be established under license from the British Post Office to Insac (a software expert company formed by the British Government's National Enterprise Board). The network will be nationwide, packet-switched, and accessible for $5 to $10 per hour.

The system's initial applications in this country will be oriented toward business. It will employ an alphanumeric, audio-coupled terminal rather than a television, according to John Bately of Insac Corporation. Industry sources believe General Telephone and Electronics Corporation will be the American firm behind the system.

Comments by several people in different specialized professional areas indicate great interest in current developments in communication technology. Larry J. Kimball, director, Economic Forecasting Models,

Graduate School of Management, University of California at Los Angeles, states that the home computer is introducing hundreds of thousands of people to the new technology without the mystery that sometimes surrounds the computer. The practice of data transmission over ordinary telephone, with one computer talking to another, is showing explosive growth. Kimball predicts that many changes will be introduced through the combination of television, computer, and typewriter. These will be social, political, educational. Business and scientific information, new educational materials, and even gossip will flow through the system. He also notes that instead of passively accepting the transmitted signals, the user will be an active participant, sending back reactions that can be tabulated, compared with other responses, and returned immediately (3).

Commenting on the effect of advanced communications on the local community, Thornton Bradshaw, President of Atlantic Richfield (ARCO) believes that it will produce a more efficient use of energy which, more than any other factor, will shape the future of Los Angeles. He adds that audiovisual transmission might well determine population distribution and that public and private institutions will have unprecedented flexibility in arranging work-time and place, eliminating long commutes and rush-hour jams (3,p.4). Without doubt the home computer will be featured conspicuously in the relevant communicational and educational services involved.

Another forecaster on the community impact is Harlan Ellison, author of Dangerous Visions. He predicts that in the future we will not be able to afford public transportation. All the little bedroom communities in a city like Los Angeles will become isolated, theater and culture will die, and the suburbs will acquire much more of a neighborhood feeling, as in New York (3,p.4). In view of this restricted, more limited geographical setting, the matter of communications will become much more important, and the home computer will be a vital force in the program.

Educational Use of the Computer

The use of the home computer for educational purposes will be of great value. Students will be able to obtain information from a wide variety of sources and have the information transmitted to their home electronic systems. Tests can be given and the results sent back immediately. Tapes on foreign languages, history, economics, and other subjects will be available and the home computer will become an excellent teaching tool.

Potential Impact On Libraries

The use of personal computers should be of great interest to the library/information community. It will probably affect public attitudes toward libraries and may change libraries' patterns and styles of providing information. Libraries in the United States could take advantage of the work already underway in Great Britain and begin experiments with home computer services in this country.

The British Library Advisory Council was interested in the PRESTEL (earlier called "viewdata") system from its beginnings and set up a plan to study ways in which it could serve the library community. A trial database was prepared, including frames about the British Library and a sample of the British National Bibliography. This was planned for three types of use:

1) Selected frames giving information about the British Library designed to promote its services and inform potential users about the resources and services available to them;

2) Frames with selections of references from BLAISE (MARC especially) containing subjects of general or topical interest, generated by use of intelligent terminals; and

3) Frames from the British Library that might be used as teaching aids for computer-aided instruction.

The Research and Development Department of the British Library is funding a study of the implications of PRESTEL for public libraries. This research is based on six public libraries: Birmingham, Norfolk, Bexley, Hounslow, Sutton, and Waltham Forest. Each library has a PRESTEL receiver located in the reference library. The research team's plan is to explore the attitudes of the staff and users of the service; examine the management implications and effect on such items as stock requirements, budgets, and space use; and collect information on ways in which PRESTEL data may best be used in a public library.

The effects of the British experiment cannot be predicted at this time, but the concept is certainly provocative and challenging in its potential for far-reaching benefits. France is also working with personal computer services, and it is likely that announcements about experiments in the United States will be forthcoming soon. It is predicted that the cost of a small terminal will be in the $100-$200 price range within the near future.

The implications for all types of libraries are exciting. With the decreasing cost of technology and the improvement in services, the benefits of these services should be used by libraries. The services include these components: information, communication, education, entertainment, and data processing. Libraries should make use of these services to expand their functions and should work with (not against) the developers of the system. Otherwise, many of the information and reference functions of libraries may be taken over by information brokers. Thus, it is important that librarians and information specialists hurry to be among the first to take advantage of "home information services." As someone has said, "It's Now--The Information age is upon us."

Suggested Studies

What are the implications for the public of a system such as PRESTEL? Research should be done in the trial use of this type of system in the following areas: 1) exploring the attitudes and reactions of users of the service and collecting data for possible future information needs; 2) examining business management and systems implications; 3) checking budget and cost factors, and, 4) investigating ways for improving the hardware and software for maximum utility for the future delivery of information.

Literature Cited

1. Gottfried, John/A Man's Best Friend is His Home Computer. Saturday Review (Oct 13, 1979). p.64

2. Prestel Comes to the U.S. In Information World (March, 1979). p. 17.

3. Looking Ahead. "You" Section, Los Angeles Times (Oct 9, 1979). p. 6.

HOW INFORMATION NETWORKS MAY DEVELOP
AND
ACCOMMODATE TO FUTURE TRENDS

by

Alphonse F. Trezza
Executive Director
National Commission on Libraries and Information Science

This article addresses problems of network definition, and of network context and characteristics; it touches on their development, describes some current library network activity, and, finally, discusses accommodating to the future.

Libraries have long recognized the impossibility of any one library having all of the resources necessary to meet the needs of its users-- be they academic and school faculty, students and researchers, business, industrial, or professional clients, or the general public. Both the tremendous increase in information and the economic impossibility of independence have made cooperation through systems, consortia, coopera- tives, and networks inevitable. Yet, trying to trace the beginnings of these networks really depends on one's perception and understanding of the term. The Oxford English Dictionary states that the term "network" has been in existence since 1560. Perhaps the development of infor- mation networks can be traced to even earlier days of civilization. Tribes communicated information to each other by sound (drums) and/or sight (smoke). Messages were transmitted to "users" who were remote from the main source and the communication was, at least, bi-directional if not multi-directional. Information was shared freely, and the only "protection" for the originator of the information was the code used to transmit it. These early information exchange "networks" were relatively slow and geographically limited when one considers today's nationwide telephone system, but they apparently were more than adequate, for they served for many centuries. Was this early communication system really a network? One of the problems we face, of course, is one of defini- tion--just when does the sharing of information by two or more individuals or organizations develop from a cooperative into a network?

There is agreement on some of the elements that are included in a network. The National Commission on Libraries and Information Science (NCLIS), for example, in its definition of networks, suggests that it includes two or more libraries and/or other organizations (tribes) engaged in a common pattern of information exchange (use of drums or smoke signals), through communication, for some functional purpose (survival). A network may consist of formal agreements whereby two or more different types of libraries share with their mutual users materials, information, and services. Libraries may be in different jurisdictions, but agree to serve one another on the same basis as each

serves its own constituents. Computers and telecommunication may be
among the tools used for facilitating communication among them.[1]

It might be useful in trying to understand networks to review
briefly the different contexts in which the term is used. Carl F. J.
Overhage[2] cites five different contexts in which the term is used:
1) science literature, as in networks of citation-linked papers;
2) organization structures as in the ERIC clearinghouses;
3) cooperative arrangements as in interlibrary loans;
4) communications systems as in press wire services;
5) computer-communication systems as in the NASA Recon System.

Becker and Olsen divide the definition first by <u>class of equipment</u>
such as in telephone, teletype, facsimile, and computer networks; second
by <u>form of data</u>, as in digital, audio, video, and film networks; and
third by <u>functions</u> as in financial, library, education, and management
networks.[3]

Swank defines the network concept as including "the development of
cooperative systems of libraries on geographical, subject, or other
lines, each with some kind of center that not only coordinates the
internal activities of the system, but also serves as the system's
outlet to, and inlet from, the centers of other systems."[4]

The concept is also hierarchical in that centers of smaller systems
are channels to centers of larger networks at state, national, and even
international levels. A familiar analogy is the telephone service, in
which systems were first locally coordinated, and then hooked up into
national and international networks.

Swank also identifies characteristics of an information network as:
1) Information resources--collections of documents or data in
whatever medium; the data bases; the input.
2) Readers or users--usually remote from the main sources of
information.
3) Schemes for the intellectual organization of documents or
data--as directories for use by readers or users.
4) Methods for the delivery of resources to readers or users--the
output.
5) Formal organizations--of cooperating or contracting formations,
representing different data bases and/or groups of users.
6) Bi-directional communications networks--preferably through
high-speed, long-distance electrical signal transmission with switching
capabilities and computer hook ups.[5]

Becker, in a paper he gave at a conference on the structure and
governance of library networks cosponsored by the NCLIS and the University
of Pittsburgh in 1978, points out that the problem of trying to define
a network is that "we are dealing with a concept rather than a word.
Concepts are explained; words are defined." He suggests that it is
important to be specific about the type of network under discussion--it
is essential to use the descriptive adjective along with the noun.
"Networks," Becker reminds us, "are perceived from many points of view
such as:
--By the signals they carry:
digital network
video network

      analog network
      communications network
--By their logical structure:
      star or centralized network
      decentralized network
      distributive network
      hierarchical network
--By their institutional focus:
      public library network
      academic library network
      special library network
      and even, intertype network
--By the functions they perform:
      cataloging network
      bibliographic network
      interlibrary loan network
      reference information network
--By the subjects they treat:
      medical information network
      agriculture information network
      energy information network
--By the equipment they employ:
      teletype network
      telephone network
      radio network
      television network
      computer network
--By the geographic area they encompass:
      statewide network
      regional network
      multi-state network
      national network
      international network

"Is it any wonder the word defies definition? Although we can explain the concept and even describe the characteristics of different types of networks, the likelihood that we will ever be able to define the word 'network' with precision in a library context seems remote."[6]

In reviewing the development of networks, a look at the major components and factors influencing their development may help set the background for a discussion of some of the future trends in nationwide networking. Some of the major components of a nationwide full-service network are resources that include all types of media and formats, such as serials, monographs, documents, newspapers, print and non-print materials, and online data bases; activities that include identification, acquisition, processing, preservation, and delivery of all bibliographic entities; resource sharing through cooperative acquisition, broad and direct patron access to resources, and sharing of staff and facilities; an integration of services of all types of libraries and segments of the information and library community including abstracting and indexing services; education and training in areas of planning and evaluation, the use of online data base services (both those for library materials processing and those for

user information services), in the philosophy of cooperation and
sharing, the understanding and ability to use new technological developments and in educating the user to exploit the library as an educational, informational, and recreational center, research and
development to keep up with the impact on library and information
centers and providers of the rapidly changing and expanding technologies in the fields of communications, computers, micrographics,
home delivery of information services, etc.; and the development of
standards required for linking systems for computer operations, for
data description, data collection, etc.[7]

Before speculating on future trends, it might, additionally, be
useful to review briefly where we are and how we got there. Norman
Stevens, in a paper on the historical perspective on the concept of
networks, reminds us that the concept of library networks like all
concepts "did not suddenly emerge as a new idea." It evolved out of a
number of events and ideas. He cites three major elements in the
development of the network concept: "First the concept of library
networks came from a long tradition of cooperation in American
librarianship...second...was the use of automation to handle library
routines...third...was the work that took place in the related area of
information science." In his view, the most significant development
affecting library networks in the United States was the reiteration
in the 1960s by the Library of Congress that "its primary function is
to meet the needs of the U.S. Congress and that its responsibilities
to other American Libraries are secondary and incidental."[8] (But, in
the late 1970s, William Welsh, Deputy Librarian of Congress, said that
the Library of Congress would participate in network development.) As
a result of this emphasis, MARC tapes were made available. Experimentation on the use of the MARC tapes culminated in the online technology
used by OCLC and in its director's belief that a bibliographic data base
not only could support cataloging and card reproduction, but could also
serve as the base to support many additional library functions.

"The long tradition of cooperation" was clearly evident in the
first half of this century as many libraries and organizations entered
into voluntary arrangements, both formal and informal, to share resources
and services. These arrangements were generally limited to interlibrary
loans, permission for patrons to use the collection for reference and
research, and, in some cases, the issuance of courtesy borrowing cards.
There was a great deal of discussion of cooperative acquisitions and
some efforts at developing cooperatively sponsored workshops, seminars,
etc. Special and academic libraries were most active in these voluntary
informal or semi-formal cooperative arrangements. Public libraries
tended to move in the direction of formal arrangements, usually through
contractual arrangements as a result of state legislation. In fact,
major developments in this movement occurred in the sixties when New
York, Illinois, New Jersey, Michigan, California, Pennsylvania, and
others adopted laws establishing statewide cooperative public library
systems. Participation was voluntary, funding was provided by the state,
and services were traditional. There were two basic patterns--the New
York-Illinois and the Pennsylvania-New Jersey. The former required the
legal establishment of a regional (within state) public library system
with its own staff and board. The system had no authority over its

member library budget, staff, or collection development. It provided coordination for cooperative services, which were determined by system members. The statewide systems provided backup resources, technical assistance, and continuing education opportunities.

The Pennsylvania-New Jersey pattern was also regionally based, but was organized around an existing library whose collection and staff were deemed to be the "strongest" in that particular area. Some additional staff was added, there was usually an advisory body, but basic govern-ance rested with the "host" library. Both patterns were productive and successful, and, as a result, all but five states today have a state-funded, partially in most cases, fully in a few, statewide public library system.

Another major development was the passage in 1965 of the Medical Library Assistance Act and the establishment of the Regional Medical Library Network. Under the leadership of the National Library of Medicine, the medical library network has provided a service that is vital and successful. It is also the prime example of a federally-supported network, although in the last few years it has moved toward encouraging states to pick up the costs of requests that can be met at the state level, leaving the use of federal funds for those requests that must be met at the regional and national level.

The Regional Medical Library Network consists of eleven regional libraries and over 100 resource libraries. Funded and coordinated by the National Library of Medicine, the regional libraries share their resources through bibliographic access to journal, monograph and audio-visual materials. The regional libraries promote network participation among medical and hospital libraries through programs of online services, training and workshops, continuing education, and consultation.

The unique elements of the Regional Medical Library Network that have been basic to its success are that it was initiated by the federal government and, in its early years was completely federally funded. It was highly structured, requiring performance standards, and was based on a distributed workload concept and organized, coordinated and supervised by a national library--the National Library of Medicine. One other major factor was the intent of the U.S. Congress to equalize access to the nation's biomedical information resources for use by health pro-fessionals in health services delivery, education and research. The network was designed to try to satisfy the users' needs and demands in their efforts to deal more effectively with the nation's health. The Regional Medical Library Network is a prime example of a federally planned, operated, and funded nationwide network that is successful and that did not develop accidentally or by guesswork. It is a model that the critics of federal participation in nationwide networking still fail adequately to recognize or understand

The growth of both single type and multitype library systems has been slow and uneven, and their use of new technology limited. The most dramatic change in the use of the new technology came through the develop-ment of functional or subject networks. The National Library of Medicine is the example of the latter. The establishment of the Ohio College Library Center (now OCLC, Inc.) first as a state-based operation and later as a national organization, is an example of the former. OCLC, along with BALLOTS (now Research Libraries Information Network),

Washington Library Network (WLN), and others revolutionized shared
cataloging, made MARC a "household" word and spawned a number of
regional (multistate) computerized networks such as NELINET, SOLINET,
Amigos, BCR, CLASS, MIDLNET, etc. These networks began as single type
systems developed to serve, at least initially, single functions, and
they tended to ignore the cooperative systems being developed through
the state library agencies--which served primarily public libraries.

OCLC, Inc., for example, began in the late 1960s as a network for
academic libraries within the State of Ohio. Contrary to the fate
experienced by many single-library attempts to automate in the 1960s,
OCLC did not fail. (Notable exceptions to the single-library automation
"failures" are the University of Chicago, Northwestern University, and
the New York Public Library, each of which has developed largely successful institution-based computer systems for library functions and services.) It has, in a mere decade, become the single largest network in
the country. And it continues to play a leadership role in developing
new technology applications to the delivery of library and information
services.

There have been growing pains. OCLC is a not-for-profit organization: its income is derived from the institutions it serves. Federal
funds were used only in the initial development stages, though it could
be said, considerable federal money still flows to OCLC, albeit indi-
rectly, through its members, some of whom do use federal funds to
support their participation in OCLC. Thus, cash flow has, at times,
been a problem. As OCLC grew from a state-level to a national network,
problems also developed with its original governance structure, and a
considerable wrenching occurred before changes came into place that
satisfied its many and diverse members. OCLC has gone through several
generations of hardware in its growth process--indeed, its first
terminals were designed solely for OCLC use, and it continues to make
use of specially adapted terminals and related equipment. And, due to
its rapid growth, it has had to change the physical site of its location
several times.

Yet OCLC is now firmly in place as the largest computer-based network in the United States, serving thousands of libraries of all types
(primarily through "subsidiary" regional networks, rather than directly)
across all political jurisdictions. Basic to its services is interactive, online, shared cataloging (based on the Library of Congress'
MARC tapes), whereby catalogers in any library can take advantage of
cataloging done by any other staff in defining their own cataloging
products. Since libraries that used OCLC for this purpose were identified through the system, an unanticipated spin-off benefit soon became
evident: the system could be used to identify book locations--and thus
served as an interlibrary loan finding tool. This application was
eventually more formally and fully developed to accommodate the record
keeping function (among others) associated with interlibrary loan.

OCLC--often referred to, among networks, as a "utility" since it
supplies the service other networks then make use of--maintains its
lead in developing new technology applications. It has undertaken
experiments in providing access to library bibliographic data directly
to the home, it is exploring the use of satellites as a delivery system,
and it is broadening its applications to include acquisition and

circulation. Most noteworthy is its recent agreement with a commercial venture, The Source, to promote access to a broad variety of information sources and services, such as access to national news wires, airline reservations and teleconferencing, directly to the individual home.

Two other such "macro-networks" deserve at least brief mention. The first is RLIN (the Research Libraries Information Network), a Research Libraries Group (RLG) service which began at Stanford University as a single-library automation effort known as BALLOTS. This system is based on the belief that the needs of large research libraries are different from those of smaller academic and public libraries, and thus, different aspects of bibliographic control (such as authority file control, and "pure" MARC) received greater emphasis in system development. RLG, originally composed of the libraries at Harvard, Columbia, Yale, and the New York Public Library, has since expanded to include other ARL (Association of Research Libraries) members, but lost Harvard as a member.

WLN (the Washington [state] Library Network), while not focusing on the needs of research libraries per se, also subscribed to a belief in the importance of "pure MARC" as a system base, and has developed separately from OCLC. WLN, moreover, has declared it does not wish to serve as a national utility, as OCLC is doing, but to serve only institutions in its own immediate geographic area. WLN, however, in contrast to OCLC, is promoting the "replication" of its system in other areas.

The OCLC phenomenon has spawned a number of regional "sub-networks" as its policy, from the very beginning, was to provide services only through regional "brokers" which would, in turn, service the needs of their individual institutional/library members, rather than itself servicing individual libraries. (Until recently, OCLC did continue to serve its original Ohio members directly, but these, too, have now formed a separate "network," Ohionet.) Some networks, like NELINET, were preexistent and were already offering cooperative services to their members; others, like MIDLNET, developed in response to OCLC.

Except in the case of RLG, each of these networks has brought into its sphere libraries of all types (albeit not without difficulty!), and even RLG includes a public library with a strong research component. They have spurred not only inter-type, but also inter-state network development. And while each originally developed individually, work is now underway to find ways of connecting the networks, so that cooperation on an even higher level--on an inter-network, rather than inter-library basis--will become possible.

Starting in the early seventies and as a direct result of the Library Services and Construction Act (LSCA) Title III, the movement for multitype library cooperation grew. The new federal title provided modest funds for the state library agencies to use as stimulus for the development of multitype services, often on a demonstration basis. Some of the funds were earmarked for experimentation with new technological developments, such as participation in OCLC or the purchase of electronic circulation systems.

The 1970s saw the broadening of the public library systems in some states to include academic, special and school libraries. This expansion was usually limited and usually did not include changes in existing laws. The libraries were permitted to share in networking services, but not in

network governance. An evolutionary integration into full network
participation appeared to some to be the best strategy. In some states
such as Colorado, Indiana, and Washington, new laws were adopted that
were specially designed to develop multitype systems and services. In
all of these cases, participation was voluntary, funding was limited,
and the use of computers and telecommunications was a factor.

A major influence in the development of networks was the increased
demands on libraries for information and services to meet the social,
scientific, technological, commercial, vocational, educational,
cultural, and recreational needs of the community. In our complex and
shrinking world, the growth of knowledge, the accelerated pace of technological development, the changing sociological revolution all make it
imperative for individuals to have access to information in an organized
and efficient mode, in a timely fashion and objective manner, and at a
cost that guarantees equal opportunity of access for all.

The National Commission on Libraries and Information Science,
established in 1970, gave early consideration to developing a nationwide network of library and information services. It addressed the
problem of bibliographic and resource support for a nationwide library
program in a 1974 report undertaken by Westat, Inc. The Commission's
National Program Document, developed after national and regional hearings and much debate and discussion, viewed nationwide network development in a long-range mode. In the Program Document, "Toward a National
Program for Library and Information Services: Goals for Action," the
NCLIS stated that existing patterns of libraries and information
services serving limited geographic areas or various special interests
lead to costly, uneven, needlessly duplicated, and wasteful services.
The time, the document asserts, has come to develop a nationwide program that would weld together today's collections and services into a
nationwide system of library and information services. The overall
goal of such a nationwide network is to serve the needs and desires of
the people of the United States by eventually providing "every individual...with equal opportunity of access to that part of the total
information resource which will satisfy the individual's educational,
working, cultural, and leisure-time needs and interests, regardless of
the individual's location, social or physical condition or level of
intellectual achievement."[9]

All of the advances described above will have an impact on the way
libraries and information centers serve people. The library's role in
providing community information and referral services will increase.
Its role as an intermediary between the user and the new technology
will not only continue but will increase significantly. More and more
we will have to blur the lines of types of libraries and institutions
and look to providing services that are needed by any and all users.
Perhaps during the next 20 years, the time for the demise of distinction
between academic, school, public, and special library will arrive. Their
places will be taken by a new institution called a library and information service that is not "part of the institution" but an information
service center. It will be a library finely tuned to serve the needs
of users at whatever level is needed. The library's own physical
collection will be limited, but tailor-made to serve any "primary
"clientele," with a guaranteed backup collection of the world's

knowledge accessible and available through the new technology, terminals, television screens, reproduction equipment.

Access to the nationwide system will be available to anyone who desires it. No credentials or special requirements will be necessary. The network will be a three-level funded organization, local-state-federal. Its financial stability will be assured because needless duplication will be a thing of the past. Multiple copies of an item or rapid reproduction of individual items will be available on demand. Support at the local level will not be significantly different from the present. Local and state taxes will provide the support for schools at all levels, and public library users and a combination of taxes and fees will provide support for the for-profit organization users. Student tuition and fees will include funds for the network at the local level. The significant difference is that all funds will go for the support of an overall nationwide system made up of a multiplicity of nationally provided services through local, state, and regional service points--the library and information center. This will necessitate changes in library school curricula and will spur the rapid growth of an effective continuing education program.

This suggested scenario of what may come to pass in the next 20 years, like all predictions, will probably come to pass in a very different way. Many of the suggestions are already a reality in some limited instances. Others are inevitable because the chain of events triggered by technology or by activities of national services and organizations (OCLC, RLIN, LC, ARL, ALA, SLA, ASIS, etc.) has already started. What needs discussion and debate and, hopefully, agreement is the recognition that we live in an interdependent society. Working together, sharing resources and services, and believing in each other's motives can make it possible for us to consider the possibility of blurring individual types of library lines to the point when we're all one type of library, i.e., a user-oriented library--not a collection-centered library; a service-centered library, not a process-centered library. What we own will not be so important as long as we can get what we need when we need it. Through sharing and reliance on national centers, we can be freed from the slavery of the institutional library. In the future we will require a different mindset as well as a different use of staff. We will need a group of library and information scientists who provide the technical expertise that will provide the mechanisms for the network and a staff of public service librarians who will interface with the user. They will devote all of their time and energy in locating, understanding, interpreting, and delivering information and knowledge to those who seek it. We will need administrators with vision and the ability not only to provide leadership but successfully to obtain the necessary financing to support the network. There will be plenty of work and challenge for all who want it.

How information networks can be developed to accommodate to these future trends is, of course, difficult to predict accurately. Most of the predictions that were made in the 1950s, 1960s, and 1970s have just not come to pass. Technological advances, especially in the later part of the 1970s, have been dramatic, but they have not caused the demise of the book or other printed material. Microforms are more in evidence but are still used with reluctance. We do not have whole library collections available to all on microforms. Even with the success of computerized online shared cataloging (OCLC, RLIN, WLG), there are still many libraries engaged in manual and local cataloging that is redundant and wasteful. Technology is always far ahead of our human ability to accept and adapt to change.

Just how will information networks develop to accommodate to future trends? Marc Porat and others all point to the fact that we are now in the information age. We are very much information-dependent for our very survival: Is there an oil shortage? Can we develop a viable cost effective energy substitute? Is the peaceful use of atomic energy really an option? Can the power of the oceans and the sun be harnessed? How do we cope with the world's food problems especially in developing nations if pesticides are to be barred? Are certain drugs useful or harmful? Are our government's actions and policies wise and sound? Experts, scientists, specialists, and scholars seem to disagree, almost violently, on these social, environmental, and technical issues. Access to current, accurate and complete information is vital to their solution. Not only must our experts have ready access to such information, but full and free interchange of information between government and citizens is also essential if the decision makers are to know what the public wants and how effective and practical their decisions have been. Moreover, citizens need to know what the government is doing so they can hold officials accountable.

There are many problems and constraints involved in network implementation to provide such access. Some are perceived and some are real. Four basic problems that it seems will always be with us are fear of loss of autonomy and control, lack of adequate funding, the need for creative and effective use of technology, and the effective development of network organization and governance. If we are to work toward resolving these problems, we must understand and accept the fact that the solution depends on political action at all three levels--local, state and federal. The art of the possible is the best politics, but knowing what is possible is the trick. If we set our sights too low we can succeed, but our achievement may not be worth the effort. If we aim too high and try to resolve all of our problems in one leap forward, failure is almost inevitable. An evolutionary process, bold in concept, reasonable in its means, methods, and implementation schedule offers the best hope for success.

Social and institutional acceptance of change is low. In the next 20 years, we will see major achievements in technology and telecommunications that will affect all types of libraries regardless of the size or depth of their collection, their geographic remoteness or the sophistication of their users. Librarians will have to drop their defensiveness and fears and embrace the changes with willingness and confidence. The changes will still be evolutionary although at an increased pace.

There is one basic problem that will require constant attention and understanding. It will always be with us, will always be imperfect, and will always defy resolution. The problem, of course, is you and me--the human problem--the people problem--the behavioral and attitudinal problem. We always have our fears, our deficiencies, our possessiveness, our egos. We can overcome many, if not all, of these problems to a limited extent.

The saving virtue of this imperfect nature, however, is that it helps assure us that we will not be overwhelmed with technology and machines-- we will not become automatons. The human factor will generate a national system that is sensitive to the needs of people, not of institutions, businesses, industry, organizations, or government at any level. The human factor will insist on analysis of the interface between a possible flow of information that will overwhelm society, and its effective and intelligent use for meeting the needs and desires of the user. Libraries and information centers, participating in networks at the local, state, and federal level must exist to serve the users at their levels of education and understanding, their levels of need, their levels of entertainment, pleasure, and escape. We can harness the best of the information and technology revolution to serve mankind in our quest for peace and a better quality of life. What we need is commitment to our cause, faith in our ability to succeed, and the willingness to work and give of ourselves, unselfishly, to the needs of others.

Obtaining reasonably accurate and relatively objective information necessary for average individuals to analyze and understand the issues so they can cope with and participate in the decision-making process in our democratic society is increasingly difficult. Working toward the resolution of this problem is the function and responsibility of today and tomorrow's libraries and information centers. How to sift through the mounds of subjective and detailed information is, of course, the problem and the challenge. The role of the library and information center is to provide the public with the latest, most objective, accurate information organized so as to provide various viewpoints and levels of sophistication so that users at all educational, social, and economic levels can have the opportunity to learn and understand the issues. Only then can intelligent and reasoned decision making take place.

Can we develop information networks to meet that challenge? Obviously we not only can, but must. Libraries have always tried to meet the information needs of their users. Today's demands are such that no library is information self-sufficient. All libraries are information dependent, and must cooperate with other libraries of all types. Unfortunately, many libraries are not really aware of just how dependent they are. The development of networking these past 10 to 15 years has been evolutionary, but the rapid change in technology resulting in computer-based limited function networks has almost been revolutionary. We have learned that through linking libraries we can improve not only the cataloging of library materials but interlibrary loan, access to online data bases, circulation, authority control, and, in the not too distant future, serials control, acquisition, management services, subject access to bibliographic data bases, etc. Even more exciting are the experiments providing access to information by direct linking to the home with interactive television.

The experiments in Columbus (Ohio), Dade County (Florida), and McLean (Virginia), will provide us with much needed experience in learning and understanding what recreational, informational, and educational services will be available to us through home terminals, computers, and our television sets. How these will interface with the library and alter our role of delivering library and information services will be our challenge.

The cost effectiveness and capability of information technology is advancing exponentially. The personal or hobby computers available today for less than $1,000 are faster and hold more information than the early core-memory equipment. Storage capacity of semi-conductor chips and magnetic bubbles can now store billions of bits, which is the digital equivalent of thousands of pages of text. Laser printers can now produce a number of pages of text per second. Communication satellites and fiber optics will transmit or carry many millions of bits per seconds--the equivalent of a few books of text.

Research collections of the knowledge of the past will remain whether they be manuscripts, rare books, or pre-2000 print and nonprint materials. Access to bibliographic and location information will be available on home and school terminals, as well as in libraries and information centers. Information experts will be prepared to assist the user to sift through the information deluge. National information and resource centers will be the backup and backbone of a nationwide system. Institutions will be less interested in duplicating holdings or building large institutional collections of seldom, if ever, used materials and, instead, will concentrate on meeting the user's immediate needs, knowing confidently that meeting the long-term and research requirements is assured through the network. The network will assure comprehensiveness, as well as timely delivery. Much of the information will be provided in hard copy or on a screen almost instantly, unless the volume of copy required can better be met through physical delivery from the centers.

The advent of the video discs that can hold 54,000 frames or images will have a major impact on libraries, especially when they hold digital information. The cost of the discs and the playback equipment when mass produced will be well within the cost range of every library. Will this development reverse the trend of networking cooperation and resource sharing? If all of the journal articles in science and technology published in any one year are available on six or eight videodiscs at a cost that is within the limited budget of the average library, what is the need for a national center of current journal articles? Will this mean that we will only need a last copy center of journals for pre-videodisc years? Will technology advance to the stage where we can reproduce the current holdings needed by major research libraries on a series of videodiscs including appropriate indexing for easy retrieval? Would this "advance" make it possible for libraries to be self-sufficient on a current basis, slowing, if not stopping, the development of local, state and regional networks?

Obviously, many issues need to be resolved if an effective nationwide full-service library and information service network is to become a reality. Self-sufficiency, network services, multitype library cooperation, governance, standards and, of course, universal access are some of the basic issues. Some research librarians remind us that research libraries' participation in cooperative activity helps meet only 10% or less of their service needs. Interdependence, therefore, is exaggerated. In view of the greatly increased volume of printing, the escalating costs of library materials, increasing salaries to meet economic conditions, and the shrinking (in purchasing power) budget, will not research libraries become more interdependent? The rapidly developing technological advances will, in the next 20 years, have a marked influence on research library developments.

In view of the telecommunications, micrographics, and technology advances, will network services only need to be provided at the national level?

Just what services will be provided at the national network level? Cataloging, bibliographic data bases, authority files, automated inter-library loan, serials location, and online data bases are presently provided with acquisitions, a full-serial service, and circulation and management data are on the horizon. Will these services be offered directly, thus eliminating the state and regional networks such as NYSILL, ILLINET, NELINET, SOLINET, etc.?

Will the national network be one that is controlled at the federal level? Or will it meet the criteria stated in the NCLIS National Program Document, that the nationwide network not be "a monolithic and authoritarian superstructure, but . . . form a shelter and frame-work for families of geographic and functional networks, developed and interconnected according to a comprehensive plan."[10]

Will there be an overall multitype library and information service network or are the requirements and needs of academic and special libraries so different from public and school libraries as to necessitate separate networks? Current thinking favors diversity but within one overall coordinated network.

This logic leads to the difficult and controversial question of governance. Obviously, all participants want to play a role. Is the formal structure a federal government agency, a not-for-profit quasi-federally funded corporation? Or will there just be a loose federation of multitype networks?

There is a strong need for a more active role both in funding and in coordinating the operation of a nationwide network. Is the time for a national capping agency long overdue? The Regional Library Medical Network under the National Library of Medicine is an example of a suc-cessful nationwide subject network that can serve as a model in estab-lishing an overall national capping agency. Such an agency can be set up without endangering the legitimate limits of local autonomy as well as providing the opportunity for shared decision making.

The need for standards to assure the compatibility of our plural-istic network development is, obviously, of major importance. How do we develop standards that serve our needs without inhibiting diversity and experimentation?

In the final analysis, all of the efforts at building a nationwide network are aimed at serving people. Can we reach our goal of equal opportunity of access? Or is this just a cliche--an unrealistic aim? Many people refer to equal access rather than equal opportunity of access. Distance, funds, limited intellectual ability, differing educational levels, language difficulties, complexity of certain subjects are all barriers contributing to inequality. Working toward a goal of equal opportunity of access can help to narrow the extremes of information inequality. The individual and not the institution, or an intermediary, must decide when the opportunity of access to information is feasible and when the inequities are not arbitrary or imposed.

To prepare for these changes, the emphasis in library school curricula will have to be on educating students to be planners and evaluators: on goal setting, developing objectives, and specific ways of achieving them within a reasonable and realizable time schedule. Continuing evaluation to measure both the service effectiveness of the programs as well as their cost will become commonplace. A major part of library school education and continuing education will have to focus on the developing technology. Understanding computers, terminals, video equipment, programming, search language, and interfacing standards will all have to be addressed in depth if students are going to be able to cope with tomorrow's library. And, more importantly, library schools will have to help educate future library and information scientists in the philosophy of cooperating, of sharing, of interdependence. Helping to develop attitudes is one of the most important contributions library schools can make.

To work toward achieving our goal we must not lose sight of the principal focus--the users, their needs as _they_ perceive them--not as we interpret them. A nationwide network must not only be capable of meeting the individual needs of its users realistically, conveniently, and for their personal enhancement and achievement, but must protect their constitutional right of personal privacy and intellectual freedom. It must preserve basic local, state, and regional autonomy. The rights and interests of authors, publishers, and information providers in the private sector must be respected and protected. The network must make the maximum use of the new technology in a creative and effective manner. We live in a technology-driven society, but we must strive to use technology to serve our needs and not let it become our master.

The long-range goal, as we have said, is to develop a comprehensive full-service network--a network not restricted to bibliographic information or computerized data but encompassing all methods and techniques that can improve access to information for all of the nation's residents. The resources, both human and material, of a full-service network must be of sufficient scope, depth, and quantity to satisfy the needs of people in an effective and timely fashion. The successful implementation of a network depends on a basic attitude of willingness to cooperate and participate for the good of society as a whole. A nationwide network is not a substitute for the local library--it is complementary and supplementary. The immediate and usual needs of the library's primary clientele--students, faculty, researchers, the general public--must be met by effective and efficient services from the local library. A fundamental principle is the provision, at the local level, of an adequately funded institution that can provide a level of service that meets reasonable service standards. Networking at the state, regional, and national level can only be effective and successful if built on such a base. The network must consist of libraries of all types voluntarily cooperating, having communication links, using computer-based services, providing comprehensive reference services, and resources of all kinds. It must provide for the delivery of services through a variety of mechanisms such as interlibrary loan, reciprocal borrowing, electronic transmission, U.S. Postal Service, telephone, teletype, local vans and delivery services, etc.

To meet the challenge of the information revolution requires a recognition of the problems and needs, and a willingness to serve the common good. The rapid development of telecommunications, micrographics, and computers has certainly had, and will continue to have, a major and dramatic impact on the development of networks. The problem is not technological, but human. We must be willing to overcome our fears and doubts. We need to take action and not just debate issues. Perfection is just not possible. We must continue our efforts to move forward, improve our coordination techniques, and develop mechanisms not only to discuss major problems and issues but to make decisions and to learn to accept them.

Notes

[1] U.S. National Commission on Libraries and Information Science. Toward a National Program for Library and Information Services: Goals for Action (Washington, D.C.: NCLIS, 1975), pp. 82-83.

[2] Carl F.J. Overhage, "Information Networks," in Annual Review of Information Science and Technology, C.A. Cuadra, ed. (Chicago: Britannica, 1969), pp. 339-41.

[3] Joseph Becker and Wallace C. Olsen, "Information Networks," in Annual Review of Information Science and Technology (Chicago: Britannica, 1968), pp. 209-91.

[4] R.C. Swank, Interlibrary Cooperation Under Title III of the Library Services and Construction Act (Sacramento: California State Library, 1967), p. 51.

[5] R.C. Swank, "Interlibrary Cooperation, Interlibrary Communications, and Information Networks--Explanations and Definition," in Interlibrary Communications and Information Networks, Joseph Becker, ed. (Chicago: American Library Association, 1971), pp. 19-20.

[6] Joseph Becker, "Functions of Existing Networks--A Reaction," in Structure and Governance of Library Networks, Allen Kent, ed. (New York: Dekker, 1979), pp. 86-89.

[7] Alphonse F. Trezza, "The NCLIS View--A Full Service Network," Journal of Library Automation, 10 (June 1977), p. 2.

[8] Norman D. Stevens, "An Historical Perspective on the Concepts of Networks: Some Preliminary Considerations," in Networks for Networkers: Critical Issues in Cooperative Library Development, Barbara Evans Markuson, ed. (New York: Neal-Schuman, 1980), pp. 29-48.

[9]U.S. National Commission on Libraries and Information Science, Toward a National Program, p. XI.

[10]U.S. National Commission on Libraries and Information Science, Toward a National Program, p. IX.

Bibliography

ALA Yearbook: A Review of Library Events, Chicago: American Library Association, 1976, 1978.

Becker, Joseph, ed. Interlibrary Communications and Information Networks: Proceedings of the Conference. Chicago: American Library Association, 1972.

Kent, Allen, and Thomas Galvin, eds. Structure and Governance of Library Networks. New York: Marcel Dekker, 1979.

Markunson, Barbara Evans, and Blanche Woolls, eds. Networks for Networkers: Critical Issues in Cooperative Library Development. New York: Neal-Schuman, 1980.

Patrick, Ruth J., Joseph Casey, and Carol M. Novalis. A Study of Library Cooperatives, Networks and Demonstration Projects, Volume 1 Findings and Recommendations. New York: K.G. Sauer, 1980.

United States. National Commission on Libraries and Information Science. Toward a National Program for Library and Information Services: Goals for Action. Washington, D.C.: NCLIS, 1975.

THE PLACE OF THE AUTHOR IN THE COMING INFORMATION SOCIETY

by

Wayne I. Boucher
Senior Research Associate
Center for Futures Research
Graduate School of Business Administration
University of Southern California

Most serious students of the future have agreed for at least a decade that something odd, profoundly important, and largely irreversible is happening throughout the industrialized world--and probably throughout the world as a whole. Hundreds of labels have been devised to characterize this ineffably complex phenomenon, ranging from "the new dark ages" to "the third wave." No doubt later historians will coin a phrase of their own to capture the essence of this apparently global transformation and thereby relate it neatly to comparable transitions in the past, such as the Renaissance. However they name it, a good deal of evidence suggests that they will be obliged to give special attention and weight to the astonishing developments occurring at an increasingly rapid rate in the collection, processing, storage, retrieval, dissemination, and use of information. Fueled largely by advances in technology, including particularly the marriage of computers and telecommunications, these developments have led authors like Daniel Bell to speak of the coming "post-industrial" society, in which information, rather than the production of manufactured goods, is the basis of human activity, the "axial principle" of society.

Many justly exhuberant words, as well as many foolish ones, have been written about the nature of the information age that is coming into being and to which every reader of this book, for example, is connected online in real time. The physical technology has been forecast repeatedly; the need for new social technologies (e.g., new privacy protections) has been studied endlessly; the economics have been evaluated again and again (though always on an insufficient data base); the societal consequences have been explored even down to the level of the individual home, office, school, or governmental agency; much effort-- often footloose--has gone into the design of "ideal" information systems; specific inquiries have been conducted into the outlook for data bases, the broadcast media, and every sort of print outlet, from newspapers to technical books and journals; extensive research has been done on the future role of publishers, libraries and information centers, abstracting and indexing services, and users--especially the users.

Curiously, one important group has been generally ignored in all that has been said and done on the brave new information society. But this group is the one that will provide the very life-blood of post-industrialism; without its contributions, all the dazzling capabilities of the information age will serve at best only to make us excellent antiquarians. This group is the authors.

This paper speculates (sometimes seriously, sometimes not) on three important questions regarding authors in the future. First, will their motives for writing change and, if so, how? Second, will their motives come into conflict with those of other players in the information process such as publishers or users, and, if so, with what likely consequences? Finally, to what extent are future authors likely to adopt the various hard and soft technologies of the information society—and what might this mean for the production and distribution of knowledge?

In a sense, everyone who writes (or who speaks for later transcription or for publication on film, tape, or disc) is an author. To make the discussion here somewhat more tractable, we will exclude from consideration the writers of letters, notes, diaries, fiction, poetry, advertising copy, insurance policies, technical manuals, questionnaires, news, parts lists, laws and regulations, tracts, and graffiti. All will no doubt experiment with the new technology, and some may come to benefit from its power. All, as will be seen, could be subjects of observations made later in this paper. But we exclude them in order to focus better on the main drivers of the information age: the scientists and engineers who create scientific and technical information (STI). This is not a small group. Today in the United States it includes well over 2 million persons, and collectively in 1980 it may account for an estimated 172,000 scholarly articles, 18,000 dissertations, 17,000 books, and some 90,000 technical reports,[1] to say nothing of other forms of communication and publication.

Ignoring the scientist and engineer _qua_ writer has a long tradition. In modern times, signs of the problem can be traced back to one of the classic papers of the information age, Vannevar Bush's 1945 essay, "As We May Think."[2] In this paper, Bush explains the need for, and forecasts the features of, a device he dubbed "memex":

> A memex is a device in which an individual stores all his books, records, and communications, and which is mechanized so that it may be consulted with exceeding speed and flexibility. It is an enlarged intimate supplement to his memory.

Its memory is enormous; 5000 pages of material could be added every day and yet not exceed the system's capacity for hundreds of years. The key to the system, however, is not its capacity. Nor indeed is it the fact that the device is housed entirely in a desk (with special screens, keyboard, buttons, and levers). The essence of the memex is that it provides access to all records by means of associative indexing, "whereby any item may be caused at will to select immediately and automatically another."

This is possible because as the user of the memex consults the file, he has the opportunity to code pieces of information and then to link items together by means of the codes. Thereafter, when he recalls an item, he may also instantly retrieve the others to which it has been linked. Thus, "trails" can be established through the literature, trails that reflect the workings of the mind and are not constrained by the hierarchical indexing and storage systems in use then and now. Moreover, in a later version of this vision, Bush gives memex the ability not only to keep track of the user's method of following trails (thereby deciding that items frequently skipped should become side trails), but also to "build trails for its master," following search strategies given by the user and zipping through the file in his absence to prepare a report for his subsequent return.[3]

Someday, Bush's memex may actually be built; it would appear that the personal computer is another of many steps that have already been taken in this direction.[4] And it is easy to see how a trained user could become a much better researcher with a device of such power at hand--given, of course, the patience to develop all the links that the machine itself (or outside specialists, whom Bush calls "trail blazers") could or would not develop.

But what use would such a machine be to the scientist or engineer as author? In a positive sense, probably not much, except, say, in mundane ways like verifying usage in grammar or mechanics. Negatively, its uses could be quite serious, a point to be considered later. Bush himself deals with authorship as if the memex had never been conceived. In 1945 and again in 1967, he observes that:

...to make a record, we still push a pencil or tap a typewriter. Then comes the business of digestion and correction, followed by an intricate--and largely cockeyed--process of typesetting, print- ing, and distribution. To consider the first stage of proceeding, will the author of the future cease writing by hand or typewriter and talk directly to the record?[5]

The answer is: very probably, at least for first drafts. To the extent that these prove incomplete or otherwise unacceptable, record making of the conventional type could follow. As Bush remarks (in a statement that bears remembering outside the memex), "For mature thought there is no mechanized substitute."[6]

Thus endeth the discussion of the author. It is worth noting that it goes no further than did Quintilian in the first century A.D.: "Writing is of the utmost importance....But a sluggish pen delays our thoughts, while an unformed and illiterate hand cannot be deciphered-- a circumstance which necessitates another wearisome task, namely the dictation of what we have written to a copyist."[7] Writers since Bush have added little; in fact, the strong tendency, as suggested earlier, has been to omit any reference to authorship. A good example is pro- vided in a recent study that describes a "new mass medium, where an infrastructure encourages the interaction of communications facilities, computers, and intelligent terminals" in a "synergistic" and highly "convivial" way, and in which Bush's associative memory scheme resurfaces on the network level as a "serendipity machine." In this system, the phonetic language might even be replaced by one that is ideographic. But, alas, things are interacting with things, and the business of writing is nowhere mentioned. It is somehow taken for granted as an aspect of the "infrastructure" and associated gadgetry.[8]

It is useful to look directly at authorship in the information society because every advance in user technology would seem to imply that writing would indeed become easier and perhaps better. Another possibility can also be argued--namely, that improvements in ease are very likely to swell the waters of mediocre and worthless STI. Finding good works may thus become more difficult. Worse yet, the potential flood of bad or indifferent works may subtly and slowly help to reduce the quality of the better works, relatively and absolutely. In the end, the new information technology may thereby actually undermine important parts of the foundations of the information age itself.

To appreciate how this may happen, consider first the question of what motivates the STI author. Why does he write? Very little research has been accomplished on this question (no doubt because most people, including authors themselves, assume they know the answer). More important perhaps, what will motivate the author in the future? There appears to have been only one study in recent years that has attempted to gain an insight into the answers to both questions.[9] In this study a fairly large group of persons was interviewed individually. At the opening of the interview, each participant was asked to evaluate a list of possible authors' motives and to estimate their importance (on a subjective scale running from 0 to 10) over the preceding 25 years. The larger part of the interview then focused on possible technological, social, economic, and political developments that might affect the nature of STI communications (particularly the scientific journal) in the years up to 2000. On the basis of this conversation, the interviewees--all of them persons intimately familiar with the types of participants in STI--were then asked to estimate the importance of the authors' motives to the year 2000. The results from these questions are summarized in the table on the following page.

What this table indicates is that the objectives of authors in STI are very unlikely to change in the next 25 years from what they have been in the last 25. Statistically, the two sets of answers are essentially the same. Thus, the top-ranking item, "Establish intellectual ownership of work," was judged by the group not only to have been the most important objective of authors over the past 25 years, but also to retain top priority in the future. This idea has, of course, been suggested by other students of the STI system, notably by de Solla Price, who has shown that the probability that discoveries will be made simultaneously by two or more scientists working independently of each other is unexpectedly high, and that prior publications in such cases can be a strong indication of first discovery.

Historically and in the future, the second most important objective for authors, according to the group as a whole, is "to gain fame and recognition." It might be emphasized that the commercial publishers who were among those in the group felt that this was by far the most important author objective.

The third-ranked objective, "Enhance career mobility and flexibility," was referred to most often in the interviews when discussing the role of authors in the journal system. It was pointed out that establishing intellectual ownership of work and gaining fame and recognition are important only because they are means for enhancing career mobility and flexibility.

Author Objectives

Objectives	Past 25 Years		Next 25 Years	
	Group Average	Rank	Group Average	Rank
1. Establish intellectual ownership of work.	8.2	1	8.4	1
2. Gain fame and recognition.	8.0	2	8.1	2
3. Enhance career mobility, flexibility.	7.0	3	7.3	3
4. Establish contacts with workers in same field (especially, to gain entree into the invisible college).	6.2	5	6.2	5
5. Get invited to conferences and meetings.	5.8	6	5.8	6
6. Fulfill obligations to an employer.	5.1	8	4.8	8
7. Fulfill a contractual obligation.	3.2	10	2.7	11
8. Fulfill obligations to a professional society or other group.	3.1	11	2.9	10
9. Share information with colleagues.	6.4	4	6.5	4
10. Adhere to scientific tradition and standards of publishing one's findings.	5.4	7	4.9	7
11. Educate the next generation of practitioners in the same field.	4.9	9	4.5	9

Though the next objective, "Establish contact with workers in the same field," was ranked fifth in importance overall, a number of participants commented that it is much more important for the younger scientist. Established scientists have already become members of an invisible college and have usually developed extensive personal contacts in their field.

"Share information with colleagues" and "Get invited to conferences and meetings" were viewed as related objectives and were closely ranked in importance. Again, it was felt that the younger scientist might find these motives more compelling than would the more senior scientist. The remaining author objectives were considered less important and were not discussed in detail. It is of more than passing interest, however, to note that two of the more or less noble motives (i.e., Items 10 and 11) ranked low.

If these results are to be believed, it seems that many STI authors have written and will continue to write for reasons of self-interest: to establish a claim, to move ahead, to avoid perishing. In a future environment in which opportunities to become an author are very likely to increase, the forecasted continued importance of these motives--and the others--suggests that the amount of drivel in the system could well increase accordingly. Protection against this outcome is now provided principally by the integrity of authors and the reviewing procedures instituted by publishers, neither without flaw. But suppose the standards of integrity changed or the reviewing systems were made obsolescent. Either could happen as a result of developments in information technology. Even today, for example, there are computer-based network systems to which admission is moderately easy, and in which anyone can say almost anything (except to attack the policies of the president if the federal government is paying the bill), there are no quality control measures, and the fruits of this sort of authorship have turned up as signed articles in scholarly journals.

Years ago, Arthur Wellington pointed out that "high efficiency in any art or calling in which many minds of no phenomenal gifts are engaged requires that every man's work should be readily comparable either with a certain uniform standard or with the work of his fellows."[10] Wellington argued that this is easy enough to accomplish in, say, "constructive engineering," where one 100-foot bridge is not much different from the next. But, he said, it is extremely difficult in the case of projects that superficially resemble each other, though they are vastly different in their individual nature and implications, such as the laying out of railway lines. Only detailed expert evaluation can help in the latter case. Increasingly, it would seem, the production of STI, which one might hope would be like the laying out of railroads, is being treated like the building of 100-foot bridges. And the volume of material, plus the extraordinary delays in getting it reviewed even on that less stringent basis, is producing pressures for less restrictive means of publication.

Something of this sort of pressure can be inferred from other results in the study cited earlier. In addition to exploring the motives of authors, the same group of persons was also asked to estimate the importance of various objectives of publishers and of users of the scientific and technical journal. The results are presented in the following two tables.

Publisher Objectives

Objectives	Past 25 Years Group Average	Past 25 Years Rank	Next 25 Years Group Average	Next 25 Years Rank
1. Increase revenues (to ensure continued existence, to stay ahead of inflation, to increase service to readers).	7.0	7	7.6	5
2. Decrease operating costs.	5.7	10	6.6	9
3. Capture desired level of readership.	6.9	8	7.3	7
4. Serve as the primary, fastest intermediary between originators and users of written scientific material.	7.3	6	7.0	8
5. Publish work of the highest intellectual quality (by reviewing and editing).	8.8	1	9.0	1
6. Uphold and maintain the scientific tradition of open information exchange.	7.6	5	7.4	6
7. Present information in a form and style acceptable to the scientific community.	7.9	4	8.0	4
8. Achieve a reputation or status as being a publisher of a superior journal.	8.0	2-3	8.1	3
9. Attract good authors, editors, reviewers.	8.0	2-3	8.2	2
10. Communicate information which has no other outlet.	6.5	9	6.0	10
11. Serve archival function (organized repository for articles, etc.).	4.8	11	5.5	12
12. Improve information retrieval capabilities of users (especially of the publisher's own journals).	4.7	12	6.0	11

User Objectives

Objectives	Past 25 Years		Next 25 Years	
	Group Average	Rank	Group Average	Rank
1. Keep up-to-date in field (for teaching, research, planning, policy formation, etc.).	8.9	1	8.9	1
2. Follow relevant developments in other fields	5.4	6	5.9	7
3. Get ideas for new research.	4.9	7	5.8	8
4. Identify members of the invisible college or other scientists.	4.8	8-9	5.1	9
5. Keep track of colleagues' progress.	5.9	4-5	6.2	6
6. Have ways of screening out irrelevant material (when needs are specific).	4.8	8-9	6.7	5
7. Have ways of retrieving all relevant material (when needs are general).	5.9	4-5	7.2	4
8. Minimize cost, time, and inconvenience in any retrieval of data and information.	6.6	3	7.8	3
9. Obtain data and information in a usable, convenient physical form.	7.7	2	8.4	2

The tables are worth examining closely, but it might suffice to call attention to only two findings. In the data on publishers' objectives, note that Item 5, "Publish work of the highest intellectual quality (by reviewing and editing)," was considered to be the most important motive both in the past and in the future. This is not surprising and it may even be encouraging. Unfortunately, however, the journal publishers as a subgroup within the entire panel of interviewees ranked this objective fifth in importance, in a tie with Items 3 and 4. Similarly, the overall group assigned a low value to the importance over the past 25 years of "increasing revenues" (Item 1) and only a slightly higher value for the coming 25 years. The journal publishers, in contrast, ranked "increasing revenues" the highest of the motives. Even without a totally new, convivial infrastructure, these findings seem to represent a formula calculated to promote survival at the expense of quality.

In contrast, the user objectives seem likely to lead to the fix for everybody's problems, for they are entirely congruent with the forces that happen to be moving information technology in the direction of the memex. After all, why should anyone care about adding even 5,000 pages of garbage a day to the memory if the cost of doing so is vanishingly small and if it is also possible to use machine-assisted techniques to sort out quickly what appears to be relevant? And, of course, this is a worst case. One can readily imagine a scenario in which, say, only 1,000 pages a day would not have gotten into circulation if traditional methods of quality control and publication were still in general use. But the user is inspired by clear and significant needs; the means of achieving them need not matter greatly.

In general, therefore, it would seem that the motivations of the principal actors are compatible with each other and with the continued accelerating rush of a benign techology toward providing greater accessibility, storage capacity, and processing speeds, with greater convenience, and at lower and lower costs. Accordingly, increasing numbers of scientists and engineers (as authors) can be expected to take advantage of these capabilities. One 1975 source, for example, forecasts that the percentage of S&T publications authored online would probably grow from zero in 1975 to more than 40% in 1990--and perhaps exceed 80%.[11] This is still a reasonable forecast, given today's trends and the possibility of any one of several conceivable technological breakthroughs--notably, an acceptable voice input system. The nature of authorship would surely change as a result of such a development.

In a sense, authorship is already changing through such a cause: the increasing use by writers of keyboards or dictation. Those who care about the language will recognize an insidious consequence of this fact. Even in the days of Quintilian (and before), it was recognized that writing by hand is preferable when style is a consideration.[12] It can readily be observed today (though, sadly, not be demonstrated) that English prose style has suffered greatly because of our newer systems of "record making." With important exceptions, writers who compose on the typewriter or who dictate their material seem to lock themselves up in a routine diction, a standardized sense of rhythm and sentence structure, a narrow view of what a paragraph can be, and a weak sense of the need for comparison, elaboration, and imagery. Writing by hand seems to open the range of opportunities. Perhaps it is the ability to introduce changes immediately (without backspacing or pushing buttons or looking unprofessional to one's secretary) that makes the difference--that is, the ability to exploit instantly the moment of deepest intellectual, creative, and physical involement. If so, the wider acceptance of other ways of composing is certain to cause further ruin in the state of the style of STI.

At the same time, there are other pressures to make every composition a 100-foot bridge. One of the great results of the formation of the Royal Society in the seventeenth century is that scientists were thereafter admonished by their peers to write simply and clearly. In this century, it would seem that this admonition has been carried to a peculiar extreme. As Sinclair Lewis said when he refused the Pulitzer Prize in 1926, "Every compulsion is put upon writers to become safe, polite, obedient, and sterile." The safe, sterile style is taught to scientists and engineers in college; indeed, it would be difficult to find two texts on technical writing that disagreed on any significant point. This lifeless style is reinforced by editors and, of course, by peers and by those who fund research. Mastery of the style leads to careless, automatic writing, and therein lie two further problems.

The first is that, in the words of George Orwell in his widely published essay, "Politics and the English Language" (1945), "the slovenliness of our language makes it easier for us to have foolish thoughts." In particular, Orwell notes that:

> ...modern writing at its worst does not consist in picking out words for the sake of their meaning and inventing images in order to make the meaning clearer. It consists in gumming together long strips of words which have already been set in order by someone else, and making the results presentable by sheer humbug. The attraction of this way of writing is that it is easy.

One might counter by arguing that this may all be true of politicians and other disreputable, ill-schooled people, but certainly not of engineers and scientists. Anyone holding such a view would do well to consider the following passage, one of thousands of incredible banality to be found easily in the S&T literature. The author, who will not be identified, is addressing senior officers in the Air Force; he himself is a distinguished engineer. The task he is dealing with is to explain the concept of a performance parameter.

> A performance parameter may be defined simply as the description of a physical property or capability of a hardware item, such as a vehicle or an airplane. A performance parameter is decidedly not a measure of the military or economic worth of such a hardware device. This can be readily illustrated by considering the most popular of all performance parameters--speed.
>
> Speed is simply the ratio of distance covered to the time required to do so, that is,

$$\text{Speed} = \frac{\text{Distance}}{\text{Time}} \; .$$

Under some conditions one desires high speed, whereas under other conditions low speed is preferred. Consider, for example, the case where one wants to cover a large distance in a specified length of time, such as a space trip to a distant planet, which is to be accomplished in a short number of years. In this instance the large distance poses the requirement for high speed. Conversely, if for a business trip one wants to cover a specified distance, say from Los Angeles to London, in as short a time as possible, this short-time requirement also makes high speed desirable. Similarly, high speed is an objective in the case of a bomber or a ballistic missile that must cover a specified distance from base to target in as short a response time as possible.

On the other hand, there are other situations (or missions, in military jargon) where one desires to cover only a small distance, or sometimes no distance at all, and to remain in a confined space for a long period of time. Thus certain reconnaissance, surveillance, or patrol missions emphasize longer endurance in a relatively stationary attitude, so that low speed rather than high speed will be desirable. It follows that the knowledge of an aircraft's speed capability, be it high or low, does not enable one to decide whether it is good or bad without knowing the purpose for which the craft is to be employed.

Having thus defined the performance parameter speed, one may wonder next what the physical limitations on speed are. The lower limit on speed is obviously zero. Yet for this statement to be meaningful, we must define speed relative to something; hence let us say zero speed relative to the earth.

And so on, and so on.[13]

The second problem that comes from sterility in style is that, as Orwell tells us, this way of writing is easy. Being easy, someone will discover sooner or later that it can be computer-assisted. When that day arrives, the author (sitting at his terminal) could do such marvelous things as direct the computer to provide a "transition, opposite," and watch the CRT display "however," "in contrast," "on the contrary," "but," "on the other hand," and the like, recommending that since past counts indicate the author's preference is for "on the other hand," this phrase be used. More sophisticated software would of course keep track of the author's current usage, so that no argument would ever have three hands.

Extrapolate today's trends and it is possible to envision a world in which the author is doubly burdened (or doubly blessed)--a world in which are available not only computer-assisted composition and word-processing capabilities, but also the memex. The former continues to corrupt style; the latter begins to corrupt the mind. The author now has prompt, cheap access to any earlier work on any subject. Constant exposure steels a writer to "the sight of trivial personalities decomposing in the eternity of print."[14] At the same time, temptations to plagiarism will be great. If avoided, there will be a deeper danger, one nicely captured in 1633 by John Earle in his <u>Microcosmography</u>, where he describes the plodding student:

> His invention is no more than the finding out of his papers, and his few gleanings there; and his disposition of them is as just as the bookbinder's, a setting or gluing of them together.

Bush foresees that the memex will make it possible for whole new encyclopedias to be created in just this way. Ordinary books and papers will look like great scholarly achievements. Networks will bring teams of authors, living and dead, together in this repackaging activity; "et al." may become the most published and cited author of the information age. At that point, the author will have become the essential--but strangely unnecessary--person in the information society.

* * *

This dismal view could become reality. All that seems necessary is the continued play of the motives discussed earlier, coupled with a few generations of advances in information technology as innovative as those of the preceding 100 years. Incidentally, it is not necessary that the pace of scientific discovery worth reporting keep up with these developments, because it will be a trivial matter to pull six different papers and a book out of each piece of research. Because the truly important will usually be known in the community well in advance of any sort of formal-looking publication--as is usually true today in well-established fields--there will be little need to read any more then than now. And memex could always be set to provide a little insurance by browsing at night for useful thoughts that might otherwise slip by.

Given the same kinds of technology, but a change in motives, the world could be far different. Authors might write because they have something to say--a fact that memex could help to verify. Authors might not write because they have learned that what they wanted to say has been said before. Redundancies in the STI corpus could be systematically weeded out, giving discoverers the place of honor. Links among research findings in the same discipline (or across disciplines) could be established, perhaps helping to establish whole new branches of science and engineering.

It is also possible that these capabilities could help both author and reader by searching for ways to simplify or clarify the text, as the Royal Society would have urged. Any student of STI will eventually encounter Frontinus' <u>The Aqueducts of Rome</u> (written about 100 A.D.), which provides a case in point. This report is still interesting because the author is clearly concerned about what he is saying. Yet the report goes flat as Frontinus provides us with obviously necessary detail about such matters as the exact routes of each of the nine acqueducts, the flow rates through the 25 nozzles, the amounts of water entering the system and the amounts actually delivered, and so on. One or two simple tables would have avoided the seemingly endless narrative presentation of these data. In tomorrow's information society, computers might be able to detect such deadly passages and signal to naive authors the possibility of restructuring them.

In general, the style of authors could be monitored and improved; for example, there is no reason why a "sterility" index could not be computed--or even something much simpler like the well-known "fog" index. (A truly convivial system would not hesitate to alert the author who is writing like a blockhead.) Quality control on both content and style could thus be exercised to a significant new degree at the author's desk, and the items that survived this scrutiny could then go to real human reviewers for their in-depth evaluation of the importance of the contribution. Finally, authors, disseminators, and users might come to see that it is not mere information that is valuable to the new age, but information that is created by the best authors.

Notes

1. D. W. King, et al., _Statistical Indicators of Scientific and Technical Communication, 1960-1980_, vol. 1 (Rockville, MD: King Research, 1976), p. 46.

2. Vannevar Bush, "As We May Think," _Atlantic Monthly_, vol. 176, no. 1 (July 1945), pp. 101-108.

3. Vannevar Bush, _Science Is Not Enough_ (New York: William Morrow & Company, 1967), pp. 95-96.

4. "No memex could have been built when that [1945] article appeared. In the quarter-century since then, the idea has been with me almost constantly, and I have watched new developments in electronics, physics, chemistry, and logic to see how they might help to bring it to reality. That day is not yet here, but has come far closer...."-- Vannevar Bush, _Pieces of the Action_ (New York: William Morrow & Company, 1970), p. 190.

5. Bush, _Science_, p. 93. The comparable passage in "As We May Think," is on pp. 103-104.

6. Bush, "As We May Think," p. 104.

7. Quoted in Moses Hadas, _Ancilla to Classical Reading_ (New York: Columbia University Press, 1954), p. 15.

8. Gordon B. Thompson, _Memo from Mercury: Information Technology is Different_, Occasional Paper No. 10 (Montreal: Institute for Research on Public Policy, June 1979).

9. Wayne I. Boucher and Dana Bramlette, _A Forecast of the Scientific Journal to the Year 2000_ (Glastonbury, CT: The Futures Group, November 1976), Appendix B, "Trends Which Can Affect the Evolution of the Scientific and Technical Journal," pp. 12ff. Portions of the following discussion are drawn with minor changes from this test.

10. Arthur M. Wellington, The Economic Theory of the Location of Railways, 6th ed. (New York: Wiley, 1900), quoted in Engineers as Writers, Walter J. Miller and Leo E. A. Saidla, eds. (New York: Van Nostrand, 1953), p. 149.

11. Audrey Clayton and Norman Nisenoff, The Influence of Technology upon Future Alternatives to the Scientific and Technical Journal (Arlington, VA: Forecasting International, Ltd., December 1975), vol. 2, "Parameter Histories and Predicted Trends," p. 29. This report was prepared in support of the study cited in note 9.

12. Hadas, Ancilla, p. 17.

13. This passage (and others like it) explain the meaning of Richard Sheridan's verse (echoed 175 years later by Ernest Hemingway), "easy writing's damn'd hard reading."

14. Virginia Woolf, The Common Reader (New York: Harcourt, Brace & Company, 1925), p. 301.

LEGAL AND REGULATORY FACTORS THAT MAY AFFECT
THE FLOW OF INFORMATION:
Privacy and Security Issues in Information Systems

by

Rein Turn
Professor of Computer Science
California State University

Privacy Concerns and Privacy Protection

"Privacy" is a concept that relates to individuals and, thus, concerns over privacy in information systems arise mostly in the context of collection, processing, storage, and use of personal information about individuals. From the point of view of overall societal information needs and information flows, personal information about individuals is a relatively small fraction and, consequently, privacy concerns may be regarded as a minor problem. The far larger part of the information in question is science and technology information (STI), bibliographic materials, economic and business information, and so forth. While these types of information at times may be sensitive and need to be maintained confidential, they are not likely to be directly associated with individuals in ways that raise privacy protection concerns.

That part of the information flows that does involve personal information on individuals could be classified as personal information records maintained for the purposes of making decisions about individuals or interacting with individuals, and as statistical data bases containing personal information. The data bases of the Internal Revenue Service and of the Bureau of Census are, respectively, examples of the two types of data bases on the level of the federal government. Financial records and social sciences research data are examples of the two types of data bases in the private sector. Privacy protection concerns arise in both types. More recently, the term "fair information practices" has replaced the term "privacy" in references to individual rights vis-a-vis personal information record-keeping systems.

Privacy, then, is a term that expresses the concern of individuals with ways that powerful organizations deal with them. While such a concern has existed ever since record-keeping about individuals began, it was greatly increased when in the early 1960s a proposal was made for the establishment of a National Data Bank (1)--an automated depository of most of the personal information collected and retained by the federal government. Even though this system was proposed for statistical purposes rather than for administrative purposes, it received a very negative response from the Congress, the media, and the population at large, and, a few years later, the proposal was abandoned. The debate continued, however, and it was argued convincingly that automation of

131

previously manual records would result in substantial increases in governments' as well as private agencies' capability to assemble personal information dossiers on citizens and, thus, intimidate them to act and live "for the records" rather than to exercise their Constitutionally granted rights and liberties. Congressional hearings also uncovered instances of information about individuals being blatantly wrong, incomplete, or irrelevant for the purposes that it was used. The need for legally enforced privacy protection was clearly indicated.

Individual privacy rights as they are used now in privacy protection legislation in the United States and abroad have evolved from a Code of Fair Information Practices, first expressed in 1973 (2), to the following set of principles that are an amalgam of ideas put forth by the Privacy Protection Study Commission in the United States (3), and the Council of Europe resolutions (4,5).

- openness—there must be no personal information record-keeping system whose very existence is kept secret, and there should be a policy of openness about policies, practices, and systems used by organizations for personal information record-keeping purposes;
- individual participation—individuals should be able to find out what personal information is kept about them, be able to gain access to personal information records about them, and be able to have corrections made to these records;
- collection limitation—limits must be established on the types of information items an organization may collect about individuals, and on the manner that such collection is accomplished;
- use limitation—there must be ways for individuals to prevent personal information about them that is collected for one purpose from being used for other purposes without their knowledge or consent;
- disclosure limitation—external disclosure by record-keeping organizations of information about individuals should be limited, and there must exist legally enforceable confidentiality obligations of record-keeping organizations for the use and disclosure of personal information;
- information management—any record-keeping organization that handles personal information about individuals must be responsible for implementing data-management policies and practices that assure quality of the personal information (accuracy, currency, relevance), provide for security, and prevent misuse;
- accountability—record-keeping organizations must be responsible for their record-keeping policies, practices, and systems, and for compliance with privacy protection requirements.

Added to these principles should be another one that was recently stated in the French data protection act (6): "No judical, governmental or private decision involving a finding or judgement on human conduct may be based solely on automatic processing of data that gives a description of the individual's profile or personality." This principle makes explicit the main concern in privacy protection—it is not the collection and storage of personal information in automated record-keeping systems

that has the greatest potential for unfairness toward individuals, but
it is their use in decision making that has this potential.

Privacy Protection Legislation in the United States

Privacy protection legislation in the United States appears at
both the federal and the state levels. A sectoral approach is being
taken on both levels—separate and different privacy protection laws
have been enacted to establish privacy protection requirements in the
public sector and in different application areas in the private sector.
This is to be contrasted with the privacy protection approach taken in
Europe where omnibus privacy protection laws apply the same requirements
on all record-keeping systems. The sectoral approach is more effective
in balancing the special requirements and problems of the various sectors
or parts of them, but this approach is also more time-consuming. Nevertheless, this approach was recommended by the Privacy Protection Study
Commission as more suitable in the United States than the omnibus
approach.

As of early 1980, four privacy protection laws have been enacted
on the federal level and several bills are pending:

- The Fair Credit Reporting Act of 1969 (7) applies to consumer
  credit reporting industry (the credit bureaus). It requires
  that anyone who is refused credit on the basis of a credit
  bureau report be informed of this fact and referred to the
  bureau in question. The latter must inform the individual of
  the contents of the credit record and permit corrections.
- The Privacy Act of 1974 (8) regulates the personal information
  record-keeping practices of the federal government and grants to
  citizens of the United States and certain aliens the right to
  inspect their records, request correction, and limit dissemination. All agencies must annually publish information about
  their personal information data bases and their use.
- The Family Educational Rights and Privacy Act of 1974 (9) grants
  students and their parents (if the student is under 21) rights
  to access to the school records.
- The Financial Privacy Act of 1978 (10) restricts government
  agencies' access to individual bank records.

The presidential privacy initiative in late 1979 proposed a privacy
protection policy based on the principles of fair information practices
and limits on government record-keeping activities, and proposed legislation to provide privacy protection to individual medical records,
financial records, insurance records, and employment records. It also
proposed legislation to provide privacy to financial records that will
be collected in connection with electronic funds transfer systems (EFTS)
and a number of amendments to strengthen the Privacy Act of 1974. At
the time of this writing the proposed bills are still pending in the
Congress. A special emphasis was placed on research records containing
identifiable personal information and their confidentiality—under the
proposed Privacy of Research Records Act personal information collected
or maintained for research purposes may not be used or disclosed in
individually identifiable form for an action that adversely affects the
individual.

On state level, privacy and fair information practices laws are in force in twelve states (11). They apply to automated and manual record-keeping systems under the states' control. Following the sectoral privacy protection legislation of the federal government, many laws have been enacted and bills are pending in the states regarding various private sector record-keeping areas: insurance, credit reporting, finance, mailing lists, employment, and so forth. In addition, unlike the federal law enforcement and criminal justice field, these fields in many states are covered by special privacy protection laws.

Impacts on Information Systems

What are the impacts of privacy protection legislation on information systems and information flows? In general, one purpose of privacy protection legislation is to grant individuals a set of enforceable rights vis-a-vis record-keeping organizations. Another purpose is to regulate and restrict these practices by the record-keeping organizations. In generic terms, the requirements placed on record-keeping organizations include the following:

- publication of notices on the existence and about the purposes of the organization's record-keeping systems;
- notification of individuals (on the letters' requests) about the existence of personal information records about them in the organization's systems, and about the ways that access could be obtained to these records;
- establishment of facilities and procedures for individuals to inspect their own records in a form that is readily comprehensible, establishment of procedures for reviewing challenges to data quality, provision of means for including in the records of rebuttal statements by the individuals, and establishment of mechanisms for notification of prior recipients of disputed records of any corrections or amendments;
- prohibition from using personal information for purposes not previously announced in public notices, unless explicitly permitted by law or agreed with by the individuals concerned, and establishment of procedures for requesting permissions from individuals;
- establishment of accountings of disclosures so that information could be traced (e.g., for the purpose of sending corrections) and so that individuals could be informed of the disclosure made;
- establishment of procedures and means for assuring that personal information is collected by lawful and fair means, and that the information collected is appropriate and relevant for the purposes it is collected for, and that it is accurate, complete and up to date;
- maintenance of confidentiality of personal information consistent with its sensitivity, and limitation of access only to those personnel of the organization who have a need to know;
- conformance with security standards that afford reasonable protection to the data processing facility, equipment, programs, and the personal information in the system against accidental

destruction, and against unauthorized access, alteration, or
distribution.

Implementation of these requirements involves policy, procedural,
and personnel matters, as well as technical considerations. The latter
arise in particular in complying with information quality, confidentiality, and security requirements. These will be examined in more detail
later in this article. In general, it must be observed that in privacy
protection, technology plays a dual role. It provides the means for
establishing automated record-keeping systems and linking these in ways
that can be used to invade individual rights, but it also provides the
means for implementing safeguards against such uses. In the absence of
privacy protection laws, however, there appears to be at work an
unconstrained technological imperative which compels organizations
to increase the efficiency and economy of their existing record-keeping
activities and systems--acquisition of data processing equipment to
store more information, to process information faster and in more
complex ways, and to provide efficient access to more users with
emphasis on maximizing information sharing. Ultimately, decision-
making functions using personal information will be automated as well.
In the future, these pressures will increase with each new generation
of more capable and more economical data processing systems. It is
essential that effective privacy protection safeguards be formulated
to constrain the technological imperative before new, harder to control
systems are implemented.

Impacts on Record-Keeping Systems

It is the intent of the privacy protection legislation to limit
collection, storage, dissemination, and use of personal information
about individuals. To the extent that such legislation will be drafted
and enacted to be effective, its impact will be to reduce the availability and flows of identifiable personal information. For example,
the collection of any information about individuals which pertains to
the individuals' exercise of their first amendment rights is prohibited
under the Privacy Act of 1974. Thus federal agencies and federal con-
tractors are not to collect information about an individual's religious
belief or political affiliation. Restrictions on external disclosure
mean that personally identifiable information about individuals will
not be available from government files. Specifically, such information
will not be made available to the direct-mail advertising industry or to
mailing list brokers. The latter are a substantial industry with
tens of millions of names, addresses, and ancilliary information available for sale (12). As a rule, these records are collected from publicly
available sources, such as telephone books. However, many states have
discontinued the practice of selling address lists from their files, the
motor vehicle department files, for example.

The main focus of federal and state privacy protection legislation
is on record-keeping activities that require individuals to submit
information under the penalty of law or in order to receive some
privilege, benefit, or service (as in the case of insurance, financial
organizations, education or health care). In the latter case, individuals are intimidated implicitly to submit any information that is

asked lest they not receive the benefit or service sought. Other
personal information is contributed by individuals freely and with
the expectation that the information will be widely circulated--various
biographic dictionaries are examples. To date, these record-keeping
activities have not been affected by privacy protection legislation.
It is likely, however, that organizations that maintain address files,
especially subscription lists to magazines, journals, or newspapers,
will eventually be required to reveal sales of these lists to other
organizations and to permit subscribers to refuse such dissemination
of their names and addresses. The net effect of legislative efforts
regarding identifiable personal information will be a reduction in the
flow of such information as intended by legislatures, which in turn
reflect the mood of the country.

Science-Technical Information

Science-technical information represents the accumulated knowledge
of mankind about the world's physical, biological, and societal
state of affairs, functions, and underlying processes. Most of this
information is not associated with identifiable individuals in ways
that would affect decisions made about these individuals. Thus,
privacy protection concerns very rarely arise. One situation in which
privacy protection concerns may arise involves peer reviews of manuscripts of papers for journals or books, or reviews with research proposals. There is a tradition in the scientific community of maintain-
ing the reviewers' identities confidential, but the author of a rejected
manuscript or proposal may claim that his or her right for due process
is violated if the reviewer can not be challenged directly.

Another privacy-related consideration arises in the social,
behavioral, and health sciences, where research deals with individuals
on some statistical basis. Researchers in these areas use surveys as
the principal means for gathering empirical information, providing data
for validating theoretical results, or providing evidence of the success
or failure of programs that may be underway. The results of research
based on the use of personal information collected in surveys and presented in aggregated form are not used to make decisions about specific
individuals, and, thus, privacy concerns do not arise from this point
of view. On the other hand, the data bases are likely to contain
sensitive information about individuals which, if available to decision
makers, could be detrimental to the individuals concerned. For example,
the fact that some individual is on a list of former sex offenders could
be very damaging if it became known to the individual's friends or
associates. The privacy questions related to statistical data bases
will be discussed in the next section.

Statistical Data Bases

Statistical data bases containing personal information on individuals are the major source of information for conducting research in
health sciences, social sciences and behavioral sciences. As scientists
in these disciplines tackle increasingly complex human problems, their
demands for personal information grow. Patterns of disease and social

relationships tend to be buried in masses of details about people's lives, and the way they go about their business. Uses of these data for research purposes can lead to strong conflicts with individuals' rights of privacy. This, in turn, can reduce the availability of personal information for research purposes.

The threat to individual privacy from research uses of personal information is essentially an indirect one. Scientists are not making administrative decisions about the research subjects (albeit the results of the research may affect the subjects as a group), but the personal information data bases they assemble may be of interest to agencies that are making administrative decisions. These agencies may be tempted to demand access to statistical data bases and to sensitive personal information they may contain. They may be able to back up their demands with investigative powers they may have (e.g., the subpoena power) or provisions in various existing laws. While it is routine for researchers to promise the respondents absolute confidentiality of the personal data they provide, in most cases such promises do not have a legal basis.

A particular incident that illustrates the problem arose several years ago during the New Jersey income maintenance project--a major social experiment designed to measure the impact of various negative income tax plans on labor force behavior and other activities of low-income families (13). Participants in the experiment were asked to complete detailed questionnaires about their income, employment, and other activities and were promised by the researchers that this information would be kept absolutely confidential. However, the local law enforcement officials saw in the experiment an opportunity to check on welfare cheating and demanded access to the data. Subsequently, the local officials were persuaded to drop their demand, but then the state officials issued an access demand of their own. While this, too, was eventually resolved, a great deal of damage had been done to the experiment. The dilemma of a researcher when faced with a subpoena for personal information collected under promise of absolute confidentiality is a serious one: either betray the respondents and seriously threaten future research or face contempt proceedings (14).

Several study groups have examined the problem with research data base confidentiality and are in agreement that steps must be taken to provide a statutory basis for research data (3,14,15). Without legal protection of confidentiality, individuals are not likely to reveal sensitive information about themselves. Coupled with prohibitions in existing and pending privacy protection laws against using personal information for purposes other than originally stated, the public's reluctance to participate in research could seriously hinder progress in societal research in the future. Consequently, in the United States the Privacy Protection Study Commission recommended that the Congress enact laws to provide for confidentiality of research and statistical records and establish a framework for retaining, using and disclosing such records (3). The Privacy of Research Records Act proposal in the administration's privacy initiative in 1979:

- provides for a legal standard of confidentiality that would allow researchers to release information for non-research purposes only to prevent injury to an individual or in a medical emergency;

- requires the researcher to tell research subjects of the possibility, if any, that information about them will be disclosed;
- ensures that research subjects are not recontacted by other researchers in a way that would embarrass or inconvenience them or otherwise intrude on their privacy; and
- provides criminal penalties for unauthorized disclosure of research information.

In the absence of legally enforceable confidentiality of research and statistical data, various procedural and technical approaches have been developed to make the research data less useful should they be seized by authorities (16). One approach is focused on reducing the sensitivity and the reliability of the research data by randomizing the responses or inoculating the data with errors such that their statistical properties remain relatively unchanged, but there is an uncertainty about the correctness of the information about any particularly identifiable individual.

Until laws are enacted to provide effective confidentiality protection to personal information in research data bases there is a strong possibility that individuals will be increasingly reluctant to participate in research projects and, as a consequence, flows of information important for tackling societal and human problems will diminish.

International Aspects of Privacy Protection

It is clear from the increasing international interdependence of nations and from the growth of international telecommunications systems that international flows of information will increase in the future. That is, provided that restrictions are not established by various countries to hinder international data flows. In particular, several countries and international organizations of nations have expressed concerns regarding transborder flows of personal information about individuals—when such information is transmitted abroad for processing or storage there, the individuals concerned may lose some of the privacy protection that is available to them in their home countries. Should this become the case, countries may restrict transborder data flows involving personal information. Several countries have defined "persons" to include also the "legal persons," such as associations, organizations, and corporations, and have extended privacy rights also to these entities. Transborder data flow restrictions under the broader definition would encompass nearly all types of data and, thus, could be much more serious than when only personal data about natural persons is involved.

Privacy protection is but one concern in transborder data flows. The worldwide availability of computer-communication systems and teleprocessing services has created a "trade" in these services, complete with competition between domestic and foreign vendors, taxes and duties, and regulation which may appear to favor domestic services. However, to date this trade has been unbalanced. Raw, unprocessed data are flowing to a very few highly industrialized countries where most of the international teleprocessing service vendors are located and where the largest and most important data bases are. From these countries, processed data and various "information products" flow back to the originating countries. Many of the latter are also industrialized countries, such as those in Western Europe, but most are industrially less developed countries of the Third World.

The imbalance in data flows has generated considerable concerns in the originating countries over their excessive dependence on foreign data processing services, and over the lack of development or loss of business of their own domestic data processing services and industries (17-20). As a result, transmission of certain types of data abroad is being prohibited by some governments, and efforts are underway to establish local or regional data bases in competition with those located in the highly industrialized countries, mainly the United States. Thus these sovereignty, dependence, and vulnerability concerns of a number of countries are another potential source of restrictions in transborder data flows that are likely to increase in importance in the future.

Foreign Privacy Protection Laws

Nine countries in addition to the United States have enacted privacy or data protection laws:

Austria: Federal Act on the Protection of Personal Data (October 1978)

Canada: Human Rights Act (June 1977); Provinces' Privacy Acts (since early 1970s)

Denmark: Public Authorities' Registers Act (June 1978); Private Registers, etc., Act (June 1978)

Federal Republic of Germany: Federal Data Protection Act (January 1977); Laender's Privact Acts (since 1969--Hessen)

France: Act on Data Processing, Data Files and Individual Liberties (January 1978)

Luxembourg: Law Governing the Use of Name-Linked Data in Data Registers (March 1979)

New Zealand: Wanaganui Computer Centre Act (September 1976, amended December 1977)

Norway: Act Relating to Personal Data Registers (June 1978)

Sweden: Data Act (May 1973, amended January 1977)

Despite the differing perceptions of the problem and differing political and legal systems and traditions, the privacy laws enacted abroad tend to grant a remarkably similar set of privacy rights. A principal reason for this is that, from the beginning, privacy protection discussions, studies, debates, and legislative proposals became widely known internationally. There are other dimensions of privacy protection, however, where there are considerable differences in national privacy protection laws, especially between those in Europe and the laws in the United States. Important dimensions to consider are the scope of applicability of the law and the data subjects covered, types of systems covered, and types of enforcement authorities and mechanisms. These aspects of the national privacy protection laws are briefly summarized below:

- United States. In the public sector, the Privacy Act of 1974 covers the automated and manual systems operated by the federal government, and protects the privacy of citizens and aliens admitted for permanent residence. Enforcement is through self-compliance and courts. The Office of Management and Budget has an oversight role. At states' level, privacy laws have been enacted in twelve states. They apply to automated and manual record-keeping systems under states' control, protect all residents, and are enforced in ways applicable to all laws in a given state. In the private sector, laws have been enacted to cover certain areas, such as credit reporting (Fair Credit Reporting Act of 1969), education (Family Education Rights and Privacy Act of 1974), and financial institutions (Right of Financial Privacy Act of 1978). These cover manual and automated systems and all individuals, and are enforced by agencies traditionally assigned legal oversight roles in these areas. Bills are pending in Congress to expand privacy protection to other areas of the private sector, such as employment records, health care, and insurance industry.

- Sweden. The Data Act (1973, amended in 1977) covers automated record-keeping systems in both the public and private sectors. Covered are all residents. Enforcement is through the Data Inspection Board. Permission is required to export personal data. Other provisions of the act reflect the record-keeping environment in Sweden: most of the record-keeping systems are automated, each citizen is assigned a unique personal identification number that can be used to link various records on an individual into a complete dossier; and Sweden is a very open society where, for example, the income and taxes of the citizens are published by the government for open distribution.

- Federal Republic of Germany. The Federal Data Protection Act (1977) covers automated and certain manual record-keeping systems in the public and private sectors. All residents are protected. Law is enforced by the Federal Commissioner for Data Protection. There are provisions for limiting disclosure to foreign organizations.

- Canada. A section of the Canadian Human Rights Act (1977) applies to automated and manual systems of the federal government. Protected are citizens and aliens admitted for permanent residence. Enforcement is effected through the office of the Privacy Commissioner. Certain TDF cases require Commissioner's approval. In the provinces' level, fair information practices laws are in force in several provinces. In the private sector, privacy protection is applied in certain areas (such as credit reporting).

- France: The Act on Data Processing, Data Files and Individual Liberties (1978) covers automated systems and certain manual files in the public and the private sectors. All residents are covered. Enforcement is by the National Data Processing and Liberties Commission. Permission is required for transborder transfers of personal data.

- Norway. The Act Relating to Personal Data Registers (1978) covers automated systems in both the public and the private sectors. Protection is provided to individuals, and to

associations or foundations. The law is enforced by the Data
Surveillance Service. Permission is required for transmission
of personal data abroad.

- Denmark. The Public Authorities' Registers Act (1978) covers
  government agencies that maintain automated records on residents.
  It is enforced by the Data Surveillance Authority. License is
  required for TDF. In the private sector, the Private Registers
  Etc. Act (1978) applies to automated systems in the private
  sector and protects individuals and institutions, associations,
  and business enterprises. It is enforced by the Data
  Surveillance Authority. No TDF provisions are made in this
  law.

- Austria. The Federal Act on the Protection of Personal Data
  (1978) covers automated record-keeping systems in both public
  and private sectors. It protects individuals and legal persons
  or associations. Enforced by Data Protection Commission and
  Council. TDF provisions include a requirement to obtain permission to export data, and to process data on foreign persons
  in Austria.

- Luxembourg. The Law Governing the Use of Name-Linked Data in
  Data Processing (1978) covers automated systems in public and
  private sectors, and protects individuals and legal persons.
  It is enforced by existing governmental authorities. In TDF
  situations, if the data access point is in Luxembourg, the law
  applies.

In addition, privacy protection laws are pending in Belgium, the
Netherlands, and Portugal. Privacy protection requirements have been
incorporated in the constitutions in Austria, Belgium, Portugal, and
Spain. Still other countries are in study phases that are expected to
produce privacy protection legislation in the near future (e.g., Finland,
Japan, Switzerland, and United Kingdom). It is important to note the
tendency in the more recent national privacy laws (Norway, Denmark,
Austria, and Luxembourg) to extend privacy protection to legal persons.
That is, corporations, associations, and other organizations are granted
the same rights regarding data about them as are given to individuals.
Implications of these extensions can be far-reaching (21). For example,
if transborder data flows were restricted under privacy protection provisions of some national law, a much greater proportion of data flows
would be affected if legal persons were included. The trend in privacy
protection legislation is unmistakeable--more and more countries will
enact privacy protection laws and the "second generation" features,
especially inclusion of legal persons, are going to be adopted in
future laws to a much greater degree than in the past.

International Conventions

The similarities and the differences among national privacy protection laws can become important practical matters to governments and
organizations in the private sector when transborder data flows are
being considered. On one hand there is the problem of comparisons of
various features in national laws in order to determine which laws are
"stronger"; on the other hand there is the problem to participants in

transborder data flows of complying with different implementations of the same requirements. Thus, there is a general agreement that it is desirable to standardize and "harmonize" the basic privacy protection provisions in the laws of various communities of nations. In response to this, two organizations in Europe have produced draft documents--the Council of Europe (located in Strasbourg, France) and the Organization for Economic Co-Operation and Development (located in Paris, France). The former is an organization of 21 Western European countries. OECD also includes non-European countries, such as the United States, Japan, Canada, Australia, and New Zealand.

The Council of Europe has drafted a Convention for the Protection of Individuals with Regard to Automatic Processing of Personal Data (22) in order to establish the following:

- A minimum set of privacy protection principles and rights to be adopted by all signatory countries (countries that are not members of the Council of Europe will be invited to join).
- Obligation of signatory countries to grant basic privacy rights to all individuals, regardless of nationality or residence.
- Cooperation and exchange of information between national data protection authorities in supervising compliance with privacy protection laws in international settings.
- Administrative mechanisms to handle disputes over jurisdiction when implementing national privacy protection requirements to handle TDF situations.

The convention would commit the signatory countries to enact privacy protection laws based on the principles listed in the previous section. It provides a privacy protection "floor" acceptable to the signatory countries in the sense that they would consider any country that has enacted and is enforcing these principles to be providing "sufficient" privacy protection. Then personal data could be transmitted to such a country from other signatory countries without loss of basic privacy protection. The convention is to cover automated record-keeping systems in public and private sectors. Protection is afforded to individuals, but could be extended to cover manual systems and/or legal persons by any signatory country. However, presumably the lack of such extensions in a signatory country's privacy laws would not be considered a sufficient reason for restricting transborder data flows to this country by signatory countries that do have these provisions.

A parallel effort toward standardization and harmonization of privacy protection principles, rights, and requirements in the form of a set of Guidelines Governing the Protection of Transborder Data Flow of Personal Data (23) has been completed by the OECD. The guidelines are to be voluntary (not a legally binding treaty) on the OECD member countries that accept them, but they are regarded as "morally bound" to comply fully. The United States is expected to participate.

The OECD guidelines are based on the philosophy that there are economic and social benefits to all participants in transborder data flows, and that it is very undesirable to establish unjustified barriers to TDF. Their purpose is to provide an interim standard until more formal treaties such as the Council of Europe's Convention are adopted. Again, the expectation is that there would be no need to restrict personal data flows between countries that have accepted and are implementing the guidelines' principles and requirements. For this purpose, the guidelines are similar to the Council of Europe's draft convention. That is, they are designed to be applicable to both the public and the private sectors, and to manual as well as automated systems. The protected data subjects are defined to be individuals (physical persons).

Regarding transborder data flows, the guidelines urge the participating countries to observe the following:

- Take into account the implications on other signatory countries of domestic processing and re-export of personal data, particularly when this may result in circumvention or violation of national privacy laws of other signatory countries.
- Take all reasonable and appropriate steps to ensure that transborder flows of personal data, including transit only, are uninterrupted and secure.
- Refrain from restricting transborder data flows of personal data between themselves and other countries except when these do not yet substantially observe the guidelines.
- Refrain from developing laws, policies and practices in the name of the protection of privacy and individual liberties which, by exceeding requirements for these, are inconsistent with free transborder flow of personal data.
- Ensure that their procedures for TDF of personal data and for protection of individual liberties are simple and compatible with those of other signatory countries.
- Work toward development of principles, national and international, to govern the determination of applicable laws in the case of TDF of personal data.

At this writing, there are still some disagreements in the guidelines, but it is expected that these will be ironed out by late 1980. A number of problems will remain, however, such as the question of effectiveness of voluntary compliance, and the adequacy of compliance-- some countries find that equivalence of privacy protection provisions should be the criterion for permitting transborder data flows of protected data.

Impacts of International Regulation on Information Flows

At the present time, privacy protection laws of the various countries are the principal potential "non-tariff" barrier to transborder data flows (the "tariff" barriers are those due to economics of data transmission, such as transmission charges or various taxes that may be levied). Until the international agreements will be formed and adopted, comparisons of privacy protection laws may be the principal means for a country to determine whether or not to apply the TDF provisions in its national privacy protection law.

Comparisons of the privacy protection laws now in force in the United States and those in Europe are likely to indicate that these laws in the United States are less comprehensive in the following ways:

- The scope of coverage is narrower since both the public and private sectors are incompletely covered in the United States-- even though the federal government is covered by the Privacy Act of 1974, only twelve states have enacted fair information practices laws. In the private sector, only consumer credit, educational institutions, and financial institutions are covered. European privacy laws cover both sectors quite completely.

- The Privacy Act provides privacy protection explicitly only to citizens of the United States and aliens admitted for permanent residence. Thus, foreign nationals other than specified above are not covered. European privacy protection laws appear to make no distinction regarding nationality or citizenship.

- No central, independent privacy protection authority exists in the United States to enforce compliance with privacy protection laws. Under the Privacy Act, Office of Management and Budget has a nominal role of coordinating compliance, and the president makes an annual report on compliance to the Congress. Compliance with federal privacy laws that apply to the private sector is with agencies that normally regulate the areas involved (e.g., the Federal Trade Commission, the Federal Reserve System, and the Department of Education). This distributed authority contrasts with the strong, central data protection authorities in Europe.

The differences in scope of coverage of the national privacy protection laws have resulted from differing philosophies of regulation. The European countries have adopted an "omnibus" approach that applies the same set of requirements (usually with some exceptions) uniformly to the government and all parts of the private sector. In United States and Canada, where federal system of government is strongly established, based on considerable separations in powers and jurisdiction, a sectoral approach has been taken--separate laws are enacted (or existing laws are amended) to provide privacy protection in specific parts of the public and private sectors. Each approach has its merits and drawbacks. Omnibus legislation establishes uniform requirements, but cannot handle easily any specific situations. Sectoral legislation is easier to enact and permits flexibility in handling exceptions, but is likely to result in scattering of privacy protection requirements throughout the entire legal code.

Implications of the above discussion are rather clear. There exist now mechanisms in the privacy protection laws of several European countries for restricting international information flows, personal information on individuals in some cases and on legal persons in other cases. Comparisons of privacy protection laws show that those in the United States are, at present, less comprehensive and, thus, could be considered as "weaker." If a country so deems appropriate, it could use its privacy protection law to place restrictions on data flows to the United States. However, in a few years the privacy protection in the United States can be expected to have advanced to a level comparable to that in the European laws and the "critical period" for data flows will have passed. Meanwhile, those organizations and enterprises involved in transborder data flows and desiring to continue may have to find means to convince the privacy protection authorities abroad of their commitment to privacy protection principles, and willingness and ability to implement these principles to match the requirements abroad.

Voluntary compliance has been urged by the Privacy Protection Study Commission, by the president of the United States at the introduction of his privacy protection initiatives in the Spring of 1979 (with special emphasis on voluntary compliance regarding employment and commercial credit granting records), and by industry and business groups, such as the Chamber of Commerce of the United States (24) and the Business Roundtable (25). In addition, codes of conduct or ethics have been suggested as one avenue toward effective voluntary compliance with privacy protection principles and requirements in national as well as TDF contexts. On an industry association level, codes of conduct and effective sanctions for noncompliance could discourage organizations from using personal data contrary to privacy protection principles. On the employee level, such codes could discourage improper handling of personal data, especially the personal data on foreign nationals. However, at this time codes of conduct or ethics are not sufficiently strong to be depended upon for satisfying privacy protection requirements.

The privacy protection laws and regulations thus far discussed do not address science-technology information or statistical data containing aggregate information only. However, issues dealing with national sovereignty and vulnerability erosion as a result of transborder data flows will continue to grow in importance and become the rationale for countries to restrict the flows of various types of nonpersonal information that could be considered sensitive from a national point of view, such as economic data, research results, and even basic discoveries. Information is power and even more, and its processing is the key to unlock that power. As stated at the SPIN Conference (26) in 1978: "Any nation that wishes to remain independent must achieve independence in informatics." Application of this thesis is likely to have important effects on international information flows.

Information Issues in Developing Countries

The developing countries of the world are nearly unanimous in viewing information as the most necessary prerequisite for progress, and informatics as the "instrument ideally suited to promote economic and social development." Information processing makes it possible to master the information necessary for production, management, assistance in making decisions, planning, control and research, as well as gives access to all types of knowledge. Starting with this premise, developing countries, through the Intergovernmental Bureau of Informatics (IBI, located in Rome) and with the help of UNESCO, are seeking to assure themselves access to the world's information depositories and capabilities for information storage and processing on domestic or regional bases.

At the SPIN conference in 1978 the developing countries considered strategies and policies for introducing informatics in their countries and the roles that they expect the industrialized countries to take in this process. In a series of resolutions and recommendations, the conference made the following points:
- Governments of developing countries should assess their needs in information and informatics, establish national information

policies, and make efforts to exchange experience and information in meeting their information needs.

- UNESCO and IBI should develop plans for technical, financial and educational cooperation in informatics among developing countries, and for developing information processing and computer equipment standards.
- Governments should encourage scientific and technical research in the field of informatics, in the official and private sectors, for the purpose of identifying the areas of application most suitable for local needs and the type of systems most appropriate for use in such areas.
- Governments should study the establishment of regional information systems and data processing and telecommunications capabilities.

In questions dealing with transborder data flows, developing countries realize the need for science-technology and business information for their development, but are wary of "information colonialism" that may ensue. To avoid the latter they are exploring ways to establish data bases that are under their own control or, at least, under the control of regional organizations. It is not likely, however, that these actions will lead to significant hindrances to international data flows.

Confidentiality and Security Issues in Information Flows

Confidentiality and security concerns in information flows deal with assuring that unauthorized access, modification or destruction of the data are prevented, as well as that data flows themselves are not disrupted. Confidentiality and security are required by privacy protection laws, by various national security related laws, and for protection of proprietary information. Protection is especially important in automated information systems where electronic storage of information makes detection and tracing of unauthorized accesses or data modifications very difficult--changes can be made without leaving a trace, and there are no seals or signatures to verify the authenticity of information items or data files.

In general, the need for confidentiality and security safeguards in an information system depends on legal requirements that may be imposed on the system (e.g., privacy protection laws), on the degree of management control to be implemented in the system, and on the system's attributes, such as the sensitivity, volume and frequency of use of the stored or transmitted data, the size and diversity of the user population, and the structure and operating environment of the information system. For example, security threats are more serious in automated information systems that permit simultaneous access to many users from remote terminals on a resource-sharing basis, that process unrelated tasks concurrently with sensitive data, and that permit users from several organizations to share the system resources concurrently.

After a decade of concern and research, there are now available numerous techniques for implementing physical security, access controls in computer software, and communications security (27-29). For example, it may be asserted that:

- except for international standards, physical security is well in hand for protecting computer installations against natural disasters, preventing unauthorized access to the premises, providing safe data storage, and setting up back-up facilities;
- software security techniques have made considerable advances and, while software security cannot be guaranteed completely, secure software systems with limited capabilities are evolving;
- techniques for providing unforgeable identification and authentication have made considerable progress; the development of digital signatures is especially relevant in the context of providing security in information flows;
- new developments in cryptography, such as the federal Data Encryption Standard (30) and public-key cryptosystem concepts (31) are promising improvements in data integrity and in communications security.

In the context of international data flows, there are a number of technical problems for implementing data security, such as a lack of standards and widely varying technical characteristics of data processing and communication systems. There are also several non-technical factors that may complicate the security problem in international information flows and systems. In particular, the existing international agreements on telecommunication, such as the International Telecommunications Convention of Malaga-Torremolinos, recognize the rights of all countries to regulate their telecommunications, and to monitor all communications crossing their borders. Thus, the use of encryption techniques for providing data security depends on whether or not the governments involved insist on access to the encryption keys or whether or not they may prohibit encryption entirely. Also lacking internationally is a legal prohibition of interception or diversion by private parties of data transmitted over telecommunication systems. In the United States, interception is prohibited by the Communications Act of 1934, and pending in Congress is a federal Computer Crime bill (S.240) which will prohibit unauthorized access and use of automated information systems.

A system of confidentiality and security safeguards is effective only when it is designed correctly and continues to operate correctly. Achieving this in information systems implies standards; ability to audit and monitor the overall system's operation; access to the equipment, which in international situations may be located in several countries; and cooperation from all parties involved. While certain procedures can be established by contractual agreements, other aspects of enforcing compliance with confidentiality and security requirements may require international agreements and support.

Literature Cited

1. C. Kaysen, Report of the Task Force on the Storage and Access to Government Statistics (Washington, D.C.: Bureau of the Budget, 1966).

2. Willis H. Ware (Chairman), <u>Records, Computers and the Right of Privacy</u>, Report of the Secretary's Advisory Committee on Automated Personal Data Systems (July 1973) (Washington, D.C.: Department of Health, Education and Welfare).

3. David F. Linowes (Chairman), <u>Personal Privacy in An Information Society</u> (Washington, D.C.: Privacy Protection Study Commission, July 1977).

4. <u>On the Protection of Privacy of Individuals Vis-A-Vis Electronic Data Banks in the Private Sector</u>, Resolution (73)22 (Strasbourg, France: The Council of Europe, 1975).

5. <u>On the Protection of Privacy of Individuals Vis-A-Vis Electronic Data Banks in the Public Sector</u>, Resolution (74)29 (Strasbourg, France: The Council of Europe, n.d.).

6. Rein Turn, ed., <u>Transborder Data Flows. Vol. 2, Supporting Materials</u> (Washington, D.C.: AFIPS Panel on Transborder Data Flows, December 1979).

7. <u>Fair Credit Reporting Act</u>, 15 U.S.C., 1687 <u>et seq.</u> (1969).

8. <u>Privacy Act of 1974</u>, 5 U.S.C., 552a (Public Law 93-579) (1974).

9. <u>Family Educational Rights and Privacy Act</u>, 20 U.S.C. 1232g (1974).

10. <u>Right of Financial Privacy Act of 1978</u>, 11 U.S.C., 1100 <u>et seq.</u> (1978).

11. <u>Compilation of State and Federal Privacy Laws</u> (Washington, D.C.: Privacy Journal, 1978).

12. "Mailing Lists," in Linowes, <u>Personal Privacy in an Information Society</u>.

13. David N. Kershaw and Joseph C. Small, "Data Confidentiality and Privacy: Lessons from the New Jersey Negative Income Tax Experiment," <u>Public Policy</u> 20 (Spring 1972), pp. 257-80.

14. <u>Protecting Individual Privacy in Evaluation Research</u>, Report of Committee on Federal Agency Evaluation Research (Washington, D.C.: National Academy of Sciences, 1975).

15. <u>Does Research Threaten Privacy or Does Privacy Threaten Research?</u> Report of A Study Group, British Association for the Advancement of Science, Publication 74/1 (London: British Association for the Advancement of Science, June 1974).

16. Donald T. Campbell, et al., "Confidentiality-Preserving Modes of Access to Files and to Interfile Exchange for Useful Statistical Analysis," in Linowes, Protecting Individual Privacy in Evaluation Research, Appendix A.

17. The Vulnerability of Computerized Society (Stockholm, Sweden: Ministry of Defense, 1978).

18. Simon Nora and Alain Minc, The Computerization of Society (Cambridge, MA: The MIT Press, 1980).

19. J. V. Clyne (Chairman), Telecommunications and Canada, Report by the Consultative Committee on the Implications of Tele-communications for Canadian Sovereignty (Ottawa: the Committee, March 1979).

20. "SPIN Conference Resolution," IBI Newsletter, Nov. 27, 1978.

21. Susan H. Nycum and Susan Courtney-Saunders, Transborder Data Flow: Legal Persons in Privacy Protection Legislation," AFIPS Conference Proceedings, Vol. 49 (May 1980), pp. 587-93.

22. Draft Convention for the Protection of Individuals With Regard to Automatic Processing of Personal Data, (Strasbourg, France: The Council of Europe, January 10, 1980).

23. Draft Guidelines Governing Protection of Privacy and Transborder Flows of Personal Data, (Paris: OECD, June 1979).

24. Personal Information Privacy (Washington, D.C.: U.S. Chamber of Commerce, June 23, 1978).

25. Fair Information Practices—A Time for Action (New York: Business Roundtable, December 1978).

26. "SPIN Conference Gets Underway," Computerworld, September 4, 1978, p. 1.

27. Physical Security and Risk Management, FIPS PUB 41 (Washington, D.C.: National Bureau of Standards, June 1974).

28. Dorothy E. Denning and Peter J. Denning, "Data Security," ACM Computing Surveys, September 1979, pp. 225-49.

29. Winfield Diffie and Martin E. Hellman, "Privacy and Authenti-cation: An Introduction to Cryptography," Proceedings of the IEEE, March 1979, pp. 397-426.

30. Data Encryption Standard, FIPS PUB 46 (Washington, D.C.: National Bureau of Standards, 1977).

31. Martin E. Hellman, "An Overview of Public-Key Cryptography," IEEE Communications Society Magazine, November 1978, pp. 24-32.

LEGAL AND REGULATORY FACTORS THAT MAY AFFECT
THE FLOW OF INFORMATION:
Copyright Ownership, Reproduction, Use Conditions

by

Harriet L. Oler*
Senior Attorney-Adviser
General Counsel's Staff
Copyright Office

The United States, as it enters the twenty-first century, is in the
throes of an information technology explosion unparalled in history.
Old methods of seeking, transferring, and using information become outdated almost as soon as they are developed. New technology both spawns
great demands for more information and generates tremendous accessibility to information. At the same time, new information technology
poses potential dangers to our society. Erich Fromm, in a character-
istically sage observation, once said that the danger of the past was
that men became slaves; the danger of the future is that they may become
robots.[1] Great quanta of information are of little value unless the
creative quality of that information is rich. For that reason, main-
taining an intelligent balance between the needs of creators and users
of information in a technological society must be a top priority now as
never before. If information user opportunities are to remain throughout the next century, creator incentive must be rigorously protected.

One hope for keeping information demands and availability in some
sort of order, while preserving the reasonable interests of both creators
and users, is federal copyright law. A primary goal of copyright law is
to provide an economic incentive for authors to create literary,
artistic, musical and sculptural works, and to assure them some control
over the subsequent marketing and use of those works. Copyright stimu-
lates the creation and dissemination of intellectual works by assuring
authors the economic reward afforded by the market.[2] That economic
reward, gleaned from copyright protection, likewise enables publishers
and other distributors of intellectual property to invest their resources
in bringing copyright works to the public.[3]

Our Founding Fathers, familiar with British history and the Colonies'
early experience, were keenly aware of the benefits to society from copyright. They framed a Constitutional copyright provision expressly

---

*The views expressed here are those of the author, and do not necessarily
reflect official positions of the Copyright Office or the Library of
Congress. Footnotes in this article are in standard legal citation
format.

designed to foster creative authorship. Article I, Sec. 8 of the
United States Constitution grants Congress the power to enact copyright
laws:

> The Congress shall have Power...To promote the Progress of Science
> and useful Arts, by securing for limited Times to Authors and
> Inventors the exclusive Right to their respective Writings ....[4]

Since 1970, the United States has attempted through federal legislation to safeguard intellectual property rights of authors as an
inducement for them to create cultural works. But, with the rapid
development of new modes of disseminating information, federal law has
frequently become an anachronism. As a result, creators have lost
control over their property; and, where legal rights have been recognized, they often benefited copyright industries far more than
individual authors.

In 1976, after more than a decade of careful legislative consideration, Congress supplanted the previous sixty-seven year old copyright
statute with an entirely new, contemporary federal statutory scheme.
It attempts to resolve some of the most explosive controversies between
creators and users created by the clash of new technology with a copyright law long outdated and severely inflexible. The new copyright law
was signed by then-President Ford on October 19th, and became effective
on January 1, 1978.

Public Law 94-553, 90 Stat. 2541 (1976), governs the legal rights
and responsibilities of creators and users with respect to all copyrighted works created on or after January 1, 1978. The purpose of this
article is to discuss generally some of the new copyright law's provisions that influence and regulate the creation and flow of information.
Specifically, the article focuses upon provisions that may affect printed
materials and computer accessed data, as well as issues of current concern to researchers, librarians and other users. The article is meant
merely to indicate statutory terms and unresolved issues. It in no way
eradicates the need for expert counsel in this highly specialized, and
frequently uncharted, legal field. Nor does it discuss in any detail
provisions of the previous copyright law that may be of continuing
relevance in determining questions, including the use of a work in
automatic storage and retrieval systems,[5] the resolution of pre-1978
causes of action,[6] or the copyright status of works published (but not
registered with the Copyright Office) prior to the effective date of
the revised law.[7]

Subject Matter

Copyright protects all "original works of authorship, fixed in any
tangible medium of expression, now known or later developed, from which
they can be perceived, reproduced, or otherwise communicated, either
directly or with the aid of a machine or device."[8] The term "original
works of authorship" is not defined in the statute, but the House of
Representatives Committee Report that accompanied the copyright bill
explains that it was intended "to incorporate without change the
standard of originality established by courts under the [1909] copyright

statute."[9] Case law, in turn, makes clear that copyrightable works
need not be novel, in the patent law sense,[10] nor aesthetically
pleasing.[11] But, they must possess at least a minimum amount of
independent, creative authorship.[12] Copyright covers both published
and unpublished works.

General categories of copyrightable subject matter are enumerated
in the law. They include literary works; musical works, including
accompanying words; dramatic works, including accompanying music;
pantomimes and choreographic works; motion pictures and other audiovisual works; and sound recordings.[13] Mindful of the rapid expansion
of new information technology, and the need for copyright legislation
sufficiently stable to provide guidelines for copyright creators and
users, Congress drafted this section largely in terms of genres of
expression, rather than media formats. Because a particular format is
not mentioned in the law as copyrightable subject matter does not
necessarily preclude its inclusion under the copyright umbrella. On
this point, the House Report observed:

> The history of copyright law has been one of gradual expansion in
> the types of works accorded protection, and the subject matter
> affected by this expansion has fallen into two general categories.
> In the first, scientific discoveries and technological developments
> have made possible new forms of creative expression that never
> existed before. In some of these cases the new expressive forms--
> electronic music, filmstrips, and computer programs, for example--
> could be regarded as an extension of copyrightable subject matter
> Congress had already intended to protect, and were thus considered
> copyrightable from the outset without the need of new legislation.
> In other cases, such as photographs, sound recordings, and motion
> pictures, statutory enactment was deemed necessary to give them
> full recognition as copyrightable works.
>
> Authors are continually finding new ways of expressing themselves,
> but it is impossible to foresee the forms that these new expressive
> methods will take. The bill does not intend either to freeze the
> scope of copyrightable technology or to allow unlimited expansion
> into areas completely outside the present congressional intent.
> Section 102 implies neither that that subject matter is unlimited
> nor that new forms of expression within that general area of subject
> matter would necessarily be unprotected.[14]

Copyright covers works embodied in a myriad of artistic formats:
books, periodicals, maps, technical drawings, paintings, sculpture,
photographs, jewelry designs, fabric designs, musical compositions,
phonorecords of sound recordings,[15] printed speeches, dramas, television
programs, motion pictures, and videotapes are some of the most common.
Utilitarian works may also be copyrightable, if some artistic element
can be conceptually separated from the functional design of the
article.[16] Purely utilitarian articles, even though of pleasing
design, including those whose form is dictated by function, such as
the configuration of computer chips, must be protected by some means
other than copyright.

Some works are considered for registration by the Copyright Office even though the extent of their protection has not been legally settled. For example, the Copyright Office will register claims to copyright in computer programs and data bases if the elements of assembling, selecting, arranging, editing and literary expression that went into the compilation of the work are sufficient to constitute original authorship.[17] But no court has directly decided the scope of protection for these works.[18] The Office registration policy is in accord with the 1978 recommendation of the President's Commission on New Technological Uses of Copyrighted Works (CONTU)[19] that the copyright statute be amended to clarify that computer programs are subject to copyright protection.[20]

The law also expresses the traditional principle that, whatever the format of a work may be, protection extends only to the original creative expression it embodies.[21] Copyright pertains to the literary, musical, graphic, or artistic form in which the author expressed intellectual concepts. It does not prevent the use by others of information or ideas found in an author's work. Ideas, systems, processes, formulas and methods of operation, as distinguished from the manner used to explain, describe, or otherwise express them, are not subject to copyright.[22] For example, the House Report makes clear that copyright protection for computer programs is not intended in any way to impair user access to the ideas they reflect.

Some concern has been expressed lest copyright in computer programs should extend protection to the methodology or processes adopted by the programmer, rather than merely to the "writing" expressing his ideas. Section 102(b) is intended, among other things, to make clear that the expression adopted by the programmer is the copyrightable element in a computer program, and that the actual processes or methods embodied in the programs are not within the scope of the copyright law.[23]

The federal statute does not embrace works that have not been fixed in a permanent form. To enjoy federal copyright protection, a work must be fixed in a tangible medium of expression that enables it to be reproduced or communicated, either directly or by a machine or device. The medium of expression may be one "now known or later developed." This provision means that an unfixed work of authorship, such as a live performance, an unrecorded broadcast or an impromptu dance, could be eligible for protection under State common law or statute,[24] but would not be copyrightable under the federal statute.

Section 101 of the law defines "fixation" in a way that permits live broadcasts that are simultaneously recorded to enjoy federal statutory benefits.

A work is "fixed" in a tangible medium of expression when its embodiment in a copy or phonorecord, by or under the authority of the author, is sufficiently permanent or stable to permit it to be perceived, reproduced, or otherwise communicated for a period of more than transitory duration. A work consisting of sounds, images, or both, that are being transmitted, is "fixed" for purposes of this title, if a fixation of the work is being made simultaneously with its transmission.[25]

Again, the House Report explains Congress' intent:

When a football game is being covered by four television cameras, with a director guiding the activities of the four cameramen and choosing which of their electronic images are sent out to the public and in what order, there is little doubt that what the cameramen and director are doing constitutes "authorship." The further question to be considered is whether there has been a fixation. If the images and sounds to be broadcast are first recorded (on a video tape, film, etc.) and then transmitted, the recorded work would be considered a "motion picture" subject to statutory protection against unauthorized reproduction or retransmission of the broadcast. If the program content is transmitted live to the public while being recorded at the same time, the case would be treated the same: the copyright owner would not be forced to rely on common law rather than statutory rights in proceeding against an infringing user of the live broadcast.

Thus, assuming it is copyrightable--as a "motion picture" or "sound recording," for example--the content of a live transmission should be accorded statutory protection if it is being recorded simultaneously with its transmission. On the other hand, the definition of "fixation" would exclude from the concept purely evanescent or transient reproductions such as those projected briefly on a screen, shown electronically on a television or other cathode ray tube, or captured momentarily in the "memory" of a computer.[26]

Certain types of works, in addition to those discussed above, are not eligible for copyright protection. Among these are titles, short phrases, slogans, familiar symbols and designs. In addition, copyright does not cover works that consist entirely of information that is common property, such as standard calendars, tape measures and rules, and lists or tables taken from public documents.

Ownership of Copyright and Transfer of Rights

One of the great advances of the recently enacted copyright law over earlier laws in legislating copyright goals involves those provisions that strengthen property rights of individual authors as against publishers, distributors and other commercial exploiters of artistic property. In most cases, the new law provides that all rights in a work inure to the author, endure for a term based upon the author's lifetime, and ultimately must be traced back to that author. Section 201(a) of the law states this premise simply: "Copyright in a work protected under this title vests initially in the author or authors of the work."[27] Coowners of a joint work likewise own the copyright jointly.

One important exception to this general rule governs works made for hire. Copyright rights in works made for hire are presumptively owned by the employer rather than the employee, and the employer is considered the author of such works. A work made for hire is defined in the statute as:

(1) a work prepared by an employee within the scope of his or her employment; or
(2) a work specifically ordered or commissioned for use as a contribution to a collective work, as a part of a motion picture or other audiovisual work, as a translation, as a supplementary work, as a compilation, as an instructional text, as a test, as answer material for a test, or as an atlas, if the parties expressly agree in a written instrument signed by them that the work shall be considered a work made for hire....[28]

This provision means that, unless a work is prepared within the scope of an employee's duties, or is one of the specified categories of commissioned works that can be considered "works made for hire" under a written agreement, copyright ownership vests initially in the individual or individuals who authored the work, unless the parties sign a written agreement otherwise.

One category of works that may be specially commissioned as a work made for hire, with a written agreement, is instructional texts. The law defines these texts as "literary, pictorial or graphic work(s) prepared for publication with the purpose of use in systematic instructional activities."[29] Further, the House Report establishes that the category covers "what might be loosely called 'textbook material,' whether or not in book form or prepared in the form of text matter."[30] It is intended to embrace only works prepared for use in structured teaching activities, as distinguished from works directed to a general readership.

Ownership of literary property rights in a commissioned journal article or other contribution to a collective work vests in the author of the piece unless the parties agree in writing that the work was made for hire. Absent an agreement, the owner of the journal acquires "only the privilege of reproducing and distributing the contribution as part of that collective work, any revision of that collective work, and any later collective work in the same series.[31]

Ownership provisions are coupled with statutory terms that facilitate the transfer of copyright rights. The law provides that mere ownership of a manuscript, painting, or other copy or phonorecord of a work does not give the possessor the copyright, and that transfer of ownership of any material object does not of itself convey any rights in the copyrighted work.[32]

The new law facilitates business transactions by specifying that copyrights are completely divisible and that any of the exclusive rights that constitute a copyright, including those enumerated in § 106 of the law, can be transferred and owned separately. This principle obtains whether or not the transfer is limited in time or place of effect, but it does not apply to non-exclusive licenses. All transfers (other than by operation of law) must be in writing and must be signed by the owner of the right.[33]

The law also expedites enforcement of rights. The owner of any exclusive right is considered the "copyright owner" with respect to his or her particular right, and is entitled to all of the protection and remedies accorded to the copyright owner for that right.[34] For example, a local broadcasting station who owns the exclusive right to transmit a work for a period of time in a particular geographic area is entitled to sue in its own name an infringer of that particular exclusive right.[35]

Authors and certain heirs are given a statutory "second chance" to evaluate the commercial value of their works and to market them accordingly. They enjoy an inalienable right to terminate grants that generally arises thirty-five years after execution of the original grant.[36]

Creation, Duration, Registration and Notice

Statutory copyright in a work authored by an individual vests from the moment the work is created and endures for the author's lifetime plus 50 years after his or her death.[37] Works authored by corporate bodies and anonymous or pseudonymous works enjoy a term of 75 years from publication or one hundred years from creation, whichever expires first.[38]

Registration of a claim with the Copyright Office is not a condition of protection, although registration offers certain statutory benefits in the event of an infringement.[39] Published works should contain the statutory notice of copyright from the time of publication,[40] but the statute allows a copyright owner to correct an omission of notice or an erroneous notice under certain conditions,[41] without harm to a user who innocently infringed a work that was published without the prescribed copyright notice.[42]

The notice and registration provisions mean that a user cannot be sure that a work published without a notice is in the public domain and available for unrestricted use without payment or permission. But, the user can order the Copyright Office to search its registration and recordation files and to report on the information they contain. If no information indicates that the work is protected, the law generally protects a user against liability for reasonable uses of the work.[43]

Exclusive Rights and Limitations

Copyright offers the owner a bundle of exclusive rights. These are set out initially in the statute and include the right to reproduce the work in copies or phonorecords; the right to distribute those copies or records; the right to prepare derivative works (such as translations and dramatizations) based upon the copyrighted work; the right to perform the work publicly (excepting copyrighted sound recordings); and the right to display the work publicly.[44]

These exclusive rights are modified by succeeding statutory exceptions and exemptions designed to protect the public's interest in guaranteed access to certain modes of information.[45] Unless a prospective use fits within these exemptions, or does not fall within one of the exclusive rights enumerated in the statute, a user must obtain the copyright owner's permission or risk liability for copyright infringement and the attendant penalties set forth in Chapter 5 of the copyright law.

Infringement penalties may include injunctions, actual or statutory damages, profits of the infringer, costs, and attorney's fees.

Statutory exceptions to the copyright owner's exclusive rights are designed to avoid unfair restraints on legitimate uses of copyrighted works. For example, Congress believed that certain technologies would be hampered if the author were allowed absolute control over his or her copyrighted work. Thus, it created statutory compulsory licenses to guarantee both public access to, and author remuneration for, performances of recorded nondramatic music on jukeboxes;[46] the manufacture and distribution of phonorecords of previously published and recorded nondramatic music;[47] the cable retransmission of broadcast radio and television programs;[48] and the use by public broadcasters of published nondramatic music and published pictorial, graphic, and sculptural works.[49]

Other exemptions permit certain public performances of copyrighted works in classroom teaching situations,[50] in connection with instructional broadcasts,[51] religious services,[52] agricultural or horticultural fairs,[53] broadcast reception on a single receiving apparatus[54] and for the handicapped.[55] In addition, some "non-profit" performances are exempted from copyright liability under the statute.[56]

The law further specifies limited permissible photocopying by libraries and archives for replacement, preservation, and (with restrictions) for individual users' private study, scholarship, or research.[57] Photocopying under the conditions expressed in this statutory provision may be performed without payment to, or permission from, the copyright owner.

Finally, the most intentionally indefinite exception to a copyright owner's exclusive rights is the statutory provision that a use of any copyrighted work may be judged by a court to be a "fair use."[58] The fair use exception applies to all copyrighted works and to all uses of those works, and allows a court to sanction a use that would otherwise be deemed a literal infringement of the copyright owner's exclusive rights.

Fair use is not defined in the law, but four criteria are set forth to guide courts in determining whether a particular use was a fair or free one. Courts are to consider the purpose and commercial character of the use; the nature of the copyrighted work; the amount or quantity of the work used in relation to the whole copyrighted work; and, perhaps most important, the effect of the use upon the potential market for the copyrighted work.[59] Evolving case law will further define user benefits from the fair use exception. The doctrine's vagueness allows its application to new uses, and permits the copyright law to balance authors' rights with rapidly changing user needs.[60]

The fair use provision also offers a statutory framework for private party compromises with respect to uses of copyrighted works. For example, educators, authors, publishers and other concerned interest groups have agreed to a set of "fair use" guidelines for limited classroom copying of books and periodicals and for educational uses of music.[61] These guidelines establish minimum standards of uses that, in the parties' view, are fair uses. Similar fair use guidelines are being negotiated for other uses of copyrighted works, such as off-air taping for non-profit classroom use of copyrighted audiovisual works incorporated in

radio and television broadcasts. And, unarguably, the law gives educators, librarians and other users incentive to negotiate with authors
for mutually acceptable arrangements for other uses of copyrighted
works.

These agreements are but a threshhold of adjusting copyright to
modern day needs and technologies. There is much unfinished business
in copyright, some of which begs for immediate legislative solution.
For example, the status of copyright and computer uses is still
unclear.[62] In part because of legal uncertainties surrounding copyright protection for computer software, Congress created a Commission
on New Technological Uses of Copyrighted Works (CONTU) to study and
make recommendations on computer use copyright issues. The commission
was charged with assisting the president and Congress in "developing a
national policy for protecting the rights of copyright owners and
ensuring public access to copyrighted works when they are used in
computer and machine duplication systems...."[63]

The commission's final report reviewed the economic impact and the
legal and legislative status of computer programs. It recommended that
the current copyright act be amended by deleting Section 117 to make the
law applicable to all computer uses of copyrighted data bases and other
copyrighted works fixed in computer sensible media. In addition, it
advised amending the copyright law:

(1) to make it explicit that computer programs, to the extent that
    they embody an author's original creation, are proper subject
    matter of copyright;
(2) to apply to all computer uses of copyrighted programs...; and
(3) to ensure that rightful possessors of copies of computer
    programs may use or adapt these copies for their use.[64]

These recommendations, if legislated, would clarify that computer programs are proper subject matter of copyright, but would allow courts to
decide the ultimate scope of that protection.

Conclusion

This brief overview of the complicated new copyright law hopefully
will persuade readers that copyright is one of the fundamental legal
principles that should direct strategies for meeting the information
needs of society. Copyright in the twenty-first century is not an
anachronism. Rather, in modern dress, the federal copyright statute
has a crucial role to play in preserving and protecting both creator
incentive and user access to information that will enrich our society.

The next century, with its clear challenges, must seek solutions
to the problems inherent in new technological advances in the creation
of and the need for information. And early, thoughtful resolutions are
imperative, for change is difficult once industry and user practices
have become habitual.

The law provides a legal skeleton sufficiently flexible to facilitate the generation and transfer of information in a manner that fairly
protects the rights of creators and the needs of users. Most important,
it preserves creator incentive and control against known threats from

industry and user demands. At the same time, the law is not a panacea.
Its ultimate success in achieving the copyright goals announced in our
Constitution depends upon the good will and the willingness to
compromise of all of us who value creation and who benefit from it.

Notes

1. E. Fromm, The Sane Society 360 (1955).

2. Mazer v. Stein, 347 U. S. 201,219 (1954); Washingtonian
Publishing Co. v. Pearson, 306 U. S. 30,36 (1939).

3. Report of the Register of Copyrights on Copyright Law Revision,
87th Cong., 1st Sess. (Comm. Print), at 5-6 (1961).

4. U. S. Const. Art. I, § 8.

5. Pub. L. No. 94-553, 90 Stat. 2541 (1976) codified as 17 U.S.C.,
§§ 1 ff.,·at § 117 (1978).

6. Pub. L. No. 94-553, Transitional and Supplementary Provisions,
Section 112.

7. The legal status of works published prior to January 1, 1978
may be determined by the previous copyright law, Copyright Act of
Mar. 4, 1909, as amended, 17 U.S.C. §§ 1-236 (1970 and Supp. V. 1975),
and by common law, since the new law does not revive copyright in works
in the public domain as of December 31, 1977. Pub. L. No. 94-553,
Trans. and Supp. Prov. Section 103.

8. Pub. L. No. 94-553, § 102(a).

9. H. R. Rep. No. 94-1476, 94th Cong., 2d Sess. 51 (1976). This
report is cited hereafter as H. R. Rep. No. 94-1476.

10. Id., at 51. See also, M. Nimmer ON COPYRIGHT at § 2.01[A]
(1979 ed.).

11. Bleistein v. Donaldson Lithographing Co., 188 U. S. 239 (1903).

12. Baker v. Selden, 101 U. S. 99 (1879); Bailie v. Fisher,
258 F. 2d 425 (D. C. Cir. 1958).

13. Pub. L. No. 94-553, § 102(a).

14. H. R. Rep. No. 94-1476, supra. n. 9, at 51.

15. Dubbing rights were legislated for sound recordings by the Act
of Oct. 15, 1971, Pub. L. No. 92-140, 85 Stat. 391, and were made
permanent by the Act of Dec. 31, 1974, Pub. L. No. 93-573, § 101,
88 Stat. 1873. Protection is available only for sound recordings

first fixed after Feb. 15, 1972. Pub. L. No. 94-553, § 201(c). Note
that the law distinguishes between copyrightable sound recordings, and
phonorecords, or the physical objects in which the sounds are fixed.

16. See Esquire v. Ringer, 591 F. 2d 796 (D. C. Cir. 1978), cert.
denied, 440 U. S. 908 (1979) (Copyright protection is not available for
the design of a utilitarian article).

17. See Copyright Office Circular No. 61 "Computer Programs"
(April 1978).

18. For a complete bibliography of cases, articles and treatises
on the issue of copyright protection for automatic information storage
and retrieval systems, see National Commission on New Technological Uses
of Copyrighted Works, Final Report, at pp. 135-38, 141 (July 31, 1978).

19. See n. 63, infra.

20. See n. 64, infra and accompanying text.

21. H. R. Rep. No. 94-1476, supra n. 9, at 56-57.

22. Pub. L. No. 94-553, § 102(b); See, Baker v. Selden, 101 U. S.
99 (1879).

23. H. R. Rep. No. 94-1476, supra n. 9, at 56-57.

24. Pub. L. No. 94-553, § 301(a) preempts, after Jan. 1, 1978, all
legal or equitable rights that are equivalent to any of the exclusive
copyright rights within Section 106, in fixed works of authorship within
the subject matter of copyright, whether created before or after 1978,
and whether published or unpublished.

25. Pub. L. No. 94-553, § 101.

26. H. R. Rep. No. 94-1476, supra n. 9, at 52-53.

27. Pub. L. No. 94-553, § 201(a).

28. Pub. L. No. 94-553, § 101.

29. Pub. L. No. 94-553, § 101.

30. H. R. Rep. No. 94-1476, supra n. 9, at 121.

31. Pub. L. No. 94-553, § 201(c). Section 404, dealing with copyright notice, preserves the author's copyright in a contribution even if
the contribution does not contain a separate notice in the author's name,
without requiring an unqualified transfer of rights to the owner of the
collective work.

32. Pub. L. No. 94-553, § 202.

33. Pub. L. No. 94-553, § 204(a).

34. Pub. L. No. 94-553, § 201(d).

35. H. R. Rep. No. 94-1476, supra n. 9, at 123.

36. Pub. L. No. 94-553, § 203.

37. Pub. L. No. 94-553, § 302(a).

38. Pub. L. No. 94-553, § 302(c).

39. For example, registration within three months of publication is necessary to assure a copyright owner's entitlement to statutory damages and attorney's fees for an infringement that occurred prior to registration with the Copyright Office. Pub. L. No. 94-553, § 412(2). Registration of a claim within five years of its publication also guarantees that a court will regard the certificate as prima facie evidence of the validity of the copyright and of the facts stated in the certificate in any judicial proceeding. Pub. L. No. 94-553, § 410(c).

40. Pub. L. No. 94-553, § 401.

41. Pub. L. No. 94-553, §§ 405, 406. The corrective notice and innocent infringer provisions of § 405 offer additional incentives to prompt registration of claims to copyright.

42. Pub. L. No. 94-553, §§ 405(b), 406.

43. H. R. Rep. No. 94-1476, supra n. 9, at 148.

44. Pub. L. No. 94-553, § 106.

45. Pub. L. No. 94-553, §§ 107-118.

46. Pub. L. No. 94-553, § 116.

47. Pub. L. No. 94-553, § 115.

48. Pub. L. No. 94-553, § 111.

49. Pub. L. No. 94-553, § 118.

50. Pub. L. No. 94-553, § 110(1).

51. Pub. L. No. 94-553, § 110(2).

52. Pub. L. No. 94-553, § 110(3).

53. Pub. L. No. 94-553, § 110(6).

54. Pub. L. No. 94-553, § 110(5).

55. Pub. L. No. 94-553, § 110(8) and (9).

56. Pub. L. No. 94-553, § 110(4).

57. Pub. L. No. 94-553, § 108. See also the CONTU guidelines for photocopying as part of interlibrary arrangements under § 108(g)(2), H. R. Rep. No. 94-1733 (Conference Report), 94th Cong., 2d Sess. at 72-74 (1976).

58. Pub. L. No. 94-553, § 107.

59. Pub. L. No. 94-553, § 107.

60. The 1976 House Report confirms Congress' intention in this regard:

The statement of the fair use doctrine in section 107 offers some guidance to users in determining when the principles of the doctrine apply. However, the endless variety of situations and combinations of circumstances that can rise in particular cases precludes the formulation of exact rules in the statute. The bill endorses the purpose and general scope of the judicial doctrine of fair use, but there is no disposition to freeze the doctrine in the statute, especially during a period of rapid technological change. Beyond a new broad statutory explanation of what fair use is and some of the criteria applicable to it, the courts must be free to adapt the doctrine to particular situations on a case-by-case basis. Section 107 is intended to restate the present judicial doctrine of fair use, not to change, narrow, or enlarge it in any way.

H. Rep. No. 94-1476, supra n. 9, at 66.

61. Id. at 68-71.

62. Section 117 of the law froze the posture of a copyright owner's rights with respect to the use of copyrighted works in conjunction with computers and similar information systems. Pub. L. No. 94-553, § 117.

63. Pub. L. No. 93-573, Title II; 88 Stat. 1873 (1974); Final Report of CONTU, supra n. 18, at 3.

64. Id., at 1.

THE FINANCING AND GOVERNANCE OF
INFORMATION NETWORKS OF THE FUTURE:
The Public Sector

Dr. Fred Weingarten, Senior Analyst
Director of National Information System
Overview Assessment
Office of Technology Assessment
U. S. Congress

Introduction

Government has not been immune to the information revolution.
Indeed, it has been confronted by a series of difficult challenges
presented by the need to deal institutionally with a pervasive new
technology, and to perform its basic functions in a society more and
more organized around the collection and use of information.

Information has become central to our economy, both as a commodity
in its own right and as a factor of production for numberless goods and
services. It is a basic medium of exchange between government and citizens. We send information to the government which collects it, voices
decisions on it, and sends services back to us, increasingly in the form
of information.

This section will discuss briefly some of the problems, peculiar to
government, in the management of information systems. Some unavoidable
emphasis will be on the federal level. Most of the same concerns are
parallel at the state and local levels, although the particular forms of
problems taken are idiosyncratic to each state, county or municipality.

The discussion will focus on problems rather than solutions. Government at all levels is just beginning to appreciate the idea that information processing technology is not just another tool, but that it creates
a fundamental change in the way agencies are organized to make decisions
and relate to their constituencies. Daily reports in newspapers and magazines bring new horror stories of the failure of billion dollars systems
or the tribulations of a citizen trapped in an automated labyrinth of
Kafkaesque proportions. The General Accounting Office of the U.S.
Congress has been issuing a steady stream of reports criticizing federal
procurement and management of information technology.

We are only now starting to realize that these problems are often
endemic to information management in the public sector rather than the
result of government stupidity or malfeasance. But what is wrong?

<u>Trends</u>

Data Collection

Government at all levels is becoming a voracious consumer of information. Despite attempts to check data collection by means of legislation such as the Privacy Act of 1974[1] and despite exhortations by groups such as the Federal Commission on Paperwork, federal agencies continue to expand their information files. The Privacy Commission has pointed out that the Privacy Act's requirement that data be directly relevant to the purposes for which it is collected, has had little effect on agency practice.[2] Relevancy of data has nearly disappeared as an element of privacy policy, not only because it is an attribute that is difficult to prove or disprove, but also because irrelevancy is not a major cause of the swelling government data banks. Of course, any data bank, private or public, contains some amount of useless, redundant or erroneous information, but this problem arises from information system management rather than policy.

A new bill[3] recently submitted to Congressman Jack Brooks (D. Texas), attempts to centralize authority for reducing federal information keeping by setting up a program in the Office of Management and Budget.

Government is motivated by several forces to collect more information:

<u>Continuing Establishment of New Programs</u>. Even when the total budget expended for certain purposes remains the same, government tends to originate new programs and to draw new procedures for old ones. Regulatory agencies continue to promulgate new rules, often with attendant new reporting requirements on individuals and organizations.

<u>Regularizing Decision Making</u>. There are continual pressures on government programs to regularize and justify decisions in such areas as eligibility for programs such as Aid to Dependent Children or for competitive awards such as research grants and purchasing contracts. A bureaucracy tends to collect more and more information from the applicants so that decisions have the appearance as well as the form of being fair.

<u>Enforcement</u>. Related to the above decision-making problem is that of catching errors and fraud in the creation of government programs. Such auditing generates heavy reporting requirements for the recipients of government services.

<u>Evaluation</u>. Ultimately, the question always arises whether a program is having its desired effect, whether it is meeting such goals as alleviating poverty, improving the environment, or stimulating scientific research. Such questions lead to program evaluation studies which, once again, can collect erroneous amounts of information.

<u>Planning and Management</u>. Societal areas such as the national economy, the state of science or public health are monitored and influenced by government agencies for the national good. As overseer, the government creates information collection and storage in order to monitor performance, enforce laws, and evaluate the effects of programs.

<u>Government Production of Information</u>. It is often not recognized that government, in addition to being a collector of information, also

generates it. Government research projects and studies result in countless reports. The Census Bureau, Commerce, the Treasury, the FBI, for
example, all generate reports and statistical data bases in support of
their work.

This set of pressures on government agencies to enlarge their
information activities ensures that this growth will probably continue
at a fairly high rate. Efforts to cut back this process will retard
information gathering only to a small extent. Unless some radical new
approach to the practice of government is devised and implemented,
bureaucratic and even authentic needs for information collection will
exist.

Information Technology

Much has been written lately about the "Information Revolution,"
and it would not be profitable to go into detail here about the panoply
of new technology available to government agencies to do their work.
Just a partial list of such technology would include:
- Microprocessors
- New data storage technology
- New Data Communication Services
- Satellite Broadcast
- Videodisc/videocassette
- New technology for visual and voice input and output of data.

In an automated society, more information is collected generally
and more exists, principally in machine-readable form. These changes
facilitate a government agency's <u>collection</u> of data, providing a greater
potential and a more economically useable form. In some communication
based systems, for example law enforcement data files, the information
may be submitted to the system from a terminal at the principal part of
data capture, the local law enforcement office. Information technology
also provides governments with potential tools to <u>retain and organize</u>
better all of this data flowing in, and to use it for better or for
worse in decision making. Finally, information technology provides
government with new tools to disseminate information back to society
through automated data banks, television broadcasts,[4] videodisc and
tapes, and other media, in addition to the continued publication of
printed documents.

Improved collectability leads to increasingly aggressive government
demands for more and more data, placing large burdens upon the private
sector to respond and raising fears of an approaching era of "Big
Brother" government surveillance of the citizenry. Increasing use of
automated data systems for decision making leads to concerns about due
process and equity in the relationship between individuals and government agencies. Finally, increased technology for dissemination leads
to problems such as privacy and government competition with a new
growing electronic-based information industry. We will consider these
problems in more detail later.

The Problems

Government information system management faces many issues and problems that are identical to those faced by management in the private sector. However, of principal interest are problems that either differ from non-government operation or lack the solutions available to the private sector. These problems in general arise in two ways.

- Through dissonance between conflicting views of information held by society and by the legal system.
- Through the unique relationship between government agencies and their ultimate bosses, the tax payers, and those self-same citizens as recipients of services.

Dissonance of Views

Society has demonstrated ambivalent conceptions about the nature of information. In general, these views, while contradictory, have been accommodated in the past. Now, as the "information society" approaches, they are more difficult to ignore. In a simple model, there are three basic views of information:

- Information as a commodity--as a thing of value. Information costs money to collect and keep. It occasionally represents assets, for example, in the form of a bank account or ownership of securities. It can be used to achieve economic benefit by increasing productivity of workers and improving management decisions.
- Information as a public good. Free public education, the public library, and free commercial television are highly visible realizations of the view that a literate, informed public is essential to any society, particularly one that governs itself democratically. The Freedom of Information Act also reflects the view that access to public information is a right of all citizens.
- Information as a sensitive material. Whether motivated by sheer cussedness or by fear that information may be used against data subjects, public attitudes continue to support data privacy strongly. Individuals, private organizations, and governments (from concerns about National Security) all insist that some kinds of information (medical, financial, marketing, etc.) should not be collected or, if collected, not distributed.

The conflict between these views has presented government institutions with difficult dilemmas. For example, in Iowa recently libraries were faced with an interpretation of the state Freedom of Information Act requiring them to release records showing what books their users were checking out. This requirement flies in the face of traditional attitudes held by American society and espoused by librarians, that such information is private. In the past, these records were protected by the difficulty of extracting information from manual files. Computerized circulation systems remove that barrier.

Managers of government information systems must be constantly aware of the conflict between "freedom of information"[5] and the demands of both privacy and National Security. At the federal level, these conflicts have involved the criminal justice community in disputes over release of files that might disclose informants. Regulatory agencies collect information about companies under their purview which, if published could be used to advantage by their competitors. In the National Security arena, the debate over the proper use of classification has never been satisfactorily settled. Rights of some agencies to control even the unclassified publications of ex-employees has been brought to intense debate by a recent Supreme Court decision.[6]

In the same way, the freedom of information requirement that the government provide public access to data it possesses can conflict with the views of information as a commodity. That is, government information systems can slide over the line from public service into direct competition with the private sector information industry. Government operated or subsidized banks of economic data banks, medical data banks, scientific literature abstracts services, all have similar offerings in the private sector.

Information is becoming an important factor of production, and thus, its nature as a commodity is growing in importance, matched by the growth of a computer- and communication-based information industry. This industry is developing exciting new products and services to be introduced over the next decade or two. The dilemma facing government is to obey its duty to provide information for the public good, yet not inadvertently muscle out small entrepreneurs.

Special Relationships

Government information systems must be designed and operated with constraint imposed by the unique relationship they have with society. The citizens-taxpayers-voters are in the positions of being both managers and recipients of services.

Over the centuries, accumulated traditions, values, and rules directed the operation of any government bureaucracy. Information centers, although they are a new service using new technology, cannot avoid entanglement with these habits. In some cases, the rules lead to irritating red tape that inhibits the orderly development of the information systems and prevents their efficient use. Other times, the rules, although uncomfortable and unfamiliar in the technological management represent important social values and imperatives which must be acknowledged by government. The successful information system manager in the next decade will be able to integrate such social and political imperatives into the system and at the same time, exploit the new technologies discussed earlier.

Procurement

Government shares with the private sector the desire to get the most for its money, albeit with perhaps a more Spartan attitude. Unlike the private sector, government does have the mandate that, since public tax money is being spent an elaborate competitive bidding procedure must be undertaken for any major procurement.

These two factors combine with a rigid government contracting system to make the procurement of computer systems a major headache. Some experts now estimate procurement of a major information system, from conception to installation, can take ten years. Often, when the system is delivered, the hardware is obsolete,[7] and attempts to upgrade meet with the same delays.

In addition to delay, these procedures can create other problems. In the face of a rapidly evolving technology, such decisions can lead to continual selection of systems at the end of the effectiveness curve, even when the projected application is the state of the art. Furthermore, government procurement rules make it difficult to consider long-term, less predictable system costs in their decisions. Thus, false short-term economies are won at the expense of long-term financial cost. This problem is inherent to most government procurement and seems to reflect the very short-range perspectives of the political sector.

Personnel

Management of information systems in the public sector presents a variety of particular difficulties with staffing, both at the operational level and at the policy level. In the private sector, turnover of programming staff is traditional, but management often tries to stabilize operations by reducing losses of key people, especially at critical points in projects. However, there are benefits to staff turnover. Above all, it allows for influx of new knowledge and brings a fresh perspective to operations--essential processes that enable an organization to keep abreast with a sophisticated and rapidly changing technology. Conversely, the organization with no turnover of personnel might maintain a staff with obsolete skills no longer marketable outside. This is not to argue, of course, that management should not strive to hold on to good personnel or not seek for other ways to keep their skills upgraded.

Although high job turnover is widespread in private industry, the picture is different in the public sector. Civil service rules, low pay, and low incentives have combined to form in many cases stagnant operations. The incentives to work in the public sector do not reward the most creative and productive information systems personnel. Studies of federal and state data processing operations have often pointed out the following civil service disincentives for competent talent:

- Job rotation is not encouraged.
- The status of programmers remains low. They are considered to be a highly skilled clerks rather than a professionals analagous to engineers.
- Procurement lags cause professional staff to spend time keeping obsolete and inefficient operations patched together, rather than working on advanced applications and new technology.
- Data processing under the management of incompetent directors who are difficult to remove because of civil service regulations.
- The federal government has yet to emulate the private sector by viewing information systems and information policy as a senior management function. Most agencies lack an important senior management perspective in planning and policy setting. No agency yet has the equivalent of an Assistant Secretary for Information

Systems. The lack of opportunity for advancement to senior management drives the brightest people to private industry or to other specialties,

In an article on troubles with the Defense Department's WIMEX system, Science Magazine quoted an Admiral as saying "I'd really wonder about an officer who wanted to make his career in computers."[8] Yet the modern military depends totally on advanced information and communications systems.

Conclusions

While many problems beseige public sector information systems managers, there are challenges and vast opportunities for improvement. Prodded by such stimuli as the Brooks Bill, government may be ready to respond to the needs. At present, the following conclusions seem apparent:

- Government information systems are by and large obsolescent. It is common to compare the U.S. data processing technology with that of foreign countries, and point out with pride the wide lead. A similar exercise comparing the capabilities in the private sector with practices in the government would be less encouraging.

- This decade will see a confluence of new demands and technological opportunities. Agencies will be required to make delivery services more efficient and effective, and to accommodate social imperatives such as privacy and due process in their system operations. At the same time, a wealth of new information technology based on the microprocessor and on new data communication services will offer a host of opportunities to improve service and, conversely, temptations to apply technological fixes to uncovered operations. Good, high level planning is necessary.

- It is imperative, given the environment depicted above, that agencies create high level executive positions for information management, and fill them with individuals who have the proper expertise and perspectives.

- Long-term studies of the impact of information technology on the organization operation and decision-making authority in government agencies are needed. Such research has been underway in the private sector for some time, and the results have been striking.[9] Similar studies on the government side have been few.[10] Yet experience from the private sector indicates that we have much to learn about how to use information systems to improve government without incorporating the worst anti-human features of bureaucracy.

Notes

[1]U.S., U.S.C. 5, 5220.

[2]U.S., Privacy Protection Study Commission, <u>Personal Privacy in an Information Society</u> (Washington, D.C.: Government Printing Office, 1977).

[3]U.S., Congress, H.R. 6410, 96th Cong., 2nd Session.

[4]Proceedings of the House of Representatives are currently made available through some in-house cable networks.

[5]U.S., U.S.C. 5, 552.

[6]U.S., Supreme Court, <u>U.S. v. Frank W. Snepp</u>, No. 78-1871 and No. 79-265.

[7]William J. Broad, "Computers and U.S. Military Don't Mix." <u>Science</u>. vol. 207 (March 14, 1980), pp. 1183-87.

[8]Broad, "Computers," pp. 1183-87.

[9]Henry C. Lucas, <u>Why Information Systems Fail</u> (New York: Columbia University Press, 1975).

[10]J. Danziger, Dutton, Kling, and Kramer, "A Survey of Local Government EDP Practices," <u>Governmental Finance</u>. vol. 6, no. 3 (August 1977), pp. 42-51.

Bibliography

Broad, William J. "Computers and U.S. Military Don't Mix," <u>Science</u>. vol. 207 (March 14, 1980), pp. 1183-87.

Danziger, J., Dutton, Kling, and Kramer. "A Survey of Local Government EDP Practices, <u>Governmental Finance</u>. vol. 6, no. 3 (August 1977), pp. 42-51.

Lucas, Henry C. <u>Why Information Systems Fail</u>. New York: Columbia University Press, 1975.

U.S., Congress, H.R. 6410, 96th Cong., 2nd Session (<u>Paperwork Reduction Act of 1980</u>).

U.S., Privacy Protection Study Commission. <u>Personal Privacy in an Information Society</u>. Washington, D.C.: Government Printing Office, 1977.

U.S., Supreme Court, <u>U.S. v. Frank W. Snepp</u>, No. 78-1871 and No. 79-265.

U.S., U.S.C. 5, 552 (<u>Freedom of Information Act</u>).

U.S., U.S.C. 5, 5220 (<u>Privacy Act of 1974</u>).

THE FINANCING AND GOVERNANCE OF
INFORMATION NETWORKS OF THE FUTURE:
The Private Sector

President and Secretary
Information Industry Association

Depending on the context involved, information can be described in many ways, not the least of which is as a commodity. In fact, in the context of this volume information qualifies very much as a commodity, not exclusively as a commodity, but as a commodity, nonetheless.

The information industry is best understood in terms of information as a commodity, or an economic good, like furniture, shoes, food stuffs, liquid oxygen, etc. The industry structure is like the structure of any other industry. There are producers (of data bases or market research studies, for example), distributors (Lockheed, SDC, BRS), retailers (FIND, Information on Demand), and systems companies capable of assembling the pieces to make up the previous three sectors.[1] An exhaustive survey of the information industry places its total annual U.S. sales at $9.4 billion in 1979.[2]

Yes, information is a commodity.

An electronic assumption underlies this volume. That is, a premise for this volume is that the distribution of information is now or soon will be essentially dependent on the new electronic media. I do not entirely agree. Rather, I see a vastly enriched information infrastructure offering citizens more than a limited electronic diet, literally a surfeit of information content in an array of alternate media.[3] In other words BOOKS ARE HERE TO STAY! So are magazines, newsletters, and more. "Look-up" tools certainly run the risk of becoming all-electronic as do a variety of reference tools. But even for some of these other non-electronic media may be superior,[4] more cost effective[5] or more "user engineered."[6]

Notwithstanding such minor quibbles, the advent of information networks is beyond question as is the need to address their funding and governance. Networks exist to serve different purposes, are organized and operated on different funding bases, and are either special purpose or general systems. The ultimate general network system is foreshadowed, of course, by the telephone systems, but cable television, broadcast television, and direct broadcast satellite systems are rapidly developing from special purpose (news and entertainment) to more general systems as videotex and teletext capabilities are added. These operate in a regulated environment. While their application to what the House of Representatives in the Communications Act Rewrite labels "mass media" services, largely electronic delivery of information formerly available

only in an "ink-on-paper medium," raises pricing, funding and governance
issues, the framework for dealing with those issues in this environment
is well established and will not be discussed further. Suffice it to
note that with the exception of the WETA and NTIA initiative in teletext the players are all in the private sector.[7]

Turning then to the special purpose of "knowledge related" networks, three financing and governance models suggest themselves:
government, quasi-government (or quasi-private) non-profit, and
private. Each exists to serve a slightly different purpose, and this
is reflected in its organization and operation. It is not my purpose
nor probably is it within ability to analyze in detail each of these
three types. I would like to suggest that each exists to attain certain
objectives for society, that all three exist in an atmosphere of dynamic
tension and that, indeed, all three are necessary in our free enterprise
economy, republic form of government, and democratic society.

What are the objectives to be served by these networks, alone or
in combination? The hallmark of a free open society is a competitive
marketplace of ideas. This requires not only the availability of
competitive sources of information, but also a foundation of an informed,
literate populace. This, in turn, depends not only on the traditional
western liberal requirement of a free flow of information, but also a
willingness and capability to give form and substance to the concept of
information justice. The economic and social mobility, in which America
takes such great pride, will increasingly depend on our ability to
extend information literacy from the specialized information audiences
of the information elite to the general population.

A healthy pluralistic information structure is like a three-legged
stool. Each leg is indispensible to the functioning of the structure.
The legs are interdependent. The functions of the government leg are
numerous. It is responsible for establishing the basic framework within
which the structure functions. In some respects it referees the operation of the framework. In other respects it is an essential player.
Much information work--gathering statistics, monitoring compliance--
requires actions only the sovereign can take. Similarly, private sector
activities are numerous. While the government is responsible for establishing a functional framework, it is the private sector that gives the
functions substance. From book, magazine, and newspaper publishers to
market researchers and data base creators, from book jobbers to online
data base distribution services, and from bookstores to information
brokers or retailers and newsletter publishers, the great majority of
information transactions are performed by private citizens with private
risk capital creating jobs and new revenue sources. Together, government and the private sector form a formidable information force capable
of serving the complex information requirements of our national economy.
Together they are creating a cerebal society and economy. Upward mobility increasingly depends on the individual's ability to master the many
dimensions of information literacy.

Libraries form the third leg offering society an escape valve for
the economic and social pressures raised by this government/private
sector information movement. Libraries have served to alert the community at large to the information resources generated for specific
audiences. They have also made these resources available without charge,

within their finite budgets. For many upward mobility begins with a mastery of library provided intellectual property resources.

Each of the three legs complements the others in similar fashion. The private sector is a fail-safe device to prevent government and libraries from combining to dominate the sources of information by controlling what information, government generated and library distributed, is available. Similarly, government provides an alternative view of what information is important to society as a whole bringing balance to the range of information resources available through libraries and the private sector.

As part of the pluralistic information structure there is a need to promote redundance rather than to eliminate it. Not only is there the old "garage sale" philosophy of "one person's junk is another person's treasure," but redundancy is necessary to assure that information, concepts, and ideas, reach the people for whom the information has value, is important, or can work to help them to be and to become.

The fundamental human condition redundant information addresses is our "cognitive screen." Each of us is the product of the past. Our minds automatically screen out that which our brains recognize to be irrelevant to our current concerns. In one sense futurists are people who are constantly striving to open their cognitive screens, consciously seeking to see new relevancies in events and ideas not immediately or obviously relevant.

Information must be creatively packaged in a wide variety of packages and presentations for it to penetrate the cognitive screens of all the people for whom it has value. No one source of information can possibly imagine all the ways in which information must be packaged in order to be useful to all the people for whom it has value. Our pluralistic information structure, which assures competition in the delivery of information, is most important for this "cognitive screen" reason.

In European countries, not only are radio, television, and communications state-run monopolies for the most part, but the economies of many countries are also less dependent on the free market system like the one we know here in the United States. It is interesting to observe what has happened in these countries with the advent of videotex and teletext. Almost universally, the creation by the PTT authorities of these new electronic media has precipitated a vast outpouring of private sector initiative and innovation. Large numbers of companies have come forward in England, for example, offering to become providers of information over the new systems. This is what the government had hoped to do: to stimulate economic growth, new product development, jobs, and increased tax base.

Indeed, the European Economic Community as well as many of its constituent countries has embarked on comprehensive programs to stimulate private sector development in key information and information-related businesses and ventures. When the EEC concluded that European countries needed to increase the world market share of the chip industry, the computer industry, and the data base business, from its current 12-15% to 33% by 1985, it logically concluded that government could not itself perform that growth and development. It needed to stimulate the private sector to do so. A whole range of incentives schemes have been set in motion from subsidizing data base development to aggregating new markets. New jobs are being created. New capabilities are being developed, and innovation is being stimulated and supported.

Another matter in a free enterprise system needing understanding is the function of price as a vehicle to recovering the cost of innovation, R&D, and market development. A new information product is a costly undertaking. It must be designed, tested, retested, put on the market, market tested, and finally sold to a skeptical public. In many cases the public has to be retrained before the product can serve its purpose. If it is priced immediately at or near the cost of producing individual units, how will such costs designing, testing, market testing, be recovered? If they are not recovered, how are new innovations in this area to be obtained?

With the introduction of a new product, the producing company may choose to "value-price" the product, that is charge a price for the product based on its value to the customer rather than on the cost to create each unit. Over time, two things happen: the innovator regains the product development costs back which can be reapplied to further innovations of use to individuals. Others, in addition, see the new product, ·benefit from the market acceptance achieved, and create and sell competitive products. Competition ultimately brings cost pricing to these products.

In a democracy, we must pay very careful attention to who controls the switches of information.[8] This also involves first amendment issues.[9] Without belaboring the point, in an age of decentralized printing activities citizens were almost guaranteed access to a variety of viewpoints. Many printing presses were run by many different people assuring Americans many competitive sources of ideas, news and information. With the advent of centralized communications capabilities, much of the control over content delivered through such systems will belong to fewer and fewer people and be subject to governmental regulation. One needs only look at the homogeneity, if not the quality, of current television programs delivered through such controlled, regulated centralized capabilities. This is becoming the central issue in the attempt being made in Congress to rewrite the 1934 Communications Act. AT&T which has operated for years under a consent decree limiting its business activities is now intent on expanding into the business of creating and marketing information content over the communication system it operates.

Can our national objectives be achieved if the operator of the network also is the owner of information content delivered by the network? Is it fair to other suppliers to the implicity unfair competition of the network itself? Will other suppliers be able to compete effectively or will such networks become the principle of sole providers of information? If such networks are regulated and thus dependent on the government, what assurance will be possible that government actions are fully explored, discussed, and evaluated? More fundamentally, who is to say such a network is capable of providing the creative packaging needed to penetrate cognitive screens?

We can see that the governance of information networks needs to be structured to preserve some fundamental objectives of our society:

- Create and nurture a free, open, informed, and literate society.
- Maintain a strongly pluralistic information structure and capability.
- Stimulate innovation, develop jobs, and economic growth.
- Establish clear rules to protect society from misadventures arising from the use of controls over the switches of innovation.

By definition, these embody the objectives of our society as a whole. In a large sense, the entire U.S. economy is involved in the financing and governance of information networks. The issues in each network environment must be matched with this national economic, political, and social system. There is a real hazard to the health and vitality of our nation if the planning of its subparts fails to take into account how these subparts fit together to create the whole, in this case the U.S. information society.

Notes

[1] Paul G. Zurkowski, "Information and the Economy," Library Journal, September 15, 1979, pp. 1800–1807.

[2] The Business of Information Report, A report of the Survey of the Information Industry, November 1, 1980.

[3] The Harvard University Program on Information Resources Policy has tagged the coming together of computers and communication with the title "Compunications." These are but two elements of the information handling infrastructure of the country. In addition to non-electronic media "compunications" does not comprehend the people engaged in the creation and delivery of content. A more comprehensive word covering the totality of information handling resources is "infostructure." The Information Industry Association published in 1979 an eleven chapter infostructure handbook entitled The Information Resource, providing a catalog of the policies, players, and background involved.

[4] For some materials evanescent electronic storage and display is inadequate to assure a permanent audit trail or record of the information, its source and its accuracy.

[5] Vast quantities of essentially static data can more easily be stored and searched on microfilm. Videodisc technology may also serve in these cases.

[6] A book is a convenient probable medium, which, for many applications, defies electronic competition.

[7] In view of the heavy involvement of government in European countries not only in the networks, but in the development of videotex and teletext systems, it was inevitable that the apparently slow, deliberate and often-times expressly skeptical approach of the private sector to these developments would produce some government involvement on the basis of "market value."

[8]Paul G. Zurkowski, "First Amendment Implications for Secondary Information Service," Communications and the Law, Spring 1979, pp. 49-64.

[9]Ithiel de Sola Pool, "The First Amendment and Information Policy," First Annual Information Policy Address, delivered at the 11th Annual Meeting of the Information Industry Association, October, 1979. See Richmond Newspapers, Inc., et al., v. Virginia, et al., decision of the U.S. Supreme Court No. 79-243, decided July 2, 1980 for a review of the law on citizen access to "important" information.

CONCLUSIONS AND RECOMMENDATIONS

by

Martha Boaz

This section will attempt to summarize and generalize from the preceding material. Information technology has developed more rapidly than anyone would have predicted or believed possible 25 years ago. It has also become vastly more sophisticated, cheaper and faster than anyone could have anticipated. The world of education and libraries will increasingly be changed by information technology and the trend toward an information-based society will continue to expand.

Problems, Trends

Information is in large supply. As a matter of fact, it is in quantitative surplus, and there are problems in getting specific facts from the masses of material available. In spite of this, there are many people, many individuals, who are information poor. How can these conditions be changed? In the complex world of today it is imperative that people everywhere have quick, ready, objective, and economical access to information, with equal opportunity to all. This will be a fundamental requirement for satisfactory societal adaptation to change.

There will be many problems. Not all problems will be in the future. They are present, now, and have existed for many years. Some of the results of technological discoveries have created serious situations, one being the pollution of the environment. Many of the problems exist because inventions were discovered in isolation, and planning has been piecemeal, not comprehensive. All new discoveries should be considered in relation to the total scene and in a framework of inter-dependence not independence. As John McHale points out, there should be a "process-orientation in which ends/means, issues/questions, problems/solutions all look back upon one another in interweaving and overlapping sets of feedback systems."[1] In plans that are made there should be incentives that will provide for individual and social goals and rewards. High priority should be given, at the national level, to serious efforts for planning and managing the development of information services for both public and private use. Government at all levels is affected by the information processing technology that is bringing about fundamental changes in the way organizations are managed, in the way decisions are made, and in the exchange of information between government and citizens and between governments and governments. There are and will be major national and international societal problems and issues whose resolutions require information services. These will include personal, industrial and business, educational and professional, political and governmental, and many others. There will be problems in

177

the development of information systems which will involve their financing and governance as well as consideration of policy issues and value
systems.

Due to its wide-reaching influence, the management of human-to-
machine interface is one of the most important points of attention
today. Great progress is being made and active efforts should be continued in this area. We know, because we live in a practical world and
are realistic in planning, that the information needs of business, with
particular attention to managerial decision making, will be of utmost
importance in the further development and refinement of information
delivery systems. Along with the refinement of larger systems, it is
expected that personal, public, and business use will be expanded to be
more inclusive than now by home/business information systems on the so-
called "personal" computers. These will soon be in wide use in several
countries and will thus extend opportunities for information to
countless numbers of people.

Legal and Regulatory Factors

In the whole area of information services there are legal and regulatory factors that may affect the author and the flow of information.
Privacy and security issues are of concern in both the public and private
sectors. Copyright is a fundamental legal principle that should direct
strategies for meeting the information needs of society. Associated
with this are inherent problems in the new technological advances in the
creation and the need for information. Individuals will need protection
from political abuses of distortion or manipulation of information. At
the same time, increased access to information is a basic requirement
for both individual and social progress. In all of this the place of
the author will be an important factor and will receive attention from
authors, publishers, and readers.

Rapid Advances in Technology

Advances in technology, in the handling and use of information,
have brought about many changes in the working habits and attitudes of
people in political and governmental processes. Advances in computer
and communications technology are continuing at a very rapid pace.
There is dramatic evidence of lowered cost and improved performance
in the computer field. A Stanford University economist, Edward
Steinmuller, talks of the dizzy pace of computer progress: "If the
airlines had progressed as rapidly as this technology, the Concorde
would be carrying half a million passengers at 20 million miles an hour
for less than a penny apiece."[2] Although the advances already made in
technology seem unbelievable, the anticipated changes in the processes
by which information will be generated and disseminated, some years
from now, almost "boggle" the mind.

Information made possible by technology assists society to advance
to higher levels of progress and to acquire more control over the future.
The actual technology machinery itself will not change the future. It
will do what it is programmed to do. So, it is man who is responsible
for the commands given to the machine. Information technology, if so

directed by man, will provide speedy, accurate information, on which man can make decisions.

There is and will be fear of and opposition to the expected effects of new information and communications possibilities. John McHale has an answer for this:

> Whereas many analysts have lamented the decline and disappearance of earlier cultural (and other) modes due to their displacement by new technical means, this has not, in fact, happened. Enhanced communications have not wholly displaced physical transportation or face to face meetings for similar purposes. The telephone has not ousted letter writing. The obsolescence of the printed word long predicted as a result of the visual 'video-culture' has almost doubled in the past ten years. The increase in availability of mass-produced artifacts is accompanied by an increase in handcraft products, and even by the revival of older crafts. Video art is accompanied by the revival of painting, drawing and engraving; electronic music co-exists with the harpsichord and the string quartet.[3]

As McHale points out, human beings in general seem to have great capacity and inclination for diversity and for alternative overlapping modes.

International--Transnational Aspects

Within a few years, society has moved from local, state, regional, and national to international and transnational viewpoints. This is not necessarily a voluntary matter; there is now no choice. Idealistically, idealogically, this might have been brought about by political, governmental action, but in reality it cannot be otherwise in this age of technological information transfer. The world becomes one small community. No longer is it possible to consider issues and problems as independent or isolated events. Current and future decision makers will have to think in terms of interdependent systems. Planning for the general welfare, on a global basis, will require great statesmen who are concerned and committed to universal progress and universal well-being. Do we have such statesmen now? Will we have in the year 2000?

As a result of changes in education, brought about by information technology, there will probably be a leveling effect on traditional social strata, and this will bring about a change in the distribution of power. If the platitude, "Knowledge is power," has meaning, it stands to reason that those who have knowledge of the new technology will form a new elite and will exercise power. The term, "the third revolution," may then be more significant than a casual use of it indicates. There will probably be a re-distribution of power--away from bureaucratic control to lower-level decision making and more general participation in organizational management, because of the information environment.

Cultural Impacts

Radical cultural changes will take place as the technological information revolution proceeds. John McHale comments on this:

Whatever actual trends may emerge, it can be stated with some certainty that the potential cultural configurations of an 'information society' will be quite different from the kind of cultural forms which have preceded it; the cultural configurations will differ more from our present print-oriented societies than the societies of the past five hundred years have differed from those more dependent upon oral communication. As the novel differs from the tribal storyteller, so television and cinema differ in form, content and pace from the novel. With more interactive communications media, such as two-way television, there will again be different possibilities.[4]

The library's role is likely to change from present special institutional connections of academic, public, and special to information service centers, and with emphasis on user-needs not collection-centered libraries. F. W. Lancaster predicts that "libraries as collections of physical artifacts will rapidly decline in value; many will disappear. Librarians will be deinstitutionalized. Some will become essential components of teams performing in industry, in law, in academia, in health care and elsewhere, while others will work in a more freelance capacity from offices or the home." But, Lancaster adds, "the decline of the library does not necessarily imply the decline of the librarian...." Instead, "the great potential value of professional persons familiar with the multitude of information resources available in electronic form and able to exploit these resources efficiently and effectively will become more widely recognized."[5] Information networks will function at local, state, and federal levels. Library schools will be responsible for educating future professionals with the philosophy of service and with the concept of interdependence.

There are times when it would seem desirable to discard much of technology and return to a simpler way of life. This is not possible. There is no real choice but to go forward. So it is important that we use technology and science to achieve goals and objectives that will benefit, not destroy, man. We should heed Albert Schweitzer's gloomy admonition that "Man has lost the capacity to foresee and to forestall. He will end by destroying the earth."

Need for Planning

The importance of planning for the future is emphasized by thoughtful people, in written articles, and in speeches, and in general conversation. Many problems have developed from the inventions of the Industrial Revolution. Progressive though they were, they have resulted in social conflict, environmental pollution, and other problems. Had inventors and planners investigated thoroughly the effects of automobile exhausts, the current pollution problem might have been averted.

Nobody can draw an exact picture of the future. The only thing that is certain is that it will be different. In order to try to make it as good or better than the present it will be necessary to try to plan for it--to build carefully, to become architects of fate. This requires a careful, reasoned, visionary assessment of both the good and bad possible trends, as well as directions and impacts of current action and plans. Good management is a key factor in the process.

Authorities in management identify the components of a good management system: 1) a problem identification section, 2) a planning and decision-making system, 3) an implementation and control system, and, 4) an information system. New technological innovations should be planned in advance as part of a package with new organizational and institutional changes, all planned as a whole.

Joel D. Goldhar says organizations must change in response to new technology. He points out that this is a three-stage process as follows:

Stage 1 The organization adopts (or purchases) the new technology and uses it to perform old functions faster and cheaper.

Stage 2 The organization begins to reorganize, change policies and procedures, and acquire new types of people to take increased advantage of the new technology's ability to perform existing functions faster and cheaper.

Stage 3 The organization begins to use the new technology to perform new functions and to offer products and services not previously possible.[6]

Involve User Population

Representatives of the user population should be involved in any projected plans for using new technology. We can make all kinds of predictions and guesses--it is the users, and only the users, who will be able to evaluate information and their own needs for further developments in the field. Carole Gantz and Joel Goldhar comment on the need for user-input in this statement: "It becomes increasingly clear, that the success of information services is more likely to be achieved through adjusting services to meet the specific needs of individuals rather than trying to adapt the individual user to match the wholesale output of an information system."[7]

In line with these comments, it is strongly recommended that representatives of the user population of society be involved in the design of any system that is planned. This will mandate initial, continuing, and intensive interaction with designated persons in different user offices and segments of the population. User-input and reaction to inventions and plans will encourage experimentation, feedback, and early improvement and modification of design in the system in its beginning stages. In this way there should be avoidance of problems, with resulting cost savings and more user-oriented systems.

User groups should be identified on the basis of their different information requirements. These groups should include known individual information users as well as untapped populations. This will involve reaching out to these people, educating them, organizing them, and involving them in the planning of future information activities.

Efforts should be made to get both public and private commitments to support the development and advancement of information technology.

There is also need for feedback in information transfer devices. Gantz and Goldhar say that "current information systems have been described as a bunch of answers looking for questions. The information is there, but the system receives less than optimum use because it is not geared, either formally or functionally to users."[8] An important matter in all of this is the use of information for its own sake. Technologists have spent years, money, time, and energy in developing ways and machinery to manage and dispose of information, but have had little concern about understanding information. How is information transmitted? With whom is it shared? How does it help individuals, families, companies, corporations, governments, the world? The use, not the form or medium, is the major item to be considered in the development of information programs.

Other matters to be considered are the standardization and compatibility of information systems. By experimentation and careful management, machinery and systems could be designed to be compatible; this would result eventually in lowered costs, and more efficient use of communication between people, and the use of systems would be greatly enhanced. The cost item will be of great importance and the financing of networks may be a deterrent to their extensive use, although the decreasing cost of machinery is a favorable item.

People in the business world are looking favorably at the development of computer machinery and at knowledge-based industries. Peter Drucker, expert on management, says, "as the U.S. reindustrializes-- struggles to regain or maintain its competitiveness [it should] go with the knowledge-based industries and not mistakenly try to save blue-collar, mass production employment."[9]

We are not ready, at this time to outline a specific course for action on information technology. We are not ready on a personal, or corporate, or governmental or educational level. How will we muster the forces and the strength to proceed?

Some group should be set up to coordinate and direct the decisions that will guide information technology. Work is being done in this area by the National Science Foundation and the Office of Technology Assessment, but a great deal more needs to be done. Research is also needed; this need is underscored and emphasized. Policy making, whether related to technology or government or education or anything else, depends on organized information flows--all the more reason for careful direction of information technology development. A lack of planning, study, research, and experimentation, and failure in establishing sound policies may negate any benefits that accrue. The ultimate objective is to develop technology that can be controlled and at the same time used constructively and efficiently.

Conclusion

Used wisely, information technology and information access can be a giant step forward for individuals and society. Misused, it can have destructive results. Man will be the master in command; technology will be the servant--man is responsible for the best use of information technology.

History has been the story of man ascending a stairway in rough-shod boots, of getting to the top and descending in white satin slippers. Civilizations on the build, going up, have been eager and industrious and hard-working, but inevitably when they reach a peak they, their governments, seem unable to plan and achieve regulations that are in the public interest. This requires independence and statesmanship and cooperation from the whole group. Can this, will this ever be achieved? Will our present society continue to rise or will it fall?

Notes

[1] John McHale, The Changing Information Environment (Boulder, CO: Westview Press, c.1976), pp. 105-109.

[2] Thomas O'Toole, "Computer Services About to Skyrocket," Los Angeles Times (June 21, 1980), Part I-A, p. 2.

[3] John McHale, Changing, p. 53.

[4] John McHale, Changing, p. 50.

[5] F. W. Lancaster, "The Future of the Librarian Lies Outside The Library," Catholic Library World, vol. 51 (April 1980), p. 391.

[6] Joel D. Goldhar, "Obtaining and Using Information in the Year 2000," IEEE Transactions on Professional Communication, vol. PC-20, no. 2 (September 1977), 127.

[7] Carole Gantz and Joel Goldhar, "The Role of Scientific Communication in the Process of Technological Innovation," Information News and Services, vol. 7 (October 1975), p. 245.

[8] Gantz and Goldhar, "Role," p. 245.

[9] James Flanigan, "Advice from Drucker," Los Angeles Times (July 27, 1980), Part VI, p. 1.

BIOGRAPHICAL SKETCHES OF THE AUTHORS

Martha Boaz

Martha Boaz is a Research Associate, Center for Study of the American Experience, Annenberg School of Communications and Dean Emeritus, Graduate School of Library Science, University of Southern California. Prior to her long tenure as library school dean, she had held positions in school, college, and public libraries. She has also served as a consultant in various aspects of librarianship both in the United States and the Far East. She has been president of the Association of American Library Schools, the Library Education Division of the American Library Association, and the California Library Association. She has been author and editor of numerous books and articles, with special interests in library education, research methods, administration, and new developments in technology and information retrieval.

Wayne I. Boucher

Wayne I. Boucher is Senior Research Associate at the Center for Futures Research, University of Southern California. A member of the futures research community from its beginnings in the mid-1960s, Mr. Boucher has conducted studies and consulted extensively on a variety of strategic problems. His books include, The Study of the Future (1977) and Systems Analysis and Policy Planning, with E.S. Quade (1968).

Richard Byrne

Richard Byrne, acting dean of the Annenberg School of Communications, University of Southern California, is an international consultant in the field of communications. He has lectured and consulted on urban communication problems, communication technologies, cable television, communication management, and graphic design and production. He has produced TV public affairs programs, and multimedia presentations for government and industry, and has been architectural design consultant for communication facilities throughout the United States.

Vincent E. Giuliano

Vincent Giuliano, after receiving his Ph.D. from Harvard in Information Processing Methods, joined Arthur D. Little, Inc. in 1959. He has had extensive experience working with large and small information storage and retrieval systems, ranging from libraries to telecommunications-based computer systems. He has been responsible for several studies, among

them one relating to the organization and governance of the Ohio College
Library Center; another study was for the National Science Foundation,
another for the United Nations Dag Hammarsjold Library, and a variety
of others relating to applications of new communications technologies.
He is author of some sixty publications and reports and of twelve film,
videotape, and mixed media presentations, holds three patents, and has
served in a variety of government committee and consulting appointments.

Paul Gray

Paul Gray is Chairman of Management Science and Computers at the
Edwin L. Cox School of Business at Southern Methodist University. His
recent research has been in the areas of telecommunications substitution
for transportation, futures scenarios, technology assessment, and the
application of advanced technologies for decision making. His doctorate
is in Operations Research from Stanford University and he has taught at
Stanford, Georgia Tech, and the University of Southern California, where
he was a member of the Center for Futures Research.

Henry S. McDonald

Henry S. McDonald is an Assistant Director and Systems Architecture
Research Consultant at Bell Laboratories, Holmdel, New Jersey. He is
currently working on the impact of computers and very large scale
circuit integration on the communication plant of the future.
Since joining Bell Laboratories in 1955, Dr. McDonald has engaged
in research work. He was initially concerned with speech and television
research and basic studies of vision. He pioneered the work on digital
signal processing leading to the practicality of digital filters. For
many years he has specialized in computer research including the use of
computers to simulate electronic systems, computer graphics, computer
design, and the application of digital technology to telephone switching.
Dr. McDonald is presently a consultant for the Department of Defense
on matters of communications and computers.
Dr. McDonald is the author of published articles on speech, encoding,
and digital instrumentation. He has been granted nine patents relating
to communications.
He is a Fellow in the Institute of Electrical and Electronics
Engineers and in 1978 he received the Society award of the Audio,
Speech and Signal Processing Society of that Institute. He is also
a member of the American Association for the Advancement of Science,
the Association for Computing Machinery, and Sigma Xi.
Dr. McDonald received the B.E.E. degree from The Catholic University of America in 1950 and M.S.E.E. and Doctor of Engineering degrees
from Johns Hopkins University in 1953 and 1955, respectively.

John Naisbitt

John Naisbitt is publisher of the Trend Report, a division of
Yankelovich, Skelly & White. Before joining YSW in 1979, he was
Chairman of the Board of the Center for Policy Process in Washington
for four years. He was Chairman and President of Urban Research
Corporation in Chicago from 1968 to 1975.

He served on the White House staff as special assistant to
President Lyndon Johnson. He was John W. Gardner's special assistant
when Mr. Gardner was Secretary of HEW. Prior to that, he was for two
years assistant to the then U.S. Commissioner of Education, Francis
Keppel. Mr. Naisbitt has served as assistant to the Chairman of the
Commission of Presidential Scholars, Dr. Milton Eisenhower. He has
also worked for IBM and Eastman Kodak Company (he has a total of 20
years of business experience). His studies at Harvard, Utah, and
Cornell were in political science.

Burt Nanus

Burt Nanus is a Professor of Management and Policy Sciences and
Director of the Center for Futures Research at the University of
Southern California, which he founded in 1971. He is the co-author of
three books, the most recent one entitled The Emerging Network
Marketplace, and his articles on long-range planning and multinational
computers appear in more than 50 leading journals and books in these
fields. Prior to joining USC, he spent 10 years in various management
capacities in the System Development Corporation, the UNIVAC Division
of Sperry-Rand Corporation, and his own consulting firm.

Harriet L. Oler

Harriet L. Oler is an honors graduate of both Dickinson College,
and the University of Pennsylvania Law School. She is a member of the
Pennsylvania and District of Columbia bar associations. Ms. Oler has
practiced copyright law for more than a decade and is currently Senior
Attorney on the General Counsel's Staff of the Copyright Office. She
has published numerous articles on copyright law, including a chapter
in a recently published book: Fair Use and Free Inquiry.

John E. Richinskas

John E. Ruchinskas, research associate in the Annenberg School of
Communications, University of Southern California, has studied the
social impact of new communications technology both in home and
organizational settings. He is currently focusing upon the social
effects of information technology in the office, including implementation
and adoption of video-conferencing.

Alphonse F. Trezza

Alphonse F. Trezza is the Executive Director of the National Commission on Libraries and Information Science. He was formerly Director of the Illinois State Library and Associate Executive Director of the American Library Association. He organized, and was the first Chairman of, the Chief Officers of State Library Agencies. He will shortly join the Library of Congress to direct a joint NCLIS/ Library of Congress project, within the framework of the Federal Library Committee, on Intergovernmental Library Cooperation.

Rein Turn

Rein Turn is a professor of computer science at the California State University, Northridge. He has published extensively on the issues of privacy protection in the age of automated record-keeping systems, computer security, and technology forecasting. He chaired a panel on transborder data flows of the American Federation of Information Processing Societies (AFIPS) and edited the panel's report. He is now chairing an AFIPS working group on transnational information flows. He is the author of a book Computers in the 1980s.

Fred W. Weingarten

Fred W. Weingarten is a private consultant in the area of information technology and public policy. He has conducted policy analyses for such organizations as the Congressional Office of Technology Assessment and the National Telecommunications and Information Administration. For several years, he was responsible for a program of research in computers and society, run out of the National Science Foundation. He has several publications in computer science and in public policy. He is a graduate of the California Institute of Technology and of Oregon State University.

Paul G. Zurkowski

Paul G. Zurkowski, President and Secretary of the Information Industry Association. He has served as Legislative Assistant to Congressman Robert W. Kastenmeier of his home state of Wisconsin, as the Judge Advocate at the U.S. Army War College, Carlisle Barracks, Pennsylvania and Fort Irwin, California, as attorney in the Office of General Counsel, Housing and Home Administration (forerunner of Department of Housing and Urban Development) and as attorney/examiner at the Interstate Commerce Commission. As the first employee of the newly formed IIA in 1969, he has since watched over the growth of their new industry.

INDEX